Also by Paul E. Johnson

A Shopkeeper's Millennium:
Society and Revivals in Rochester, New York, 1815–1837

The Kingdom of Matthias:
A Story of Sex and Salvation in 19th-Century America
(with Sean Wilentz)

Sam Patch,

the Famous Jumper

Sam Patch,

THE FAMOUS JUMPER

Paul E. Johnson

HILL AND WANG

A DIVISION OF FARRAR, STRAUS AND GIROUX

NEW YORK

Hill and Wang
A division of Farrar, Straus and Giroux
18 West 18th Street, New York, 10011

The Library of Congress has cataloged the hardcover edition as follows:
Johnson, Paul E., date.
    Sam Patch, the famous jumper / Paul E. Johnson.— 1st ed.
    p. cm.
    Includes index.
    ISBN 0-8090-8389-2 (hc : alk. paper)
    1. Patch, Sam, 1807–1829.   2. Daredevils—United States—
Biography.   I. Title.

GV1839.J65 2003
791'.092—dc21
[B]

                                                            2002191306

Paperback ISBN: 0-8090-8388-4
EAN: 978-0-8090-8388-6

Designed by Jonathan D. Lippincott

www.fsgbooks.com

14 12   13 15

Cover illustrations: (*front*) Horseshoe Falls at Niagara Falls, colored engraving, English, after W. H. Bartlett, courtesy of The Granger Collection, New York; (*back*) Genesee Falls, Rochester, N.Y., courtesy of Culver Pictures

For Alice Styles Johnson

CONTENTS

PREFACE

This is the story of Sam Patch, a factory hand who, in the 1820s, became America's first professional daredevil. Patch jumped from high places beside waterfalls. Journalists wrote about him, crowds came to see him, boys imagined being him, and he became a famous man.

Sam Patch was a mill boy who became a celebrity, and that is the story line of this book. (A second and surrounding story line is that Sam inhabited and helped to shape an America in which things like factory work and modern celebrity were beginning to happen.) But this is not a biography. Sam Patch and people like him did not have the linear careers that drive most biographies. When asked, they told their lives episodically, in stories that did not accumulate into a larger one. The few autobiographies written by such people—and Sam was not one of them—strike modern readers as picaresque, pointless, and, especially to readers who have not listened to the stories told on front porches, hard to follow. Sam Patch comes to us like a front-porch story: a dim and spotty family history, the dull, unrecorded events of factory work and heavy drinking, and a few spectacular events at waterfalls. This sparse and uneven record, along with my own inclinations, has led me to write about Sam in a series of stories that cannot add up to a biography. It is all that the evidence allows, and I suspect that Sam would have approved.

Sam Patch was ordinary for twenty-seven years and famous for two, but of course the anonymous years were crucial. His parents were among the first Americans to lose their foothold in the countryside and take up factory labor, and the book begins with their journey from farm to factory. It is not an easy story to tell, for the Patches were not important people: they did not keep diaries or write memoirs, they did not appear in newspapers, and no one bothered to save their mail. They did, however, leave traces in vital records, tax lists, church records, wills and deeds, records of town governments, court records, and other scattered genealogical sources. An account of their lives is fragmentary and too often speculative, but it does track one troubled family into the factory. It also helps to explain how Sam Patch became a skilled factory operative, a daring falls jumper, and a melancholy, drunken young man.

Once Sam's career as a falls jumper began, the nature of the evidence changes. We have abundant newspaper stories and editorials about Sam's leaps, yet the biographical trail goes dead: Sam did not marry, father children, buy or sell property, appear in census or tax records, or write a will—and he certainly never joined a church. After the record of his birth, there is no trace of Sam Patch in local records. We know only that he worked in textile mills and drank a lot, and that his jumping abilities attracted a lot of attention.

Working again with what is available, I have tried to situate Sam Patch's leaps in the social, cultural, and ecological histories of the waterfalls where they took place. Sam learned his leaping abilities with other factory boys at the falls of the Blackstone River in Pawtucket, Rhode Island. He moved on to Paterson, New Jersey, where in 1827 and 1828 he made the leaps at Passaic Falls that first got him into the newspapers. The papers did not mention this, but Sam's leaps at Passaic Falls were bound up with the angry industrial history of Paterson: his first publicized leap spoiled a celebration planned by an entrepreneur who had enclosed a working-class playground and turned it into a retreat for the well-to-do; his second was part of a class-based contest for control of the town's festivities on the Fourth of July; his third was tied to the first labor walkout in Paterson's history. Sam Patch performed these leaps before workmates and neighbors as well as disapproving businessmen and their friends, and his audience knew precisely what he was doing.

Sam Patch left Paterson (there is evidence that he was blacklisted), and in August 1828 he leaped into the Hudson River opposite New York City. He then disappeared for a year and emerged, drunker than ever, as the conqueror of Niagara Falls and Genesee Falls at Rochester. It was these leaps that made him a national celebrity.

At Niagara and Genesee Falls, Sam Patch leaves the factory towns and enters cultural history. Rochester and Niagara sat at the midpoint and the western terminus, respectively, of the Erie Canal—the most ambitious and successful of the internal improvements that were commercializing the northeastern countryside. Both waterfalls were sites of a busy conversation about the conquest of nature under the aegis of democratic capitalism. The falls at Rochester provided power for a manufacturing city that had mushroomed out of nothing in a few years. Along with the Erie Canal itself, Rochester in the 1820s was a national icon of rapid economic development. After a trip along the Canal and through Rochester, the wealthiest Americans reached Niagara Falls. There they stood before the power and beauty of nature, convincing themselves that their newfound sensibility and taste—not mere money—set them apart from the mass of rude and unfeeling Americans. These two waterfalls, in short, were places at which (and *about* which) the more comfortable and enterprising Americans invented, acted out, and publicized lessons about material progress and spiritual uplift that they would carry through the century.

Sam Patch thought differently about waterfalls, and about progress and uplift as well. Accompanied by boisterous crowds and a pack of popular journalists, he invaded Niagara and Rochester with sensibilities that were darker, funnier, and more playful than those of the developers and aesthetes—sensibilities that interrupted the "official" meanings of those waterfalls and called them into question. Americans who heard of Niagara and Rochester before Sam Patch's leaps thought of economic progress and the moral sublime. After 1829 many of them thought of Sam Patch. Their thoughts about Sam, celebrity, democracy, and the new world in which such things were happening form the concluding chapter.

I have spent a long time with Sam Patch, and I have run up debts. The National Endowment for the Humanities, the John Simon Guggenheim Memorial Foundation, the Gilder Lehrman Institute, the Obert C. and Grace A. Tanner Humanities Center, and the New Jersey State Historical Commission provided money and free time. Libraries that were particularly helpful include the American Antiquarian Society, the New-York Historical Society, the Library Division of the Henry Francis du Pont Winterthur Museum, the Henry E. Huntington Memorial Library, the Buffalo and Erie County Historical Society, the public libraries of New York City, Paterson, Rochester, Niagara Falls (New York and Ontario), and Reading and Wakefield, Massachusetts, the Family History Library of the Church of Jesus Christ of Latter-day Saints, and the libraries of Princeton University and the University of South Carolina. There is no way to thank all the colleagues and friends who have listened to my stories about Sam Patch, but some took on heavy burdens. These include Kasey

Grier, Katherine Martinez, Christine Stansell, Mary Strine, Richard White, Sean Wilentz, and—at the University of South Carolina—Ron Atkinson, Dan T. Carter, Mark M. Smith, and Larry Glickman. Parts of Chapters I and II appeared in *The New England Quarterly* and *American Quarterly*, and are reprinted with permission.

My agent, Geri Thoma, and Elisabeth Sifton of Hill and Wang both do good work. The dedication is to my mother. She is nearing ninety, and she still keeps a good front porch.

Onancock, Virginia
August 2002

Sam Patch,

the Famous Jumper

PAWTUCKET

Sam Patch first saw Pawtucket in 1807, when he was seven years old. It was an old village, founded in 1672 at the falls of the Blackstone River, four miles north of Providence, Rhode Island. The Englishman Samuel Slater had built America's first water-frame cotton-spinning mill there in 1790. In 1807 three mills stood beside the falls, and they were beginning to edge out the family-owned anchor forges, snuff mills, nail factories, and artisan shops of the old town. Pawtucket was becoming America's first textile manufacturing town, and the Patches were one of the first mill families.[1]

Postrevolutionary America was an overwhelmingly rural republic, and proponents of domestic manufactures insisted that factories would threaten neither agriculture nor the independence of farmers. The clear streams and abundant water power of the New England and mid-Atlantic states would encourage manufacturers to scatter their mills through the countryside, and these would provide employment for children and women from poor farm households. Alexander Hamilton explained some of the advantages of this system: "The husbandman himself experiences a new source of profit and support from the increased industry of his wife and daughters; invited and stimulated by the demands of the neighboring manufactories." Marginal farmers would continue to farm, securing their independence through new and more profitable forms of dependence for their wives and children. Thus Americans, said the promoters, could enjoy domestic manufactured goods without threats to agriculture, and without the European messiness of industrial cities or an industrial working class. There would, they promised, be no Manchesters in America.[2]

At first, Samuel Slater's Pawtucket kept that promise. His earliest mill workers were children of his partners and associates, then the children of Pawtucket artisans and farmers. Within a few years, however, he was searching beyond the neighborhood for mill hands and outworkers. Slater needed women and children, and he advertised for widows with large families. What he found was whole families headed by propertyless, destitute men. The Patches were one of these.

As the new families struggled into Pawtucket, Slater and the other mill owners began referring to the workers as "poor children," "that description of people," "those who are dependant on daily labor for support." A Baptist minister who worked with the new people disclosed that the moral "condition of the factory help was deplorable" and dubbed them "children of misfortune." Mill labor was stigmatized, and artisans and farmers (indeed any father who could manage without the wages of his children) took their daughters and sons out of the mills. A widening flood of destitute migrants took their places, and the mill families became a separate and despised group of people. The Baptist preacher recalled that these families were not only poor but prone to thievery, violence, and drunkenness: "The cotton mill business has brought in a large influx of people," he said, "who came in the *Second Class* cars. Such was the prejudice against the business that few others could be had, and the highways and hedges had to be searched even for them. A body of loafers was on hand before, who were, by turns, inmates of the tippling shops and the poor house, and not infrequently found in the gutter. . . . *Bang-all*, *Hardscrabble*, *Bungtown*, *Pilfershire*, *&c.* were . . . appropriate epithets for the place." In 1830 a travel guidebook (one that tried to be optimistic about most places) warned that in Pawtucket "the influx of strangers, many of them poor and ignorant foreigners, and most of them removed from the wholesome restraints of a better society, has produced unfavourable effects on habits and morals; which is the worst feature in the manufacturing system." America had its first little Manchester.[3]

It must have been a bewildered Sam Patch who, at the age of seven, stood with his father, mother, and four brothers and sisters and looked at Pawtucket for the first time. The Patches had spent the previous few years in the fishing village of Marblehead, in Massachusetts, but they had lost their house there, and the father had taken to drink and no longer worked. Before Marblehead, Sam's family had lived on farms surrounded by his mother's kin, but Sam did not remember those places. He would grow up in Pawtucket, shaped by his work and workmates in the mills. He would also be formed by the disorder of this new mill town, and he played his own part in making that disorder. Sam Patch was a product of family history as well—of the long train of disinheritance, uncertainty, and moral disintegration that had destroyed his father and delivered his family to Pawtucket. Sam could not remember much of that history, and his mother would try to hide it. But it shaped Sam Patch in ways he would never outrun.

Sam Patch was the son of Mayo Greenleaf Patch, a marginal farmer and cottage shoemaker from northeastern Massachusetts, who went by the name of Greenleaf.[4] The life of Greenleaf Patch was shadowed by two burdensome and uncomfortable facts. The first was the immense value that his New England neighbors placed on economic independence and the ownership of land. In postrevolutionary Massachusetts, freehold tenure conferred not only economic security but personal and moral independence, the ability to support and govern a family, political rights, and the respect of one's neighbors and oneself. New Englanders trusted the man who owned land. They feared and despised the man who did not. The second fact was that in the late eighteenth century increasing numbers of men owned no land. Greenleaf Patch was one of them.[5]

Like nearly everyone else in revolutionary Massachusetts, Greenleaf Patch was descended from yeoman stock. His family had come to Salem from England in 1636, and they worked a farm in nearby Wenham for more than a century. The Patches were church members and farm owners, and their men served regularly in the militia and in township offices. Greenleaf's father, grandfather, and great-grandfather all served terms as selectmen of Wenham. His great-grandfather was that town's representative to the Massachusetts General Court. His older brother was a militiaman who fought on the first day of the American Revolution.[6]

Though the Patches were an old and familiar family in Wenham, in the eighteenth century they were in trouble. Like thousands of New Englanders, they owned small farms and had many children, and by mid-century it was becoming clear that young Patch men would not inherit enough to enjoy the material standards established by their fathers. The farm on which Mayo Greenleaf Patch was born exemplified those troubles. His father, Timothy Patch, Jr., had inherited a house, an eighteen-acre farm, and eleven acres of outlying meadow and woodland at his own father's death in 1751. Next door, Timothy's brother Samuel worked the remaining nine acres of what had been their father's farmstead. The father had known that neither of his sons could make farms of these small plots, and he demanded that they share resources. His will granted Timothy access to a shop and cider mill that lay on Samuel's land, and it drew the boundary between them through the only barn on the property. It was the

end of the line: further subdivision would make both farms un-
workable.[7]

Timothy Patch's situation was precarious, and he made it
worse by overextending himself, both as a landholder and as a
father. Timothy was forty-three years old when he inherited his
farm in 1751, and he was busy buying pieces of woodland, upland, and meadow all over Wenham. Evidently he speculated in
marginal land and/or shifted from farming to livestock raising,
which he did on credit and on a fairly large scale. By the early
1760s Timothy Patch held title to 114 acres, nearly all of it in
small plots of poor land. These were speculative investments that
he may have made to provide for an impossibly large number of
heirs: he was already the father of ten children when he inherited
his farm in 1751, and in succeeding years he was widowed and
remarried and had two more daughters and a son. In all, he fa-
thered ten children who survived to adulthood. The youngest
was a son born in 1766. Timothy named him Mayo Greenleaf.[8]

Greenleaf Patch's life began badly: his father went bankrupt
in the year of his birth. Timothy had transferred the house and
farm to his two oldest sons several years earlier, possibly to keep
them out of the hands of creditors. Then, in 1766, the creditors
began making trouble. In September Timothy relinquished
twenty acres of his outlying land to satisfy a debt. By March 1767
he had lost five court cases and had sold all his remaining land to
pay debts and court costs, and he was preparing to leave Wenham. It was the end of his family's history in that town. Timothy's
first two sons stayed on, but both left Wenham before their
deaths, and none of the other children established households in
the neighborhood. After a century as substantial farmers and local leaders, the Patch family disappeared from the records of
Wenham.[9]

The father's wanderings after that cannot be traced with cer-
tainty. Timothy may have stayed in the neighboring towns of Andover and Danvers. A neighbor sued a Timothy Patch in Andover

(a few miles northwest of Wenham) in 1770; citizens of Danvers launched seven lawsuits against a Timothy Patch between 1779 and 1783. Some of these cases involved considerable sums of money, but the last of them accused the seventy-four-year-old Timothy of stealing firewood. That is all that we can know about the Patch family during the childhood of Mayo Greenleaf Patch.[10]

About the childhood itself we know nothing. Young Greenleaf may have shared his father's moves, but it is just as likely that he stayed with relatives in Wenham, for he eventually named his own children after members of the household of his brother Isaac in that town. We know also that young Greenleaf Patch learned how to make shoes, and as his first independent appearance in the civic records came at the age of twenty-one, we might guess that he served a formal, live-in apprenticeship. But all these points rest on speculation. Only this is certain: Greenleaf Patch was the tenth and youngest child of a family that broke and scattered in the year of his birth, and he entered adulthood alone and without visible resources.

In 1787 Mayo Greenleaf Patch appeared in the Second (North) Parish of Reading, Massachusetts—fifteen miles north of Boston and about the same distance west of Wenham. He was twenty-one years old and unmarried, and he owned almost nothing. He had no relatives in Reading. Indeed, no one named Patch had ever appeared in the town's records. In a world where property was inherited and where kinfolk were essential social and economic assets, young Greenleaf Patch had inherited nothing and lived alone.[11]

Greenleaf soon took steps that improved his prospects. In July 1788 he married Abigail McIntire in North Reading. He was twenty-two years old; she was seventeen and pregnant. This early marriage is most easily explained as an unfortunate accident, but from the standpoint of Greenleaf Patch it was not unfortunate at all, for it put him into a family that possessed resources his own family had lost. For the next twelve years, Patch's livelihood and ambitions centered on the McIntires and their land.[12]

The McIntires were descendants of Scots soldiers who had supported the accession of Charles II after the Puritans executed Charles I in 1649. They fought an English army led by Oliver Cromwell at Dunbar in 1650 and suffered a disastrous defeat. Three thousand Scots died on the field, nine thousand ran off, and ten thousand were taken prisoner. Cromwell released the wounded and force-marched the others south and imprisoned them in the cathedral at Durham. Only three thousand survived the march, and about half of those died in the cathedral. After a long and hellish imprisonment, the half-starved survivors were transported to English colonies in the Caribbean and the North American mainland.[13]

The ancestors of Greenleaf's pregnant young bride had found themselves exiled to the northern reaches of the Massachusetts Bay Colony, in what is now Maine. Some walked south, and Philip McIntire helped to pioneer North Reading in the 1650s. Over the years, the McIntires intermarried with their old Puritan enemies and joined their Congregational church, and by the 1780s McIntire households (now as much English as Scots) were scattered through the North Parish. Archelaus McIntire, Abigail's father, headed the most prosperous of those households. Archelaus had been an eldest son, and he inherited the family farm intact. He kept that farm and added to it, and by 1790 he owned ninety-seven acres in North Reading and patches of meadowland in two neighboring townships, a flock of seventeen sheep, cattle and oxen and other animals, and enough personal property to indicate comfort and material decency, if not wealth. Of 122 taxpayers in the North Parish in 1792, the estate of Archelaus McIntire ranked 23rd.[14]

In 1788, when Archelaus McIntire learned that his youngest

daughter was pregnant and would marry Mayo Greenleaf Patch, he may have been angry. But he had seen such things before. One in three Massachusetts women of his daughter's generation was pregnant on her wedding day, and the McIntires had contributed amply to that figure: Archelaus himself had been born three months after his parents' wedding in 1729; an older daughter had conceived a child at the age of fourteen; his only son would marry a pregnant lover in 1795.[15]

Faced with this early pregnancy, Archelaus McIntire determined to make the best of a bad situation. In the winter of 1789–90 he loaned Greenleaf Patch the cost of a shoemaker's shop and a small house and granted him use of the land on which they stood. At a stroke, Mayo Greenleaf Patch was endowed with family connections and economic independence.[16]

Northeastern Massachusetts had been exporting shoes since before the Revolution, for it possessed the prerequisites of cottage shoemaking in abundance: it was poor and overcrowded, many of its farmers had taken to raising cattle (and thus leather) on their worn-out land, and there was access to markets through Boston and the port towns of Essex County. After the Revolution, thousands of farm families turned to the making of shoes, for footwear was protected under the first national tariffs, the maritime economy on which the shoe trade depended was expanding, and they were still poor.

The rural shoemakers' shops were not entrepreneurial ventures. Neither, if we listen to the complaints of merchants and skilled artisans about "slop work" coming out of the countryside, were they likely sources of craft traditions or occupational pride. They were simply the means by which farmers on small plots of worn-out land maintained their independence.[17]

The journal of James Weston, a shoemaker in Reading during these years, suggests something of the rural shoemaker's way of life. Weston was first and last a farmer. He spent his time worrying about the weather, working his farm, repairing his house and outbuildings, and sharing farm labor with his neighbors and kin-folk. He went hunting with his brothers-in-law, took frequent fishing trips on the coast at Lynn, and made an endless round of social calls in the neighborhood. The little shop at the back of Weston's house supplemented his earnings, and he spent extended periods of time there only during the winter months. With his bags of finished shoes he went regularly to Boston, often in the company of other Reading shoemakers. The larger merchants did not yet dominate the trade in country shoes, and Weston and his neighbors went from buyer to buyer bargaining as a group, and came home with enough money to buy leather, pay debts and taxes, and survive as independent proprietors for another year. Weston enjoyed relations of neighborly cooperation with other men and he was the head of a self-supporting household and an equal participant in neighborhood affairs. In eighteenth-century Massachusetts, these attributes constituted the social definition of adult manhood. Mayo Greenleaf Patch received that status as a wedding present.[18]

Greenleaf and Abigail occupied the new house and shop early in 1790, and their tax assessments over the next few years reveal a rise from poverty to self-sufficiency or perhaps a little more. In 1790, for the first time, Greenleaf paid the tax on a small plot of land—land that he did not own. Two years later, his personal property had increased enough to rank him 56th among the 122 taxpayers in the North Parish. He wasn't getting rich, but he enjoyed a subsistence and a place in the economy of his neighborhood. That alone was a remarkable achievement for a young stranger who had come to town with almost nothing.[19]

With marriage and proprietorship came authority over a complex and growing household. Few rural shoemakers in the 1790s continued to work alone. They hired outside help, and they put their wives and children to work binding shoes. Isaac Weston brought in apprentices and journeymen, and Greenleaf Patch seems to have done the same. In 1790 the Patch family included

Greenleaf and Abigail and their infant daughter, along with a boy under the age of sixteen and an unidentified adult man. In 1792 Patch paid the tax on two polls, which suggests again that the household included an adult male dependent. It seems clear that he hired outsiders and that he regularly headed a household work team that (assuming Abigail helped) numbered at least four persons.[20]

During those same years, Greenleaf Patch enjoyed the trust of the McIntires and their neighbors. When Archelaus McIntire died in 1791, Patch was named executor of his estate. Greenleaf spent considerable effort, including two successful appearances in court, putting his father-in-law's affairs in order. In 1794 he witnessed a land transaction involving his brother-in-law, suggesting again that he was a trusted member of the McIntire family. That trust was shared by the neighbors. In 1793 the town built a schoolhouse near the Patch home, and in 1794 and 1795 the parish paid Greenleaf Patch for boarding the schoolmistress and for escorting her home at the end of the term. Those were duties that could only have gone to a trusted neighbor who ran an orderly house.[21]

Greenleaf Patch had found a home. But his gains were precarious, for they rested on his ties to the McIntires and on the use of land that belonged to them. When Archelaus died in 1791 and Patch was appointed executor of the estate, title to the McIntire properties fell to nineteen-year-old son Archelaus Jr., who was bound out to a guardian. At that point Greenleaf began to prey on the resources of Abigail's family. In succeeding years bad luck and moral failings would cost him everything he had gained.[22]

With Archelaus McIntire dead and his son shipped off to a guardian, the McIntire household shrank to two women: his widow and his daughter Deborah. The widow described herself as an invalid, and there may have been something wrong with

Deborah as well. In his will Archelaus ordered that his son take care of Deborah. Archelaus Jr. would repeat that order ten years later, when Deborah, still unmarried and still living at home, was thirty-five years old. It was a vulnerable household, and it became a target of Mayo Greenleaf Patch. Soon after Archelaus McIntire's death (and shortly before Patch was to inventory the estate), the widow complained to authorities that "considerable of my household goods & furniture have been given to my children," and begged that she be spared "whatever household furniture that may be left which is but a bare sufficiency to keep household." Since two of her four daughters were dead and Deborah lived with her, and since her only son was under the care of a guardian, the "children" could have been none other than Abigail and Greenleaf Patch, whose personal property taxes mysteriously doubled between 1791 and 1792.[23]

Patch followed this with a second and more treacherous assault on the McIntires and their resources. In November 1793 Archelaus McIntire, Jr., came of age and assumed control of the estate. Greenleaf's use of McIntire land no longer rested on his relationship with his father-in-law or on his role as executor, but on the whim of Archelaus Jr. Patch took steps that would tie him closely to young Archelaus and his land. Those steps involved a woman named Nancy Barker, who moved into North Reading sometime in 1795.

Mrs. Barker had been widowed twice—most recently, it seems, by a Haverhill shoemaker who left her with his tools and scraps of leather, a few valueless sticks of furniture, and two small children. Nancy Barker was the half sister of Mayo Greenleaf Patch, and in November 1795 she married Archelaus McIntire, Jr. She was thirty-one years old. He had turned twenty-three the previous day, and his marriage was not a matter of choice: Nancy was four months pregnant.[24]

Archelaus and Nancy were an unlikely couple, and we must ask how the match came about. If we note that Archelaus had grown up with three older sisters and no brothers, his attraction and/or vulnerability to a woman nearly nine years his senior becomes a little less mysterious. And Nancy had good reasons for being attracted to him: she was a destitute widow with two children, and he was young, perhaps manipulable, unmarried, and the owner of substantial property. Finally, Greenleaf Patch, who was the only known link between the two, had a vital interest in creating ties between himself and his in-laws' land. It is plausible (indeed, it seems inescapable) to conclude that Nancy Barker, perhaps in collusion with her half brother, seduced Archelaus McIntire, Jr., and forced a marriage. (Given how many young people experienced premarital sex, and how many of them faced propertyless futures, it would be surprising if some of them did not realize that they could acquire property or the use of it through seduction and the hurried marriages that often followed. Indeed, Greenleaf Patch's marriage to Abigail McIntire may not have been a case of bad luck turning to good, but a calculated strategy vis-à-vis seventeen-year-old Abigail and her family.)

Of course that may be nothing more than perverse speculation. It is possible that Nancy and Archelaus simply fell in love, started a baby, and got married, and that whatever role Greenleaf Patch played in the affair only added to his esteem among the McIntires and in the neighborhood. But that line of reasoning must confront an unhappy fact: the neighbors and the McIntires began to dislike Mayo Greenleaf Patch.

The first sign of trouble came in autumn of 1795, when town officials stepped into a boundary dispute between Patch and Deacon John Swain. Massachusetts towns encouraged neighbors to settle arguments among themselves. In all three parishes of Reading in the 1790s only three disagreements over boundaries came before the town government, and one of those was settled informally. Thus Greenleaf Patch was party to one of the two mediated boundary disputes in Reading in the 1790s. Then, after 1795, the schoolmistresses no longer stayed in the Patch household; they now boarded with his unfriendly neighbor Deacon Swain. In 1797 Patch complained that he had been overtaxed (another rare occurrence), demanded a reassessment, and was in fact reimbursed. Then he started going to court. In 1798 Greenleaf Patch sued Thomas Tuttle for nonpayment of a debt and was awarded nearly $100 when Tuttle failed to appear. A few months earlier, Patch had been hauled into court by William Herrick, a carpenter who claimed that Patch owed him $480. Patch denied the charge and hired a lawyer, and the court found in his favor. But Herrick appealed the case, and a higher court awarded him $100.52. Six years later, Patch's lawyer was still trying to collect his fee.[25]

There was also a question about land. In the dispute with John Swain, Greenleaf Patch was described as the "tenant" of a farm that does not match any of the properties described in the McIntires' deeds. A federal tax list demonstrates that Patch did not occupy any of his brother-in-law's land in 1798. It seems that, perhaps as early as 1795, Greenleaf Patch had been evicted from McIntire land.[26]

At some point the authorities had stopped trusting Greenleaf Patch, and by 1801 they made it clear. A year after Nancy Barker McIntire died in 1798, Archelaus remarried, then died suddenly himself in 1801. He willed his estate—two houses and the ninety-seven-acre farm, sixty more acres of upland and meadow in North Reading, and fifteen acres in the neighboring town of Lynnfield—to his children by Nancy Barker. Archelaus's second wife sold her right of dower and left town, and the property fell to girls who were four and five years of age. Their guardian would have use of the estate for many years. Abigail and Greenleaf Patch were the orphans' closest living relatives, and though they had moved away by this time surely authorities knew their whereabouts. Yet the officials passed them over and appointed William Whitridge, a cooper in North Reading, as legal guardian. For Patch it was a costly decision: it finally cut him off from prop-

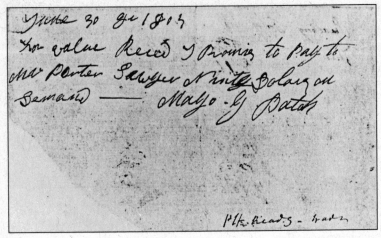

Mayo G. Patch I.O.U. (*Sawyer v. Patch,* Essex County Court of Common Pleas, March 1803, Essex Institute, Salem, Mass.)

erty that he had occupied and plotted against for many years. The promising family man of the early 1790s was, apparently, a contentious and morally bankrupt outcast by 1798.[27]

Late in 1799 Greenleaf and Abigail and their four children—including the newborn Sam Patch—left North Reading and resettled in Danvers. Famous as the hometown of the witchcraft hysteria of 1692, Danvers in 1800 was a neighborhood of farmershoemakers on the outskirts of Salem. We cannot know why the Patches selected that town, Greenleaf's father may have lived there briefly around 1780, but Abigail Patch's ties to the town were stronger. Danvers was her mother's birthplace, and she had an aunt and uncle, five first cousins, and innumerable distant kin in the town. Also, her father had owned land in Danvers. In 1785 Archelaus McIntire, Sr., had seized seven acres from John Felton, one of his in-laws, in payment for a debt. Archelaus Jr. sold the land back to the Feltons in 1794 but did not record the transaction until 1799. Possibly he agreed to allow Greenleaf Patch to use that land—an agreement that would have gotten rid of Greenleaf and provided for his sister at the same time. (Another speculation involves the troubled sister, Deborah. She disappeared from records in Reading after being mentioned as a dependent in her brother's will in 1801. Perhaps she was passed on to the Patches in Danvers, a possibility raised by the fact that a woman named Debbie McIntire hanged herself in Danvers in December 1801.)[28]

Danvers was another shoemaking town, and the Patches probably rented a farm and made shoes. They were in any case poor, obscure, and temporary residents of the town. Their names do not appear in the records of town government; late in 1799 the Danvers tax collector assessed Greenleaf for a poll tax and nothing else (no real estate, no personal property). In a census taken at about the same time, the Patch household included Greenleaf and Abigail, their children, and no one else, which suggests that they no longer hired help. But this, like everything else about the family's career in Danvers, rests on guesswork. We know only that they lived there.[29]

Late in 1802 Greenleaf Patch received a reprieve. His half brother Job Davis (his mother's son by her first marriage, and the brother of Nancy Barker) died in the fishing village of Marblehead and left Patch one-fifth of his estate. The full property included a butcher's shop at the edge of town, an unfinished new house, and what was described as a "mansion house" that needed repairs. The property was mortgaged to merchants named William and Benjamin T. Reid, and the heirs inherited the mortgage along with the estate.[30]

The other heirs sold to the Reids, but Greenleaf Patch, whether from demented ambition or lack of alternatives, moved his family to Marblehead early in 1803. He finished the new house, moved into it, and reopened the shop. In 1804 he was assessed a poll tax and listed as the resident of the house and shop and the owner of a horse and two pigs. At least on paper, Green-leaf Patch was back in business.[31]

But it was a shaky business—founded on property that Greenleaf did not truly own and burdened by debt. Some of the debts were old. Patch owed Ebenezer Goodale of Danvers $54. He also owed Porter Sawyer of Reading $92 (and paid a part of it by laboring at 75 cents a day). Then there were debts incurred in Marblehead: $70 to the widow Sarah Dolebar; a few dollars for building materials and furnishings bought from the Reids; $50 to a farmer named Benjamin Burnham; $33 to Zachariah King of Danvers; $35 to Joseph Holt of Reading; another $35 to Caleb Totman of Hampshire County. Finally, there was the original mortgage held by the Reids. Greenleaf Patch's renewed dreams of independence collapsed under the weight of these debts. In March 1803 a creditor repossessed property valued at $150. A few weeks before Christmas of that year the sheriff seized the new house. In the following spring, Patch missed a mortgage payment and the Reids took him to court, seized the remaining property, and sold it at auction. Still, Patch retained the right to reclaim it by paying his debts. The story ends early in 1805, when the Reids bought Greenleaf Patch's right of redemption for $60. Patch had struggled with the Marblehead property for two years, and it had come to nothing.[32]

With that, the Patches exhausted the family connections on which they had subsisted since their marriage. The long stay in North Reading and the moves to Danvers and Marblehead had been determined by the availability of relatives and their re-sources. In 1807 the Patches moved to the mill village of Paw-tucket, Rhode Island, nearly one hundred miles south of the neighborhoods in which the Patches and McIntires had always lived. The move was the climactic moment in their history: it marked their passage out of the family economy and into the la-bor market.

New England families did not move into Pawtucket's mills

unless something bad had happened—usually to the man of the house. A broken Mayo Greenleaf Patch fit that pattern perfectly. Pawtucket was enjoying a small boom in 1807, and if Greenleaf had been willing and physically able he could have found work. But we know that he did not work in Pawtucket. He drank, he stole the money earned by Abigail and the children, and he threatened them frequently with violence. Then, in 1812, he abandoned them. Abigail waited six years and divorced him in 1818. To the court she recounted Greenleaf's drinking and his threats and his refusal to work, then revealed what for her was the determining blow: Mayo Greenleaf Patch had drifted back to Massachusetts and had been caught trying to pass counterfeit money. In February 1817 he had been sent to the Massachusetts State Prison at Charlestown. He was released in August 1818—at the age of fifty-two—and that is the last we hear of him.[33]

The invitation to move to Pawtucket may have come from the mill owner Samuel Slater himself, who was searching far beyond Pawtucket for child workers, recruiting among the urban and rural poor. The seaports and old farming towns of northeastern Massachusetts produced such persons in abundance, and as early as 1797 one of Slater's partners reported Marblehead as a particularly likely spot: ". . . the inhabitants appear to be very Poor their Houses very much on the decline—I apprehend it might be a good place for a Cotton Manufactory Children appearing very Plenty." Slater may have recruited the Patch family on one of his periodic trips to Salem and Marblehead.[34]

Pawtucket was something new in America: a town where women and children supported men or lived without them, and where women reconstructed lives that had been damaged in the failure of their men. Abigail Patch was one of those women, and her grim work of reconstruction coincided with the childhood and youth of her son Sam.

Independence—along with its burdens, dangers, and opportunities—was something that Abigail Patch had never expected. She had grown up in a family that, judging from available evidence, was a model of eighteenth-century rural patriarchy. Her father possessed a respected family name and a farm inherited from his father that he passed on to his son; he was the steward of the family's past and future as well as its present provider. As a McIntire, he conferred status on every member of his household. As a voter, he spoke for the family in town affairs; as a father and church member, he led them in daily prayer; and as a proprietor, he made decisions about the allocation of family resources, handled relations with outsiders, and performed most of the heavy work.

Archelaus McIntire had married Abigail Felton of Danvers and had brought her to a town where she lived apart from her own family but surrounded by McIntires; her status in North Reading derived from her husband's family and not her own. She and her daughters spent long days cooking and cleaning, gardening, tending and milking cows, making cloth and clothing, and caring for the younger children—work that took place in and near the house and not on the farm. And while that work was essential, New England men assumed that it would be done and placed no special importance on it. The notion of a separate and cherished domestic sphere was slow to catch on in the countryside and, if we may judge from the spending patterns of the McIntires, it was absent from their house. Archelaus McIntire spent his money on implements of work and male sociability—horses, wagons, well-made cider barrels, a rifle—and not on the china, tea sets, and feather beds that were appearing in towns and among the rural well-to-do. The McIntires owned a solid table and a Bible and a few other books, and there was a clock and a set of glassware as well. But the most imposing piece of furniture in the house was Archelaus's desk. Insofar as the McIntire children had any quiet evenings at home, they probably

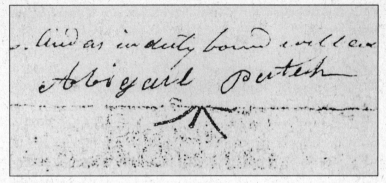

Abigail Patch signature (Petition of Abigail Patch for Divorce, Records of the Supreme Court of Providence County, Providence College Archives)

spent them listening to the father read his Bible (the mother was illiterate) or keeping quiet while he figured his accounts.[35]

As the fourth and youngest daughter, Abigail traded work and quiet subordination for security, for the status that went with being a female McIntire, perhaps even for peace and affection in the home. And as she set up house with Mayo Greenleaf Patch, it is unlikely that she expected things to change. Years later Abigail recalled that in taking a husband she expected not a partner but "a friend and protector." She spoke of her "duties," and claimed to have been an "attentive and affectionate wife." It was the arrangement that she had learned as a child: husbands supported their wives and protected them; wives worked and were attentive to their husbands' needs and wishes. All available evidence suggests that those rules governed the Patch household during the years in North Reading.[36]

Abigail and Greenleaf Patch maintained neither the way of life nor the living standards necessary for the creation of a private, domestic world in which Abigail could have exercised independent authority. The house was small and there was little money, and the household regularly included people from outside the immediate family—Greenleaf's apprentices and journeymen, the schoolmistresses, and probably Nancy Barker and her two children.

At work, rural shoemakers maintained a rigid division of labor based on sex and age, and Greenleaf's authority as a father and master craftsman affected every corner of Abigail's life. Abigail's kitchen, if indeed it was a separate room, was a busy place. It was there that she bound shoes as a semiskilled and subordinate member of her husband's work team, cared for the children (she gave birth five times between 1789 and 1799), did the cooking, cleaning, and laundry for a large household, and stared across the table at apprentices and journeymen who symbolized her own drudgery and her husband's authority at the same time. As Abigail Patch endured her hectic and exhausting days, she may have dreamed of wallpapered parlors and privacy and quiet nights by the fire with her husband. But she must have known that such things were for others and not for her. They had played little role in her father's house, and they were totally absent from her own.[37]

Greenleaf Patch, despite (or perhaps because of) his meager resources, consistently made family decisions—not just the economic choices that were indisputably his to make, but decisions that shaped the texture and feeling of life within the family.

Take the naming of children. Since the beginnings of settlement, New Englanders reinforced their corporate sense of family by naming children for their parents, grandparents, and other close relatives. As Greenleaf Patch was separated from his own family and dependent on McIntire resources, when children came along we might expect him and Abigail to have honored McIntire relatives. That is not what happened. The first Patch child—the one conceived before the wedding—was a daughter born in 1789. She was named Molly, after a daughter of Greenleaf's brother Isaac. A son came two years later, and the Patches named him Greenleaf. Another daughter, born in 1794, was given the name Nabby, after another of Isaac Patch's daughters.

A second son, born in 1798, was named for Isaac's son Samuel (or perhaps Isaac's and Greenleaf's brother Samuel, who worked the farm next to Isaac's). When that child died, the son born the following year—the daredevil Sam Patch—was also named Samuel. (The practice of giving a dead child's name to the next-born child of the same sex was a marker of customs that valued the family over the individual identity of the child, and it was falling into disuse in the eighteenth century. That Greenleaf Patch persisted in this practice at the turn of the nineteenth century suggests a firm, die-hard traditionalism on his part.) The last child, a boy born in Marblehead in 1803, was named for Greenleaf's brother Isaac. All the children's names came from the little world in Wenham—uncle Samuel's nine-acre farm, the shared barn and outbuildings, and the eighteen acres operated by brother Isaac—where Greenleaf Patch had presumably spent much of his childhood.[38]

Religion is a second and more important sphere in which Greenleaf seems to have made choices for the family. Abigail McIntire had grown up in a religious household. Her father had joined the North Parish Congregational Church a few days after the birth of his first child in 1762. Her mother had followed two months later, and the couple baptized each of their five children. The children in their turn became churchgoers. Abigail's sisters Mary and Mehitable joined churches, and her brother Archelaus Jr. expressed a strong interest in religion as well. Among Abigail's parents and siblings, only the questionable Deborah left no religious traces.[39]

Churchgoing traditions in the Patch family were not as strong. Greenleaf's father and his first wife joined the Congregational church in Wenham during the sixth year of their marriage in 1736, but the family's ties to religion weakened after that. Timothy Patch, Jr., did not baptize any of his thirteen children, neither the ten presented him by his first wife nor the three born to Thomasine Greenleaf Davis, the nonchurchgoing widow whom he married in 1759. None of Greenleaf's brothers or sisters became full members of the church, and only his oldest brother, Andrew, "owned the covenant"—a practice permitting adult children of church members to place their own families under the church's watch and governance without themselves becoming members.[40]

Among the Wenham Patches, however, there remained pockets of religiosity, and they centered, perhaps significantly, in the homes of Greenleaf's brother Isaac and his uncle Samuel. Uncle Samuel was a communicant of the church, and although Isaac had no formal religious ties, he married a woman who owned the covenant. The churchgoing tradition that Greenleaf Patch carried into marriage was ambiguous, but it almost certainly was weaker than that carried by his wife. And from his actions as an adult, we may assume that Greenleaf was not a man who would have been drawn to the religious life.

As Greenleaf and Abigail married and had children, the question of religion could not have been overlooked. The family lived near the church in which Abigail had been baptized and in which her family and her old friends spent Sunday mornings. As the wife of Greenleaf Patch, Abigail had three options: she could lead her husband into the church; she could, as many women did, join the church without her husband and take her children with her; or she could break with the church and spend Sundays with an irreligious husband. The first two choices would assert Abigail's authority and independent rights within the family. The third would be a capitulation, and it would have painful results. It would cut her off from the religious community into which she had been born, and it would remove her young family from religious influence.

The Patches lived in North Reading for twelve years and had five children in that town. Neither Greenleaf nor Abigail joined the church, and none of the babies was baptized. We cannot retrieve the actions and feelings that produced those facts, but this much is certain: in the crucial area of religious practice, the

Patch family bore the stamp of Greenleaf Patch and not of Abigail McIntire. When Greenleaf and Abigail named a baby or chose whether to join a church or baptize a child, the decisions extended his family's history and not hers.[41]

Abigail accepted her husband's dominance in family affairs throughout the years in North Reading, years in which he played, however ineptly and dishonestly, his role as "friend and protector." With Greenleaf's final separation from the family economy and his humiliating failure in Marblehead, Abigail began to impose her will upon domestic decisions. The result, within a few years, was a full-scale feminine takeover of the family.

In 1803 Abigail gave birth to her sixth child in Marblehead, a boy named Isaac. She was still a relatively youthful thirty-three, and Isaac, perhaps significantly, would be her last child. Isaac was baptized at the Second Congregational Church in Marblehead, though neither of his parents was a member. And in April 1807 Abigail and her oldest daughter, Molly, presented themselves for baptism at the First Baptist Church in Pawtucket. By then Abigail was thirty-seven, had been married nineteen years, and had five living children. Molly was eighteen and unmarried. Neither followed the customs of the McIntire and Patch families, where women who joined churches did so within a few years of marriage. Abigail and Molly Patch presented themselves for baptism not because they had reached predictable points in their life cycles but because they had decided to join a church.[42]

At the same time Abigail's daughters appear to have dropped their given names and evolved new ones drawn from their mother's and not their father's side of the family. Molly joined the church as Polly Patch. Two years later this same woman married under the name Mary Patch. (Abigail's oldest sister, who had died in the year that Abigail married Greenleaf Patch, had been named Mary.) The second Patch daughter, Nabby, joined the First Baptist Church in 1811, but by then she was calling herself Abby. By 1829 she was known as Abigail. The daughters of Abi-

gail Patch, it seems, were affiliating with their mother and sever-
ing symbolic ties with their father, and they were doing so while
Greenleaf remained in the house.[43]

For five years Abigail worked and took the children to church
while her husband drank, stole her money, and issued sullen
threats. He ran off in 1812, and by 1820 Abigail, now officially
head of the household, had rented a house and was taking in
boarders. Over the next few years the Patch sons left home: Sam
for New Jersey, Isaac for Illinois, Greenleaf for parts unknown.
Among the Patch children, only Mary (Molly, Polly) stayed in
Pawtucket. Her husband died in 1817, leaving her with two small
children and pregnant with another. In 1825 the widowed Mary
was caught sleeping with a married man and was expelled from
her church. Two years later—as the result of an extended affair,
or perhaps of a new one—Mary gave birth to a child out of wed-
lock. Sometime before 1830 Abigail closed the boardinghouse
and moved into a little house on Main Street with Mary and her
four children. Abigail and her daughter and granddaughters were
to live in that house for the next twenty-five years.[44]

The neighbors remembered Abigail Patch as a quiet, steady
little woman who went to the Baptist church. She did so with all
the Patch women and none of the Patch men. Mary had joined
with her, and Mary's daughters followed in their turn: Mary and
Sarah Anne in 1829, Emily (the illegitimate girl born in 1827) in
1841. First Baptist was a Calvinist church, subsidized and governed by the owners of Pawtucket's mills. The Articles of the
Church insisted that most of humankind was hopelessly damned,
that God chose only a few for eternal life and had in fact chosen
them before the beginning of time, that "the heart is deceitful
&c., and that the carnal mind is enmity against God, not subject
to his law &c. And that in the flesh dwelleth no good thing." It
was not a cheerful message. But it struck home among the Patch
women—and perhaps among the other Pawtucket women who
filled three-fourths of the seats on Sunday mornings.[45]

The Patch women spent most of their time in the house on Main Street. Abigail bought the house in 1842 (it was the first piece of real estate that the Patches had ever owned), and her granddaughters Mary and Emily taught school in the front room for many years. The household was self-supporting, and the women's relationships with men were either troubled or nonexistent. Abigail's daughter and the granddaughters she helped to raise either avoided men or got into trouble when they did not. Abigail never remarried. Mary also remained single for the rest of her life. Sarah Anne Jones, Mary's second daughter, was thirty-six years old and unmarried when called before a church committee in 1853. Although she married a man named Kelley during the investigation, she (like her mother) was excommunicated "because she has given this church reason to believe she is licentious." Sarah Anne's sisters, the schoolteachers Mary and Emily, were spinsters all their lives. Abigail Patch lived on Main Street with the other women until 1854, when she died, after a long and apparently trying illness, at the age of eighty-four.[46]

The women lived quietly and simply (Abigail's furniture and other belongings were valued at only $17 at her death) but with as much outward respectability as they could muster. Their pupils remembered Abigail's granddaughters with affection; Reverend Benedict recalled that Abigail was "of a most respectable character," and that the other Patches (despite the two dismissals from Benedict's church) were "of good reputation." Behind the parlor schoolroom and the kindly cover-ups, however, was a backroom world inhabited only by the Patch women. Within that world, Abigail and her daughter Mary reconstructed not only themselves but the history of their family.[47]

Toward the end of the nineteenth century, a Providence newspaperman decided to write about the mill worker–hero Sam Patch. He asked Emily Jones, Abigail's youngest granddaughter, about the Patch family history. Emily, born in 1827, knew about the family's past only through what she had picked up from her mother and grandmother. Her response to the reporter revealed the attempts at discretion and the selective amnesia with which any family remembers its past. In the case of the Patch family, however, the fabrications were sadly revealing.[48]

Miss Jones told the reporter nothing about what the Patch women did for a living, nothing of their religious or personal lives, certainly nothing about the promiscuity of her mother and sister or of her own illegitimate birth. Instead she recounted the public lives of the Patch men. Emily claimed that her oldest uncle, Greenleaf Patch, Jr., had gone off to Salem to become a lawyer. That is not true: no one named Greenleaf Patch was ever licensed to practice law in Massachusetts. About her uncle Sam Patch, Emily said that in the 1820s he operated a spinning mill of his own north of Pawtucket, but failed when his partner ran off with the funds. This is possible, but there is no evidence that it happened. What we do know about Sam Patch is that he was a drunkard with a powerful suicidal drive who succeeded in killing himself at the age of thirty. Miss Jones remembered that her youngest uncle, Isaac, moved to Illinois and became a farmer— another piece of family knowledge that cannot be verified. It seems that Abigail Patch and Mary Patch Jones embellished the careers of their men, giving them a respectability they may not have had. It may have been a way of erasing some of the pain created by Mayo Greenleaf Patch.[49]

Emily's memory of her grandfather upholds that suspicion. We know that Greenleaf moved to Pawtucket, headed the household in 1810, and stayed until 1812. But Miss Jones told the reporter that her grandfather had been a farmer in Massachusetts, and that he died before Abigail brought her children to Pawtucket.[50]

In the 1820s, when Sam Patch was a famous jumper, he did not talk about his family. He told one young friend that he had been born in Pawtucket and then orphaned, another that he had been a sailor. A girl who knew him thought that he was a foreigner, and a newsman in Providence did not even know that Sam Patch was from neighboring Pawtucket. Sam burst into public consciousness as the Jersey Jumper, the man who leaped waterfalls in the newspapers. He was a nineteenth-century hero: no past, no family connections, no firm ties to any place. It was what the public was learning to expect, and it may have been what Sam Patch wanted.[51]

There was not much family history worth remembering. Sam Patch spent his childhood in the wreckage that his father had made. He could not remember North Reading (notation of Sam's birth was the final record of the Patches in that town), and it is unlikely that he ever saw his father treated with neighborliness or respect. He knew him only as a broken man who made the house smell of alcohol, a man whose despairing silences could explode into incomprehensible and terrifying violence. When Sam was thirteen, the father abandoned him forever. In his twenties, Sam Patch was described as melancholy, verging on morose. He may have retreated into himself at an early age. He was also a heavy drinker, and that too may have begun early on. Drunkenness and melancholy: these were what Greenleaf Patch finally possessed, and what he passed on to his second son.

Sam's mother knew that children were supposed to work and obey. She was trying to keep a family together without a husband, and she counted on the money her children could earn in Pawtucket. She found jobs for them, and she doubtless took them to church and enrolled them in Sunday school. We have reason to believe that Sam Patch was not a good boy, and he probably did not pay much attention to Reverend Benedict's half-comprehensible threats about predestination, limited atonement, and human inability. At Sunday school, the teachers tried to explain: Sam was bad and could do nothing to make himself good. They taught reading from the King James Bible, then set the children to memorizing Bible verses—a pedagogical form that taught obedience and rote memory, not imagination and individual moral development. After a week in the mills and Sundays listening to Reverend Benedict and his teachers, the child Sam Patch returned to Abigail's life of work and prayer, and to her hardening insistence that much of the family's history had never happened. We do not know how Sam held up under all this. But we do know that he rejected it. Reverend Benedict tells us that "Sam Patch's course of life [was] a source of deep affliction to his mother. . . ."[52]

Sam went to work at Samuel Slater's White Mill at the age of seven or eight. The White Mill, completed in 1799 on a site directly across the river from Slater's first mill, was small and unpretentious like its predecessor. (The original floor space was only forty by twenty-six feet; in 1808 it was expanded to seventy-six by twenty-nine feet.) The wooden structure was two stories high, and, unlike the brick behemoths that mill owners would begin building in the 1820s, it blended into the neighborhood. Painted white and topped with a cupola, to the child Sam Patch the White Mill might have looked like the First Baptist Church.[53]

Inside, the mill was full of children. In the ground-floor carding room scores of boys and girls worked under an overseer. They were given raw cotton that other children, working in their homes, had cleansed of dirt and twigs, and fed it into carding machines with revolving wire teeth that combed it until the fibers lay parallel. The carding machines turned raw cotton into loose cotton ropes. More children tended roving machines that twisted and stretched the cotton into longer and tighter ropes called roves, then ran the roves upstairs to the spinning room. There skilled men worked the spinning mules, with the help of children called piecers and scavengers. Scavengers (the smaller children were best at this) crawled between the carriage and frame and under the long lines of thread, cleaning the floor and machinery and picking lint and dust balls off the threads. Piecers stood outside the frame and knotted broken threads at the end of a run, tying at a rate of five or six knots a minute.[54]

The millwork that Sam and the other children did was neither dangerous nor particularly difficult. True, Reverend Benedict reported that some of the children "had their hands terribly lacerated" by the carding machines, and none but the most nimble scavengers avoided blows from the moving parts of the machinery. But there are—apart from Benedict's—few accounts of injuries to the children. As for factory discipline, it was by contemporary standards neither brutal nor cruel. Samuel Slater himself frequently roamed the carding room, exerting what an admirer called "a strict, though mild and paternal scrutiny" over the children, and boss spinners sometimes backed up their commands with slaps and ear boxings. (A child who later worked under the boss spinner Sam Patch recalled—with no hint of resentment—that "many a time he gave me a cuff over the ears.") But routine discipline in the mill consisted of threats, humiliation, and occasional praise. The mills, after all, were in business to produce cotton yarn, not to brutalize children. While yarn was produced to the mill owners' and the spinners' satisfaction, Sam and his young workmates were relatively safe.[55]

The children's chief complaint was not injury or brutality but the deadening monotony of simple, attention-demanding tasks synchronized with machines that ran twelve hours a day. The rooms were cold in winter and hot and humid in summer, the air was filled with cotton dust, and the factories were among the noisiest places that men had ever made. A Boston gentleman who visited Pawtucket in 1801 and peered into a room full of child workers felt "pity for these poor creatures, plying in a contracted room, among flyers and coggs, at an age when nature requires for them air, space, and sports. There was a dull dejection in the countenances of all of them. This, united with the deafen-

ing roar of the falls and the rattling of the machinery," made it a
very unpleasant place. Mill children suffered from swollen ankles
and loss of appetite, and they were tired all the time. Whenever
the machines stopped, youngsters crawled into corners and fell
asleep. At the end of the day many dragged themselves home,
went to bed without supper, and awoke only to return to work. In
the mills, slaps and cuffings were used most often to keep drows-
ing children awake.[56]

Sam Patch spent his childhood and youth in the mills, picking
lint and tying knots amid the din of machinery and falling water,
passing whole days in a half-sleep punctuated by shouts and occasional slaps across the head. He seems to have been good at it:
he learned the rules and skills of the spinning room, and in the
1820s he took his place as one of the first American-born boss
spinners.

The boss spinners were a remarkable set of men. The spinning mule among the biggest machines in the world, and it
had revolutionized the making of cotton cloth. Yet before the in-
troduction of the self-acting mule in the 1840s, mule spinning
was only partly automated, and none but skilled, experienced
men operated the machines. With each cycle of the spinning
mule a long, heavy carriage rode out on tracks from the machine,
stretching and twisting the carded and roved cotton into yarn
(what we call thread). The carriage then reversed, and the finished thread wound onto bobbins attached to the machine. It
was at this final stage that the boss spinner's skills became crucial.
With one hand he depressed a wire that ran the length of the carriage, holding the threads tight and flat. With the other hand he
grasped a wheel that pushed the carriage and adjusted its speed,
and with his knee he muscled the carriage toward the bobbins,
carefully controlling the speed and keeping a lookout along the
line of threads. The work required experience, along with a practiced mix of strength and a sensitive touch: return the carriage
too slowly and the power-driven bobbins would snap the threads;

push it too quickly and the threads tangled. "The skill and tact required in the operator," said an English observer of the process, "deserve no little admiration, and are well entitled to the most liberal recompense."[57]

Before 1820 most spinners in New England mills were emigrants from the factory towns of Lancashire. They were veterans who knew that their skills were essential, and they commanded respect. Slater and the other proprietors may have owned the spinning mules, but the spinners were semi-independent subcontractors: they worked for piece rates, and it was they who hired, trained, paid, and disciplined their own helpers. (An illustration in a book praising Samuel Slater places a well-dressed supervisor behind the spinner, but in fact such men were either ineffective or absent.) Each spinner adjusted the machine to his own body and pace of work; when a spinner had labored with a mule for a few weeks, no one else could run it—a partnership be-

Mule spinning (from George S. White, comp., *Memoir of Samuel Slater*, Philadelphia, 1836, author's collection)

tween man and machine that made the man irreplaceable. Pawtucket's mule spinners earned as much as the overseers downstairs, and much more than the repair mechanics, clerks, and
other men who worked in and around the mills. The owners
sometimes branded the mule spinners as arrogant, self-
important, and often drunken and riotous. They may have been
all that, but first and last the spinners were fiercely independent—skilled, formidable artisans who had constructed a craftsman's world within factory walls.[58]

We can imagine why the child Sam Patch did well in the spinning room. There, at least, work and discipline were tied to un-
derstandable rules enforced by predictable authorities. If Sam
showed up on time, stayed awake, and attended to his tasks, he
avoided humiliation and occasionally won a bit of praise. He may
have seen being a boss spinner as a good alternative to the brute
impossibilities of the rest of his life. The spinners made what
looked like good money, they exerted a fatherly authority that
Sam did not know at home, and they commanded respect in the
mills and in the neighborhood. For their part, the English mule
spinners may have recognized Sam as an able boy (and perhaps
as a boy who needed help) and trained him up as one of their
own. Sam worked hard, paid attention, and became one of them.

The falls of the Blackstone River provided a second way out of
Sam's closed world. Travelers on the road between Providence
and Boston often paused to look at Pawtucket Falls, for the white
water cascading fifty feet over broken black rocks was a stirring
sight. "Romantic," granted Timothy Dwight, president of Yale
College. An Englishwoman deemed it "a very respectable fall,"
while a young American romantic pronounced it "a scene of astonishing beauty and sublimity." "It is a circumstance rather unusual," he continued, "that an object of such wild grandeur,
should be environed in the midst of dwelling houses, and the cot-

ton establishments which the higher surface of the water supplies."[59]

Samuel Slater and the others who built Pawtucket's factories had little use for the "wild grandeur" of their waterfall. Their mill dams and raceways diminished the falls, flooded farmland upriver from them, and damaged a valuable fishing ground, and they fought legal battles with their neighbors over their right to do that. When the manufacturers mentioned the river and falls, they talked of millsites and the volume of water and the possibilities of flooding, not of its beauty. They wanted to tame the waterfall and make it useful, and when they built a village upstream from it the buildings had the effect of diminishing the falls and then hiding them from view. By 1820 mills, workshops, houses, and fences built to keep livestock from falling into the river blocked the view of the river and falls from nearly every point in Pawtucket. Sam Patch could have passed through this densely built townscape without seeing the waterfall at its center.

A short walk through crooked streets filled with lumber, cotton bales, and foraging pigs and dogs brought Sam to the White Mill. From the windows of the spinning room upstairs he could look directly onto the Blackstone River above the falls. From that viewpoint it was Samuel Slater's river: the mill dam crossed the river a few yards upstream from Sam's window, and at the end of the dam on the far side was Slater's first mill, its machines and busy children visible through the windows. Sam's eyes could follow the river downstream to where it passed under a sturdy wooden bridge and disappeared from sight.[60]

The centerpiece of Samuel Slater's Pawtucket was not the waterfall but the bridge that passed over it. The bridge was the one point at which workaday life brought citizens of Pawtucket into contact with the falls. The bridge had been thrown—not by Slater, but by proprietors early in the eighteenth century—directly across the line of the falls, and it too hid the waterfall. The water was high to the north of the bridge and lower and more

Pawtucket Falls, by J. R. Smith (author's collection)

troubled to the south, but walkers could view the falls themselves only if they paused to lean over the south rail. In views of Pawtucket, they seldom did that. When an artist early in the nineteenth century sketched the falls and bridge he pictured a lone walker and men in a carriage passing over the bridge. Their gazes are fixed straight ahead as they pass high over the river and at a level with the village, moving resolutely through Slater's landscape while the water roars and crashes far beneath them.

An occasional visitor lamented that the bridge ruined the view of the falls. One Englishman insisted that "the scenic effect of the fall is most materially injured by the situation of Pawtucket bridge," and Josiah Quincy of Boston agreed that the bridge "hides much of the grandeur of the scene." But such complaints missed the point: while the bridge hid the waterfall, it used the falls to call attention to itself and to the built landscapes that it joined together. Pawtucket owed its growth to the technological conquest of a waterfall. The layout of the village and the placement of the bridge completed that conquest visually and emotionally.[61]

An occasional visitor explored the wilder territory below the falls. The Frenchman Jacques Milbert looked downriver from the bridge in 1818, and left a picture of what he saw:

After crossing several dams the river advances with apparent calm until it suddenly leaps sixty feet in a magnificent cascade. From this same point of vantage I could see the water boiling after its drop between massive perpendicular rocks that are remarkable for their imposing elevation. Trees growing out of these natural walls arched over the precipice, making it very dark. [Milbert found a pathway and] stood at the foot of the falls, where I could see the whole picture. My ear was deafened by the roar of the cataract and my eyes bedazzled by whirling waters and spurting snowy foam. I saw waves force their way between rocks they had rounded or break on others whose sharp points revealed their primitive character. The pressure of the falls on the air was so strong that the foliage was kept in constant motion. A brilliant rainbow touching first one bank then the other was the final poetic note in this magnificent picture, in which the rustic mills bordering the falls and the bold bridge surmounting it were not unworthy accessories.[62]

In more boisterous and less educated ways, Sam Patch and the other factory boys knew the waterfall that had dazzled Milbert. In the mills, underneath the clatter of machinery and the shouts of the bosses, the invisible falls sent up their magic and incessant roar. And at night, when the mill canal was shut down and the river ran with full force, the waterfall rattled windows and invaded the imaginations of boys all over town.[63]

Whenever they were free, the boys and young men of Pawtucket converged on the falls. The tides from Narragansett Bay brought ocean fish all the way up to that point, and men fished from the bridge and from the shore below, or threw out nets from rocks in the stream itself. The boys swam, they took boats into the pool below the cataract, and they played and fished along the banks. These were times given over to the rough, democratic companionship of boys, to the seductive roar and disorder of falling water, perhaps to the first experience of the warm, comforting blur of alcohol. Some of the boys, Sam Patch among them, took chances there.[64]

Early on, boys began jumping from the bridge into the river below the falls. It was a drop of more than fifty feet, and the bottom was rocky and dangerous. At one spot near the east bank, however, the falls had carved a deep hole, and there the aerated water was, as a local journalist put it, "nearly as soft as an ocean of feathers." The boys called it "the pot." In 1805, when the four-story Yellow Mill went up on the east side just below the falls (two stories above road level, two below), the jumpers wasted little time. That year three young men made the astounding eighty-foot leap from the peaked roof of the Yellow Mill into the pot. In 1813 the six-story Stone Mill went up on the east side, just below the bridge. In ensuing years the bravest Pawtucket boys—Sam Patch among them—regularly made a running leap from its flat roof into the pot, a descent of close to one hundred feet.

The jumpers attracted crowds, then the attention of the au-

Pawtucket Falls, by J. Milbert (Print Collection, The New York Public Library)

thorities. "Although no one was hurt by this unusual sport," reported Reverend Benedict, "yet there was a hazard, and not always a decency [some of the boys were naked?], in the performance, which, in the course of a few years, led the citizens to break it up, and young Patch wandered off in other regions in pursuit of this strange and anomalous vocation." But in fact the ban on jumping was either ineffective or came long after Sam Patch had left Pawtucket; boys leaped from the Yellow Mill at least as late as November 1829.[65]

Falls jumping, like mule spinning, was a craft. It called for bravery that verged on foolhardiness, but it required self-possession and a mastery of skills as well. The Pawtucket boys all jumped in the same way: feet first, breathing in as they fell; they stayed underwater long enough to frighten spectators, then shot triumphantly to the surface. It was truly dangerous play, but people in Pawtucket—both jumpers and spectators—knew that the leaper would be hurt only if he lost his concentration and did not follow the rules. Most of the leapers were factory boys, but sons of farmers and artisans, locals who despised the mill families, also turned up at the falls. Two of the three young men who first jumped from the Yellow Mill were blacksmiths, one of them a son of Nehemiah Bucklin, the farmer who had owned the property on the east side of the falls before the factories came. The waterfall may have been the one place in town where the prejudices, failures, and forebodings of adult Pawtucket could be forgotten—a place where boys could take the measure of each other as boys and nothing else. It was there that Sam Patch began turning himself into a hero.[66]

Mule spinning and falls jumping: they were two ways in which Sam Patch separated himself from the devastating legacy of Greenleaf Patch, and from Abigail Patch's grim struggle to make decency out of hard work and family secrets. In the spinning room and at the waterfall, Sam Patch fashioned skills, a reputation, and a sense of his own worth that had nothing to do with his family's history. He modeled himself after the most admirable men and the bravest boys he knew, and he forged an identity out of his own trained and practiced performances. Given what he had to work with, Sam Patch was beginning to make something of himself.

★ II ★

PATERSON

In his mid-twenties Sam Patch left Pawtucket and reappeared in Paterson, New Jersey—twelve miles west of New York City. We cannot know why he made the move, but Paterson was a good place for him: it was a bigger factory town than Pawtucket, and it sat beside a more famous waterfall.

Educated travelers knew Paterson as the site of Passaic Falls, one of the scenic wonders of North America. The young architect Benjamin Latrobe spent part of his honeymoon there in 1800, and suggested it as a good place for an American academy of landscape art. Passaic Falls, said Latrobe, "combine every thing in themselves and in the magic circle of which they are the Center, of which Nature forms her sublimest Landscapes, excepting the ocean." Other cultivated visitors agreed that Passaic Falls provided a rare combination of the beautiful, the sublime, and the picturesque. The Passaic River widened and slowed above Paterson, then made an abrupt turn just at the brink and dropped seventy feet (second only to Niagara in the eastern United States) into a deep shaded pool. The falls, the dark and craggy rocks, the dangerous sheer cliffs on both banks, and the ancient forest that brooded over the scene were perfect expressions of natural power and primordial gloom. The view at the falls was "grand and beautiful," "sublime—almost terrific," "frightful," "a terrible prospect," "a scene of singular grandeur and beauty." Those who wanted to escape from these sublimities into the more reassuring picturesque could turn their backs to the falls and precipice and peer through the trees onto shaped land: a broad plain of farms and country roads in the eighteenth century and, after 1815, the sprawl of Paterson along the lower Passaic River.[1]

Paterson itself possessed a well-known history. It had been founded as the "National Manufacturing City" in 1792, with the active support of Secretary of the Treasury Alexander Hamilton, and with money from a joint-stock company called the Society for the Encouragement of Useful Manufactures (SUM). Pierre Charles L'Enfant, the French architect who had laid out the federal city of Washington, designed an ambitious and costly dam and millrace for the SUM. The project took two years to complete, and the first Paterson factory opened in 1794. The enterprise was premature: capital, skills, and markets for domestic manufactures were limited, and the Paterson factory closed its doors in 1796. The company leased a few millsites in the early years of the nineteenth century, and a few more during the War of 1812. Then the commercialization of inland farming after 1815 created an exploding domestic demand for textiles and other American-made goods. Factories, mills, and forges sprang up along L'Enfant's old Paterson raceways, sending a flood of finished goods to the nearby entrepôt of New York, and from there to markets all over the United States. By 1827 Hamilton's ghost town was a manufacturing city of six thousand, described by a New Jersey newspaper (one that no longer apologized for such things) as "this flourishing Manchester of America."[2]

Sam Patch was among the thousands of workers who moved into Paterson in the 1820s. He found work as a mule spinner and,

in September 1827, he performed a leap at Passaic F...
him into the newspapers for the first time. The jump was a cha...
lenge to the ambitions and pretensions of a Paterson entrepreneur. It was also, like all of Sam's performances, a grand and
eccentric gesture thrown into contemporary conversations about
nature and economic development, class and masculinity, and
the proper uses of waterfalls.

A builder and sawmill owner named Timothy B. Crane had
bought the forested north bank of Passaic Falls in August 1827.
In September he turned it into a commercial pleasure garden,
announcing that he would reshape the forest in the name of material and moral progress: "Although Nature has done more for
this spot of earth, than perhaps any other of its size, to render it
beautiful and interesting to the visitor, it is nevertheless susceptible of very great embellishments, from the hand of ART," and
with that he improved the grounds with gravel walkways, imported bushes and trees, and a combined ice cream parlor and
saloon. Crane called his establishment the Forest Garden. During the next few summers crowds went there for ice cream and
conversation, and there were periodic circuses, Indian war
dances, and displays of fireworks as well.[3]

The Forest Garden was an outdoor restaurant with facilities
for putting on shows—a copy of Niblo's and the other summer
gardens of New York City. But Crane and his supporters advertised it as something more: an artful refinement of raw nature
that transformed a forbidding wilderness into an opportunity for
aesthetic contemplation. The *Paterson Intelligencer* praised the
Forest Garden as a retreat where "the refinements of taste and
art [are] combined with the varied and romantic beauties of nature," and later congratulated Crane on his gardens and fireworks: "This rude spot, where the lonely visitor once heard
nought but the wild roar of the noble Passaic . . . is now become
the brilliant scene of science, added to the sublimity of nature."
A satisfied customer agreed: "[Crane] has so far domesticated the

Passaic Falls and Clinton Bridge, by W. H. Bartlett (author's collection)

wilderness of nature, and blended with it the improvements of art, that the Passaic Falls is no longer a place for the melancholy retirement of the horror-stricken wanderer, who seeks solitude as the only food for his bewildered imagination, but is now become the delightful scene of social gaity and interesting contemplation." The editor gave this advice to tired clerks and workingmen: cross the river and "greet the smiles of your friends amid the enchanting groves of the Forest Garden," "bid dull cares begone," "lounge at your pleasure under the illuminated Cedars of Lebanon," and, on the way home, "take a peep at the awful chasm below—listen for a moment to the tremendous roar of the troubled Passaic, [and] contrast the scene with your own quietude of mind." Social gaiety, sublimity, scenes of science, quietude of mind—all of it across the river from the factories and tenements of Paterson, New Jersey.[4]

Before receiving customers, Timothy Crane had to bridge the falls chasm that separated the Forest Garden from Paterson, and of all the improvements that he made, Crane was proudest of his bridge. He designed the thing himself. It was made of wood, covered, and its substructure was sided to form an arch. The sides were open, with latticed railings, affording a full view of the falls and chasm. Crane called it Clinton Bridge, after Governor De Witt Clinton of New York. Few of his fellow citizens could have missed the reason why, for in the 1820s Clinton was a hero to developers everywhere. He had promoted and then presided over the construction of the Erie Canal. Completed in 1825, the Canal was a stupendous triumph of engineering that was opening the whole Great Lakes frontier to settlement and commerce. The Erie Canal stood as a magnificent icon of the triumph of American civilization over wilderness, and a lot of people were naming taverns, ferryboats, hotels, steam locomotives, and babies after De Witt Clinton. (In Portland, Maine, lived an improver named Neal Dow. In the 1820s Dow was at the threshold of activities that would make him one of the great nineteenth-century temperance reformers, and he was a man who loved progress: he owned a tannery that was as fully automated as such things could be, and his was among the first houses in Portland to have a bathroom with running water and a hot-air furnace. In 1825 Dow toured the recently completed Erie Canal, returned home, and named his horse Governor Clinton.)[5]

Through the late summer of 1827 Timothy Crane's workmen cleared land, planted bushes and trees, and assembled Clinton Bridge beside the falls. They finished at the end of September, and Crane announced that he would supervise his men as they pulled his bridge across the chasm and set it into place. He advertised his exhibition for the afternoon of Saturday, September 30. The factories would be closed. The whole town could come out and watch Clinton Bridge conquer Passaic Falls. It would be a big day for progress, and a bigger day for Timothy Crane.

Across the river in Paterson, twenty-eight-year-old Sam Patch watched Crane's improvements taking shape. Sam's life was not going well. For a time, he had operated a small Paterson candlewick mill in partnership with a man named Martin Branigan, but the partnership dissolved in 1826. Like Sam's purported enterprise with Kennedy near Pawtucket, the agreement seems to have ended in acrimony: Branigan pointedly announced that "All persons are forbid giving any further credit to the above firm, without the consent of [Branigan.]" Branigan—like Kennedy—stayed in business, and Sam Patch went off looking for employment elsewhere. In 1827 he was working as a mule spinner in Paterson's Hamilton Mills. He was also a solitary drinker who repeatedly boxed the ears of children who worked under him. (The boy who recounts these stories also tells us that Patch suffered bouts of delirium tremens, suggesting that he had been drinking heavily for a very long time.)[6]

Sam Patch, in short, was an angry and not particularly admirable victim of the huge social process that was creating places like Pawtucket and Paterson and granting money and respect to people like Timothy Crane. As he watched Crane boss his gardeners and bridge builders, an unhappy constellation of class anger and rum-soaked resentment took shape in the mind of Sam Patch. Sam let it be known that he would spoil Crane's day.

That Saturday all of Paterson turned out to watch Timothy Crane pull his bridge over the chasm. Constables patrolled the crowd looking for Sam Patch. They had locked him into a basement for safekeeping, but someone had let him out.[7]

Tim Crane swaggered through the afternoon, tugging at his whiskers and shouting instructions to his men, always with an eye on the crowd. The bridge rested on log rollers on the northern bank. Cables stretched across the chasm, and ropes and tackles waited to edge the bridge over the precipice and along the cables and to set it into place on the substructure. At last the workmen took their stations and pulled at the ropes, and Clinton Bridge edged slowly across Crane's fairy-tale landscape, moved by sweating men and by what the *Paterson Intelligencer* called "the exercise of a good deal of ingenuity and mechanical skill" on the part of Timothy Crane. As the bridge reached the cliff and began riding out over the cables, things went wrong: one of the log rollers slipped and dropped end over end into the pool below the falls, and the bridge lurched dangerously. Crane's men regained control and set it safely into place. Tim Crane looked up for applause, but the cheering was broken by shouts from the south bank. For there was Sam Patch, standing erect on a rock at the edge of the cliff. Sam spoke to the people near him. Then he stepped off.

It was a straight seventy-foot drop to the water below, and Sam took it in fine Pawtucket style. At the end he brought up his knees, then snapped them straight, drew his arms to his sides, and went into the water like an arrow. Tim Crane and his kidnapped audience stared into the chasm, certain that Sam was dead. But in a few seconds Sam shot to the surface. The crowd cheered wildly as Sam sported in the water, paddled over to Crane's log roller, took the trail rope between his teeth, and towed it slowly and triumphantly to shore.

Before he jumped, Sam Patch told the people on his side of the chasm that "Crane had done a great thing, and he meant to do another."[8]

At its simplest, Sam's leap at Clinton Bridge was an act of vandalism: Timothy Crane was an enterprising, successful man, and Sam Patch was a sullen failure who risked his life to ruin Crane's celebration. We might label the jump an act of drunken resentment and leave it at that. So it may have been. But the crowd applauded Sam Patch's leap, and the leap survived in the folklore of Paterson as an admirable performance. Something, it seems, had prepared the people of Paterson to enjoy Sam's assault on the festivities of Timothy Crane.[9]

A look into the past and future of Passaic Falls reveals the reason why: the Forest Garden was built on land that had once been a public playground, and Crane's improvements and the ways he managed them and talked about them aroused the sustained fury of his neighbors. Sam's leap, it turns out, was no isolated event. It was the opening shot in a twelve-year war over the north bank of Passaic Falls—a war that ultimately drove Timothy Crane into bankruptcy and away from the falls.

Crane and his supporters insisted that the north bank had been a useless, forbidding wilderness before he built the Forest Garden, but the working people of Paterson knew better. For them, the north bank was a valued retreat from the city and a place to play. A family named Godwin ran a tavern there about half a mile above the falls. An English gentlewoman who visited in May 1827 pronounced it "quite a cockney place and crowded with Saturday and Sunday visitors." From Godwin's tavern, pathways led through the forest toward the falls. The land along these paths was privately owned, but no proprietor had ever changed the landscape or excluded the public. The woods were dense, and the rock base was crossed by deep cracks which most people assumed were the work of ancient earthquakes. One of the ravines led all the way down to the river below the falls. Pleasure seekers drank at Godwin's tavern (tea and lemonade as well as alcohol), hiked through the woods, threw stones into the chasm and dropped them into the crevasses, carved their names on trees and rocks, fished at the base of the falls (there were legends of two-hundred-pound sturgeon), or found quiet places to sit and enjoy the summer air. The bravest boys dove and swam in the pools above the falls, and Sam Patch leaped from the cliffs into the river at least once before his famous jump in September 1827. The working people of Paterson valued the falls ground: it was a wild and beautiful spot that belonged to everyone and no one, unimproved private property that was open to free public use. A boy who grew up in Paterson recalled that "the Falls have always been looked upon with pride by the citizens, and they expected it would always remain so. Some folks . . . even demanded that free access should be had by all."[10]

Crane took the north bank out of public hands and turned it into the Forest Garden, "a place of rational amusement." Crane's later advertisements invited "the poet and the painter" and the "man of leisure;" he hoped that refined out-of-towners would patronize his gardens, and he was particularly proud of a visit from the bishop of New York. He went out of his way to offer "the man of *labor and industry* a relaxation from the toils of his occupation." But he insisted that customers behave themselves, and he reserved the right to exclude those who did not. Welcome guests included "decent people," "ladies and gentlemen," "good society," those who were "respectable and orderly," and those who maintained "good order and decorum." He wanted customers who stayed on the walkways and out of the bushes, who conversed politely and never got drunk, and who contemplated trees without wanting to climb them.[11]

Timothy Crane's transformation of the old pleasure ground, along with his talk about art, nature, and De Witt Clinton, would have caused trouble in any event. But he compounded his crimes by charging a toll at Clinton Bridge. The toll was only two pennies, but Crane insisted on it. An occasional genteel guest objected to Crane's bad manners at the tollbooth, and even Crane's friends thought his zealous toll taking was "ungentlemanly." In 1831 Crane bought space in a newspaper to justify the toll. He pleaded that he had risked everything he owned in his north-bank improvements, and could survive only if he turned a profit. Closely tied to this argument was the next one: the toll was his one means of keeping the place decent and safe. Crane knew what happened when just anyone crossed Clinton Bridge: "1st. If the bridge were thrown open, the Garden would be occupied with a set of lazy, idle, rascally, drunken vagabonds. 2d. This would drive away all decent people. 3d. We should thereby lose all our income; and 4th. Our little ornaments and improvements would be defaced, ruined, and in fact, destroyed."[12]

Crane spoke from experience, for the Forest Garden had come under attack from the beginning. First, of course, was the opening-day leap of Sam Patch. Then, in his first season, Crane had to install spring guns to discourage "Night Poachers" who defaced his tollgate and entered the grounds to steal liquor. During business hours, drunken, foul-mouthed men insulted respectable customers and threw firecrackers at ladies' feet. Others cut down Crane's trees, broke his imported bushes, smashed his glassware, stole his lanterns, and hurled his tables and benches over the falls. Rowdiness and vandalism escalated into assaults on Crane and his family and employees. Crane's boys were kicked and beaten when they worked the tollgate; some attackers threatened to throw them into the river. The boys found trouble whenever they ran errands into town, and Crane himself could not walk safely in Paterson. At night, musket balls and doses of buckshot slammed into the walls and through the windows of buildings on the old pleasure ground. One of the worst of these attacks occurred on Christmas Night in 1828—a night when the lower orders traditionally settled scores with upper-class enemies.[13]

Throughout these assaults, Timothy Crane knew who his tormentors were. Some were well-dressed sports who might have passed as gentlemen. Others were men, Crane said, "from whom we might expect better things," who condoned the violence. But most were workingmen, and Crane singled out the English weavers and spinners as the worst: "They come into my gardens, and cut down my young trees, and mutilate my seats and tables and bridge, and get drunk and curse and swear, and use indecent language," and scare off respectable women and men.[14]

The attack on the Forest Garden was an early round in the contest over recreational space in industrializing America, a contest that regularly pitted the noise and physicality of working-class recreations against the privatized, contemplative leisure pursuits of the middle class. In Paterson the contest took on a particularly personal and violent edge, for many of Crane's attackers were people who had been his friends. Timothy Crane had been in Paterson since 1812, and as an architect, builder, speculator, and sawmill owner, he had watched his fortune grow with the town. His work, his public services, and his membership in the Episcopal Church brought him into cooperation with Paterson's leading families. His joviality and love of talk won him entry into other circles as well: between 1815 and 1823 he was an elected chief of Paterson's volunteer fire companies, and he was widely known as a storyteller, a genial braggart, and a friend to traveling acrobats and circus riders. A boy from the mills recalled that people had liked Timothy Crane. A lot of them called him Uncle Tim.[15]

Crane seems to have retained the goodwill of the community until he bought the land next to the falls. His decision to turn it into a romantic retreat for ladies and gentlemen transformed his relations with Paterson. Crane's old associations—the fire companies, the sawmill and the construction sites, the storytelling groups—had been with a democracy of males that excluded women. The Forest Garden, on the other hand, catered to respectable women and their male escorts, and it pointedly excluded the working-class men who had made up much of Crane's old social world.

The reasons for Crane's decision must remain a mystery. But we should note that the purchase of the north bank was the second big event of 1827 for Crane. In February he had married Maria Ryerson, daughter of one of the old families of New York City. He was a fifty-four-year-old widower; she was twenty-four and, by the time he bought his land in August, pregnant with their first child. Crane's marriage to this polished young woman, coupled with his withdrawal from the old male democracy and his new interest in exclusivity and romantic sentimentalism, suggests that he had determined to change his way of life. Timothy Crane was no longer one of the boys. He had become an inventor of American bourgeois culture.[16]

Viewed from the factories and poor streets of Paterson, Crane's Forest Garden was a vast provocation. It violated customary-use rights to the falls ground, and that alone would have started a fight. But Crane's personal transformation made it worse. Timothy Crane was breaking with the informal, democratic society of other men and redefining respectability and right behavior. The Forest Garden translated Paterson's familiar hierarchy of wealth into a new, undemocratic, and utterly unacceptable formula for the distribution of respect. That is when Paterson changed its mind about Timothy Crane. The people of Paterson may have admired Clinton Bridge. It was a straightforward conquest of nature and a fine feat of engineering. But at the end of the bridge there were tree stumps, gravel walkways, and orderly bushes and shrubs where their pleasure ground had been, and Uncle Tim was talking in strange new ways.

Crane's bridge raising in 1827 was a truly ambivalent celebration. Sam Patch resolved the ambivalence with a little speech about the democracy of worth and a spectacular reassertion of the freedom and physicality of the old north bank. Patch's leap was the first in a continuous series of assaults upon Timothy Crane. The Forest Garden never made money, and Crane's creditors began to seize the land within a year. He stayed on as manager, dodging rocks and demanding tolls all the way, until 1839. Then he abandoned his vandalized and neglected gardens and retired to a log cabin in a forested corner of the north bank, where he died in 1845. It was the end to a long and ugly war with the neighbors, a war that began the day Sam Patch sneaked past the constables and joined the crowd that had come to see Timothy Crane conquer Passaic Falls.[17]

Months after the episode at Clinton Bridge, when he had begun to jump professionally, Sam Patch offered an explanation of his leaps. Crane and other friends of progress had been spreading rumors. Some said the jump at Clinton Bridge had been the act of a madman. Others insisted that Patch was merely drunk, and Timothy Crane himself concocted the best story of all: Sam Patch had leaped for love. Patch was enamored of a young woman, you see, and she had turned him down. He had leaped not to humiliate Timothy Crane but to kill himself. Patch countered with his own explanation. "It is no melancholy event," he insisted. "I am perfectly sober and in possession of my proper faculties, and [leaping waterfalls] is nothing more than an art which I have knowledge of and courage to perform"—"an art," he went on, "which I have practiced from my youth."[18]

Art. It was an important word in the vocabularies of Sam Patch and Timothy Crane, but it had different meanings for the two. Crane used "art" as a crucial component in what might be called the language of progress, a language that described and legitimized what he was doing at Passaic Falls. Patch's use of the word derived from plebeian-democratic sensibilities that called Timothy Crane and his works into serious question. We might look at the episode at Clinton Bridge as a confrontation between the art of Sam Patch and the art of Timothy Crane.[19]

When Sam Patch said that leaping waterfalls was an art, he tied his jumps to familiar notions of Anglo-American manhood. In Patch's world a man's art was his identity-defining skill. There was the shoemaker's art, the carpenter's art, the multiform arts of husbandry—the whole range of combined mental and manual performances by means of which trained men provided for the wants and needs of their communities. The word "art" affirmed the intelligence, learning, and dexterity that went into building a house, making a shoe, or raising a field of wheat. It also affirmed the worth of men who performed those tasks. It was the combination of knowledge (not speculative imagination but mastery of a "system of rules," as Noah Webster called it, learned from childhood under the guidance of a father or master) and skilled hands that made ordinary work an art. And it was the possession of an art that made a man independent and useful and therefore the sovereign equal of any other man.[20]

This understanding of "art" called up the yeoman-artisan republic and the ideals of manhood and individual worth that it sustained—ideals that Sam Patch and other workingmen had reformulated and extended into the industrial world of the nineteenth century. His "art" was tied to an ethos that his father had lost and that he had regained. Greenleaf Patch had been a landless farmer turned cottage shoemaker, and in his proudest days he may have claimed possession of an art. But skilled shoemakers knew better. Men like Greenleaf Patch performed clumsy work and sold it to merchants who then put it into world markets. His rented farm and his misshapen shoes were tied less to the neighborhood bases of occupational arts than to the wider commercial relationships that were dissolving them. Sam Patch's dimmest childhood memories were of his father's expulsion from even that dubious artisanship. And then there was Pawtucket and a childhood in the mills.

Yet by 1827 Sam Patch was himself master of an art. He had operated spinning machinery since childhood, and his elders on the job had recruited and trained him as one of the first American-born boss spinners. If he was anything like the other mule spinners, Sam talked and acted like a man who possessed an art: he was the master of a machine that his employers did not fully understand, he hired, managed, and disciplined his own helpers, and he demanded respect from lowlier workers and from the owners themselves. The mule spinners pioneered the effort to reshape old standards of male autonomy and to establish them within factory walls.

Patch's leap at Clinton Bridge was—indirectly but unmistakably—tied to that effort. His leaping ability was a kind of occupational skill, invented and practiced by mill boys at mill-village waterfalls. Jumping at waterfalls was an art. Patch's feet-first, knees-bent position in the air and his practice of breathing in as he fell followed the system of rules governing that art that Pawtucket boys had developed over the years. Throughout his jumping career, Sam Patch never deviated from the formal Pawtucket style. (Each mill town, apparently, developed local variations. In 1885, when a man named Odlum killed himself trying to leap from the Brooklyn Bridge, Sheriff McKee of Paterson said that as a boy in the 1850s he had known at least twenty young men who could have made the leap safely. Paterson boys, explained the sheriff, knew the secret: the jumper must keep his mouth shut and hold his breath.)[21]

No one recorded what Sam Patch wore when he jumped at Clinton Bridge or at his other leaps in Paterson. But he made his subsequent leaps in a close-fitting shirt and pants of white cotton. His garb was neat and highly visible, a good outfit for jumping waterfalls. It was also the parade uniform of the Paterson Association of Spinners.[22]

Patch's membership in the mule spinner's world was hard-won and vital, and he repeatedly talked of his jumping abilities in ways that referred to it. His remarks at Clinton Bridge (Crane had done a great thing, and he meant to do another) called up a world in which things competently done established a democracy of respect among the doers. And when the following summer Patch jumped on the Fourth of July, he said that he wanted "merely . . . to show that some things can be done as well as others"—a sideways reference to the same republic of arts. By thus insisting that falls jumping was an art—a truly traditional art, one that required knowledge and years of practice—Sam Patch spoke to the one world in which he could imagine his own worth, the world he carried with him when he confronted Timothy Crane at Clinton Bridge.[23]

When Timothy Crane used the word "art" (and he used it often) he did not mean things like shoemaking, mule spinning, or leaping waterfalls. Crane and other improvers were shaping America's revolutionary republic into new landscapes, new social hierarchies, and new uses for key English words. In Crane's vocabulary "art" stood for all the works of humankind. In particular, it referred to the works of technology and entrepreneurial vision that were transforming nature and the social order in their generation. Art was the Erie Canal, a man-made river that turned a wilderness into new farms and towns. Art was water-powered factories and mills. It was bridges and roads and steamboats. It was the whole range of projects by which civilization was refining nature and putting it to human use, and it had little to do with the skills practiced by ordinary men.

Timothy Crane used "art" as a near-synonym for civilization, and he coupled it with its ancient opposite, "nature," in two ways. The first—represented by Clinton Bridge—reiterated understandings that had come to North America with the first settlers: art was opposed to hostile natural forces. Civilization, as Keith Thomas has reminded us, was "virtually synonymous with the conquest of nature." Crane, however, inflated this meaning of "art" and used it in newly aggressive and grandiose ways, for he and others had come to believe that civilization was winning its age-old war with wilderness. In the 1790s Crane's hero De Witt Clinton had predicted that "the hand of art will change the face of the universe. Mountains, deserts, and oceans will feel its mighty force. It will not then be debated whether the hills shall be prostrated, but whether the Alps and Andes shall be levelled; nor whether sterile fields shall be fertilized, but whether the deserts of Africa shall feel the power of cultivation." Such language was self-consciously prophetic then, but by the time Timothy Crane built his bridge it seemed that Clinton's prophecy was coming true: art was conquering nature on a broad front and with unprecedented success; man's long-sought dominion over nature was being realized.[24]

The Forest Garden represented a second, newer juxtaposition of nature and art. With the final triumph of civilization at hand, educated northerners were beginning a long, complex conversation about humankind's relation to the retreating natural world. They had always seen wilderness as primordial chaos, and many continued to do so. But others began to perceive a new divinity in nature—a benign order that could be counterposed to the transitory, selfish, ugly, and artificial aspects of their own increasingly civilized world. This revolution in perception was expressed in efforts to gain access to nature through art: landscape paintings, nature books, half-wild gardens, rural cemetaries and urban parks, and journeys to a Niagara Falls surrounded by stairways and new hotels. By the 1830s the northeastern United States was dotted with landscapes that domesticated wilderness just enough to rob it of its terrors and to reveal its moral lessons, *combinations* of art and nature that were supposed to educate, renew, and uplift citizens of the world that progress was making. The Forest Garden, which, as one of Crane's happy customers testified, "domesticated the wilderness of nature, and blended with it the improvements of art," was one of those landscapes.[25]

The art of Timothy Crane's north bank had both utilitarian and spiritual connotations. It linked developmentalism and romanticism, material progress and spiritual improvement, prosperity and uplift. Simply put, it linked the material accomplishments and the spiritual possibilities of people like Timothy Crane. Other places in the Northeast juxtaposed those meanings as well. European visitors to Boston often traveled to nearby Mount Auburn Cemetery and the factory town of Lowell within a day or two of each other—possibly because their guides were rich Bostonians who had helped to build both places. Tourists on

reformist'n nature

the Erie Canal enjoyed that triumph of utilitarian art, knowing all the while that it carried them to the natural wonders of Niagara Falls. But seldom were the twin promises of utility and moral up-lift linked so dramatically as at Passaic Falls. Clinton Bridge spanned the river with technological ease, then delivered visitors into the Forest Garden, a spiritualized landscape whose very name combined nature and art. Passing through a new factory town, over a noble bridge, and into the Forest Garden, Crane's customers witnessed triumphs of art and combinations of art and nature that represented big pieces of the material and moral agenda of an emerging entrepreneurial class. It was an agenda that left little room for Sam Patch and his idea of art.[26]

The art of Timothy Crane and the art of Sam Patch were op-posed in many ways. That opposition was clearest at the Forest Garden: Crane simply excluded workingmen who did not "un-derstand" the new falls ground, thus enforcing the new social and aesthetic boundaries that such places were helping to make. The art of Clinton Bridge, however, posed subtler and deeper threats, for it assumed forms of social organization that diminished the "arts" that working people practiced. In earlier centuries the struggle with nature was carried out by the occupational arts: people turned woodlands into farms, trees into furniture and houses, rocks into chimneys and fences, cattle into food and shoes. The progress of "art" was thus little more than the sum of what the occupational arts had made, and the arts of Timothy Crane and Sam Patch were parts of one conceptual scheme. The new language of progress, however, dissolved individual skills into a larger, more interdependent, and more abstract "art." A newsman who learned what Sam Patch did for a living, for in-stance, described him as "a mechanic connected with one of the factories in Paterson." This was not an insult. Most skilled work-men called themselves mechanics, had done so for a long time, and would continue to do so for at least a generation. In their us-age, a mechanic was the possessor of an art. But in the language

→ workingmen no longer possess
art but are merely connected
to it

→ capital value
→ skill value

of progress, mechanics were more often, like the newsman's Sam Patch, "connected" with the grander designs of art.[27]

A friend of Crane's on the *Intelligencer* provided a set-piece example of how the language of progress dealt with Sam Patch and his fellow mechanics. In 1828 he described the millwrights of Paterson as "a useful class of mechanics which enables the manufacturer to render the natural elements so immanently subservient to the comfort and prosperity of this town." He did not mean that millwrights had lost their arts or skills. Indeed, the mills of Paterson were among the most complex and demanding products of the millwrights' art in North America. The abilities of millwrights were not diminished but devalued—devalued because cognitive and manual responsibilities were no longer assigned to the same people, and because capital and entrepreneurial imagination were assuming primacy over ancient knowledge. Mill-building was losing status, and the balance of respect was shifting toward the "manufacturer" who thought up projects and financed them, who organized the various "classes of mechanics" in ways that turned unruly nature into "comfort and prosperity" for the whole town—all of it accomplished through a process and with results that people like Timothy Crane called art.[28]

When Crane advertised in newspapers he seldom talked about himself in the first person. He was the "subscriber" or the "proprietor," and Clinton Bridge and the Forest Garden were made not by him but by "the hand of ART." (Sam Patch, remember, claimed his art for himself: *I have knowledge and courage to perform it; I have practiced it from my youth.*) Crane's disembodied "hand of ART" was an abstraction not only for his gardens and bridge but for the processes that such projects required. In order for art to conquer Passaic Falls, Crane had to imagine his bridge and gardens, buy the land, and exclude other users. Then he had to hire scores of laborers, carpenters, and gardeners and supervise them as they assembled the parts of his scheme. And

Crane does not claim art for himself,
but Sam Patch does
↳ Crane has merely facilitated it

then (here is where "art" was put to new uses) he had to convince the people of Paterson that the project embodied not his own capital and aspirations but the Hand of Art. The project and the process of realizing it belonged not to him but to humankind. Everyone would profit from it, everyone could be proud of it.

The owners of mills and foundries along the millrace on the south bank shared Crane's sensibilities, and they planted flower gardens between the raceway and the lower Passaic River. The result was a striking vision of nature improved by art. At the head of town stood a majestic waterfall, spanned by Clinton Bridge and abutted by the Forest Garden. Across the river and below Crane's garden, a line of factories and flower beds sloped unevenly down to the tenements and little houses of Paterson—narrow, unpaved streets filled with pigs and dirty children, with émigré English factory hands, and with the wage-earning daughters and sons of American yeomen. A traveler walking through Paterson in 1832 counted "thirty cotton-mills [and] iron and brass foundries, in the upper part of it, with gardens so tastefully laid out, and the banks of the river kept so neat, and ornamented with weeping willows, as to compensate for the broken bridges and dirt of the lower part of town." It was a picture-book balance of art, nature, and early industrial squalor. It was what American romantic capitalism had made in Paterson, New Jersey.[29]

Clinton Bridge was the linchpin in that landscape. And when Timothy Crane invited the neighbors to walk out of their part of the picture and into his, he wanted more than applause. He wanted factory hands and foundry workers to participate in meanings that he and other entrepreneurs and their friends were inventing. In oblique but profound ways, he wanted them to ratify their place within the language and landscape of progress.

Crane's spectacle almost worked. He drew a huge crowd, and when the bridge was in place most had to admit that Timothy Crane had done an impressive thing. But Sam Patch, with an anarchic leap and a mock rescue of a piece of failed engineering,

stole the day. In a split second the applause went from the art of
Timothy Crane to the art of Sam Patch. It was what some people
would call a silly gesture, existential rebellion at its most juvenile
and dangerous. But Sam Patch lived in a world where "art" was a
vehicle of self-expression within a system of recognized equalities
and reciprocities, and he wanted to show Timothy Crane how an
American man conquers a waterfall.

On July 4, 1828, Sam Patch leaped again at Passaic Falls. Later
on the same day, Timothy Crane presented a display of fireworks
at the Forest Garden. Crane's fireworks and Patch's leap were the
first commercial entertainments ever advertised for Independence Day at Paterson: they were at it again.

Independence Day celebrations had been initiated by the political parties (the Jeffersonian Republicans in particular) of the
early republic, and citizens had expressed Federalist and Jeffersonian versions of what America was about in speeches and parades. With the disappearance of the Federalists after 1815, the
celebrations became nonpartisan and local, and something went
out of them. Whole neighborhoods still turned out for the parades and nighttime fireworks, but most treated the Fourth as
a festive day off from work, complete with theatrical performances, hunting parties, circuses, boat races, and complaints
about drinking and gambling among the lower orders. The upper
classes began to stay at home, or to spend the day in church, or to
take exclusive pleasure trips.[30]

In Paterson, Independence Day celebrations in the late 1820s
were a part of what was happening in the mills, on the streets,
and on the north bank of Passaic Falls: the republic of useful arts
was confronting Progress and the new inequalities of a mill city.
The *Paterson Intelligencer*, which began publication in 1826, reported its first July Fourth celebration that summer. Representatives of the mechanics' and spinners' associations joined with

"citizens" in a general committee of the day, which planned the festivities. The day began with a ringing of church bells, the playing of patriotic airs by the town band, and the firing of a cannon. But the centerpiece was the parade, led by a uniformed company of militia. The town band came second, followed by "Ladies" (almost certainly the wives and daughters of leading men) and female schoolteachers with their pupils, then men hoisting the cap of liberty and the American flag, then the town's civic leaders and clergy. Following the dignitaries came thirteen elderly citizens carrying the flags of the original thirteen states, accompanied by ten boys bearing banners of the newer states. Militia officers in uniform were followed by the associations of spinners, weavers, and other mechanics, marching trade by trade, carrying flags emblazoned with patriotic emblems and pictures of the tools and processes of their trades. The flags and the trade-by-trade marching order, along with the mechanics' participation in the planning of the day, sustained the tradition that the individual arts, in their making of shoes and houses and cotton cloth, fashioned the nation itself. (A citizen commented that the spinners were particularly striking in their white uniforms with green badges, and their blue banner with a spread eagle and depictions of the spinning process.) Male teachers and their pupils walked behind the mechanics and were followed by a final and inclusive contingent of "Citizens generally"—any white men, apparently, who wanted to march. A second company of militia brought up the rear.[31]

The parade began at ten o'clock in the morning and carried its pomp and noise through the streets. It ended at Brick Presbyterian Church, where the inclusiveness of the morning parade gave way to selective celebration. The town's leading men and women left the ranks and entered the church, where, according to one of them, "exercises suitable to the occasion were performed with a becoming sense of the sacred character of the place, and the honor due to the day." The minister offered a prayer, a lawyer read the Declaration of Independence, and the Orator of the Day (another lawyer) spoke with (according to the first lawyer) "masterly eloquence, which, combined with the beauty of thought, the aptness of allusion, and the force of classic illustration scattered throughout the composition, rendered this Oration a mental feast not soon to be forgotten, by those who partook of it." After songs by the choir, the lawyers, factory owners, and their ladies filed out of the church and rejoined the democratic parade that had waited outside.

The procession marched to Munn's Passaic Hotel. The militiamen fired their muskets into the air and disbanded. The crowd dispersed into festivities that the newspaper ignored, the ladies went off to an entertainment of their own, and the leading men of Paterson gathered in the hotel dining room. (The newspaper reported that the dinner was open to "all who choose," but the cost was a dollar a plate—a day's labor for most Patersonians.) There were food and speeches, and toward the end the innkeeper brought in a pie. He opened the pie and a white pigeon flew out bearing a very bad poem entitled "The Herald of America's Prosperity." ("O'er fields and plains by Nature blest / On lightsome wing I came," and on and on.) Thirteen toasts were proposed, commemorative of the thirteen original states: to the Nation, the People, the Heroes of the Revolution, the Republicans of Greece and South America, the New Jersey School Fund. The thirteenth toast, as was customary, went up to "Our Fair Country Women."

In the evening the banqueters rejoined the rest of Paterson for a grand flight of rockets, staged and paid for by the general committee of the day. Later, citizens could read that the Fourth had gone off with "harmony and good order," and with "unanimity manifested by all classes." It was a fine Fourth of July of the 1820s—a parade and fireworks staged and enjoyed by the whole town, and a sermon, readings, high-minded music, and banquet for the town's leaders. The festivities demonstrated republican hierarchy and celebrated the dignity and usefulness of white men—dignity that derived from daily work.

The festivities were similar in 1827: an inclusive, trade-based parade, a church service, an elite banquet, and a civic display of fireworks. The banquet ended with the usual toasts, but this year some of the toasts folded the language of the republic into the language of progress. There was a salute to American "Mechanical Genius" as manifested by the practical inventors Benjamin Franklin and Robert Fulton, and another to the American System of sheltering infant industries under protective tariffs—accompanied by the playing of "Yankee Doodle." Volunteer toasts saluted the rise of American manufactures and of Paterson in particular, while from outside came the sounds of another wedding of patriotism and progress: the engineer who was building the Morris Canal through Paterson (the canal linked the Pennsylvania coalfields with New York) set off thirteen explosions—"not only a loud but a profitable expression of patriotic feeling," according to a bemused Canadian visitor. The town leaders acted out their bipartisanship with dueling toasts to the Democrat Andrew Jackson and the National Republican Henry Clay, and there was a circumspect toast to "the Constitution" by Timothy Crane. But there were also toasts to Paterson's artisans and mechanics, phrased in the language of mutual usefulness and mutual respect: "In their industry and ingenuity the manufacturer has found . . . the best protection"; "may they be at all times united and free, and always maintain their integrity"; "the strong pillars upon which our prosperity rests. May they long maintain that respectable rank in society which they at present so deservedly occupy." Perhaps representatives of the workingmen's associations had again taken part in the planning and thus in the dinner (the planning session went unrecorded that year), or perhaps some among Paterson's elite in 1827 (at least at a civic and festive occasion, and toward the end of a lot of drinking) continued to fuse progress and the republic with respect for labor.[32]

The Fourth of July went differently in 1828. First, Patersonians learned that there would be no public fireworks. Instead, Timothy Crane promised a grand pyrotechnic display at the Forest Garden, on the far side of his tollbooth, to be witnessed only by subscribed ticket holders. Citizens then read that "a large and respectable meeting of Young Men" had planned the civic celebration and selected its officers and other dignitaries. The "Young Men" (a common code for ambitious and well-connected young men) neglected to invite women—either "Ladies" or female teachers—or "Citizens generally" to join the parade, though they did include the mechanics and spinners. The marching workers were duly noted, but only in the language of progress. (The newspaper account noted the banner carried by millwrights, "on which is exhibited in beautiful perspective the various implements and the mode of their application, by which this useful class of mechanics enables the manufacturer to render the natural elements so immanently subservient to the comfort and prosperity of this town.") The banquet was not attended by mechanics, nor were toasts given to their usefulness and patriotism. The usual salutes to the republic and founding fathers went up, but this time they were linked principally to entrepreneurial progress: to "Roads and Canals—important links in the chain which binds our union" (accompanied by "Meeting of the Waters," a tune composed for the opening of the Erie Canal); to "Domestic Manufactures—The Only Hope for National Independence" ("Heigh ho! The Cotton Spinners"); to "Literature, Science, and the Arts—The aliment of Freedom ("Ode on Science").[33]

The day ended with Crane's fireworks, presented for an exclusive audience at the Forest Garden, "where the refinements of taste and art combined with the varied and romantic beauties of nature, to afford pleasure and satisfaction to the numerous company present."[34]

Celebrations in this new and exclusive "spirit of rational freedom," so different from the civic inclusiveness of earlier years, would continue into the 1830s. But July 4, 1828, did include one performance that the Young Men had not planned. At four-thirty in the afternoon, as advertised, Sam Patch leaped from the south side of Clinton Bridge. The plain people of Paterson, absent as usual from the ceremonies at the church and hotel, had been excluded from the planning, denied the civic fireworks show, denigrated in the parade, and ignored by the toastmasters. They marched in battalions to the falls to see Sam Patch. A New Yorker gasped that "the giddy precipices around the chasm were covered with a promiscuous multitude of both sexes whose curiosity had brought them together to see this singular feat of temerity." The local paper estimated the crowd at between three thousand and five thousand persons. (Paterson had six thousand residents.) They lined the cliffs, rank upon rank. At the appointed time Sam Patch stepped to the edge and stared down at the river. He took off his coat, vest, and shoes; perhaps he was wearing the spinner's uniform in which he had marched that morning. Some in the crowd pushed forward for a better view, nearly crowding those in front off the precipice. As the crowd regathered, Sam turned and delivered a short speech that few could hear and none recorded. Then he faced the precipice and leaped into the chasm. The *Intelligencer* granted that it was a "hazardous feat," "handsomely executed." Sam rose to the surface of the water as the crowd's anxious silence broke into wonder and a roar of applause.[35]

Though most of Paterson witnessed Sam's leap on the Fourth of July, it is doubtful that the town's merchants and manufacturers were among them, for Sam had scheduled his leap at an hour at which they almost certainly were still at the banquet, offering toasts to progress, patriotism, and each other. A news story about this leap was the first to report the phrase that became Sam's motto: "Some things can be done as well as others."[36]

Twelve days later Sam Patch announced that he would perform his "astonishing leap" once more, on Monday, July 28. On the same day as Sam's announcement—Wednesday, July 16—twenty-two Paterson manufacturers made an announcement of their own:

> Notice. The subscribers hereby give notice to their *workers* and others, that after Saturday, the 19th July, 1828, they will stop their Mills and Factories, at half past seven o'clock, in the morning, for breakfast, and at one o'clock P.M. for dinner.
>
> This arrangement we consider will divide the day in a more equal manner than heretofore, and prove of advantage to the workers.

The announcement changed the dinner hour from noon to one o'clock, and it met with resistance. A friendly newspaper stated that the owners "had the good of the children in view," though the same editor had earlier averred that they changed the lunch hour "for their own convenience." It really made no difference: the manufacturers' decree was certain to start a fight.[37]

In the mills, Sam Patch and the skilled Englishmen who were his peers read the proclamation and thought about it. It was only a small change in the routine of the working day, but a little reflection revealed what the bosses were trying to do. Signers of the decree owned all but two of the town's cotton mills and many of the foundries and factories. The new rule changed the lunch hour for nearly half of Paterson's manufacturing wage earners, and for many more than half of the job-holding children. In a mill town where most families depended on more than one breadwinner, and where workers went home for lunch, few wage-earning households would be unaffected. Put simply, twenty-two wealthy men had taken it upon themselves to complicate the domestic schedules of hundreds of Paterson families. Worse, they announced the new hour after a closed meeting and in language (they "hereby give notice") that assumed their right to dictate the conditions of work. The owners must have known that the adult male spinners and weavers would resist this attack on their authority over themselves and the children who worked under them, particularly when it came in the form of an arbitrary assertion of power by a closed-door combination of employers.[38]

The manufacturers posted their decree on Wednesday: the customary noon lunch hour would be in effect for the rest of the week, but when the mills reopened on Monday, lunchtime would be one o'clock.

Sam Patch was a boss mule spinner at the Hamilton Mills, and he must have been in the thick of the discussions that took place during the week. Many of the other boss spinners were veterans of the labor violence and repressed reform movements of industrial Lancashire. Described in newspapers as "Manchester *mobites*" subject to "the moral diseases of Europe" (the first of which, of course, was a propensity for rioting and labor radicalism), they were the terror of Timothy Crane and men like him. But in Sam Patch's world, they were the staunchest and most admirable of men. Sam was himself a twenty-one-year veteran of the mills, and three years earlier had witnessed and perhaps taken part in the Pawtucket walkout—the first textile strike in American history. While the spinners and weavers planned what they would do, Sam thought up a contribution of his own: he spread the word that on Saturday afternoon—after the factories had closed, and in the first hours of calm before what everyone knew would be a storm—he would again leap at Passaic Falls.[39]

The mills and factories closed at noon on Saturday. Workers left their machines and workbenches knowing that peace was at an end. There would be a day and a half of eerie quiet, and on Monday there would be trouble. The people of Paterson began that day and a half with a walk to Passaic Falls. They streamed out of their workplaces and out of the houses and grogshops in the lower neighborhoods, jostling and talking. Latecomers hurried past the last empty factory and around the embankment, and there stood the crowd waiting for Sam Patch. A New Yorker estimated the crowd at six to ten thousand: the whole town. At the appointed time, Sam strode out of the audience and stepped onto his rock. A part of the crowd stood at his back, with the deserted town behind them. Clinton Bridge and the falls were at his right and the basin was at his feet, and everywhere Sam turned he met the eyes of workmates and neighbors. He straightened, gathered himself, and stepped off and dropped with perfect grace into the gulf. Some person or persons had wanted to ensure that this grand gesture would be made: Sam collected fifteen dollars for the leap.[40]

(Again, we cannot know what Sam wore for this leap. But it is likely that he jumped, as he did in future leaps, in the white shirt and pants that were the parade uniform of the Paterson Association of Spinners. This uniform carried meanings—probably for Patch, certainly for the Englishmen who worked with him and witnessed his leap—that reached back to Manchester. After the defeat of Napoleon in 1815, workers in the textile towns of Lancashire, led again by the weavers and spinners, revived their demands for republican rights—in the faces of Britain's victorious aristocrats. The workers organized a great rally at St. Peter's Field, near Manchester, in 1819 to hear a speech advocating parliamentary reform. Soldiers who had been instructed to arrest the speaker charged into the crowd, killing several and injuring hundreds of others. Before the Massacre at Peterloo began, the cap of liberty [the symbol of international republicanism] was delivered to the podium by a group of women dressed in white with green trim. After the Massacre, Manchester spinners adopted white hats with green ribbons as a defiant and angry remembrance of the day. Hundreds of these men later migrated to the United States, and many of them found their way to Paterson over the next few years. The English spinners and their American compatriots marched in Paterson's July Fourth parades wearing suits of white cotton adorned with prominent green badges. The jumping attire of Sam Patch—the white uniform with the green badge removed—might have meant more to Sam's audience than the newspapers evidently understood.)[41]

On Monday the mill hands came to work on time and worked at their machines through the morning. When the clock struck noon they stopped. The spinners and weavers and the boys and girls who worked under them marched downstairs and out of doors. It was twelve o'clock. Time for lunch.

There are differing accounts of what happened next. An early report stated that the workers had gone out on strike on Monday afternoon and had become "very riotous and disorderly, and such as to keep the inhabitants of the place in continual apprehension." The same report announced (erroneously) that the militia was on its way from Newark. Another account had young strikers, encouraged by the incorrigible weavers and spinners, mobbing their opponents and threatening to throw them into the "ugly basin into which Mr. Patch jumps occasionally." The *Paterson Intelligencer* downplayed the violence, but admitted that the walkout "was indeed conducted with some noise and show of outrage." The known facts are these: the workers rioted on Monday afternoon, two hundred men and many more children and women were out on strike, and only two mills remained in operation—the two that had not tried to change the dinner hour.[42]

On Tuesday the weavers and mule spinners, joined by skilled journeymen from the smaller shops, held a meeting and issued two demands. First, they resolved to stay out on strike until the noon lunch hour was reinstated. Second, evidently enraged and emboldened by events, they demanded that the citywide workday be cut from eleven to ten hours. They would greet employers who agreed to the twelve o'clock lunch hour and the ten-hour day as "friends to their fellow citizens and to mankind in general." The others would not be friends at all. The mechanics would not work for them, and they would use "all legal means" to keep others from entering their degrading and dishonorable employment. The mechanics ended their meeting and went home.

Later that night, someone set fire to one of the struck mills. Another sneaked into the weaving room of the Phoenix Mills—one of the two that remained in operation—and cut the warps with a knife.[43]

The owners stood adamant, and the strike continued through July. Not until early August did the papers announce that "the children have yielded their position and most of the mechanics returned quietly to work, to take their dinner at one o'clock. . . . The children are now perfectly docile and appear sorry for their misconduct." With the mills running and the power of the owners to set schedules at least temporarily acknowledged, the victorious manufacturers became kindhearted: by fiat (and not by the authority of riotous workingmen) they restored the lunch hour to twelve o'clock. Their newfound benevolence, however, did not extend to the weavers and spinners who had led the strike. During the angry days of late July, the owners had sworn that they would never rehire the chief troublemakers, though they were, as an anti-strike editor conceded, "among the best workmen." They carried out their threat: a New Yorker who visited Paterson reported, "The ringleaders of the mechanics, among whom are some of the Manchester *Mobites*, have been discharged."[44]

On August 6 Sam Patch jumped from a ship's mast into the Hudson River at Hoboken, cheered on by a crowd of New Yorkers who had gathered on a hotel lawn. Sam had not made his advertised leap at Passaic Falls on July 28. The leap on the Saturday before the strike was his last appearance in the records of Paterson. An editor claimed to have "learned that Mr. Patch has resolved to leap no more from the place he has chosen heretofor. Sam felt rather 'ugly' about it the last time."[45]

The invitation to leap at Hoboken probably came from John Cox Stevens, whose father, Colonel John Stevens, had bought a confiscated loyalist estate with three miles of riverfront facing

New York Harbor in 1784. The estate occupied the one point at which a break in the New Jersey Palisades permitted easy boat traffic across the Hudson, and the Colonel laid out the village of Hoboken in 1804. Colonel Stevens was a wealthy tinkerer and an enthusiast for steamboats. He launched a primitive steam vessel at Hoboken in 1804 (three years before Robert Fulton's more successful venture), and five years later his sidewheeler *Phoenix* steamed from Hoboken to Philadelphia—the first steam vessel to venture into the ocean. Colonel Stevens wanted to establish a line between Albany and New York City and steam ferry service between Hoboken and New York, and he sued to break the monopoly held by Robert Fulton and Robert Livingston. The case went to the Supreme Court, whose decision in *Gibbons v. Ogden* struck down the monopoly in 1824. Colonel Stevens built the Hudson River Line to Albany and the ferry service to Manhattan, then began turning his attention to railroads.[46]

While his father and brother worked at their transportation projects, John Cox Stevens developed the riverside property as a promenade and a place of entertainment. Beginning about 1820 he built a shaded pathway along the river, planted a spacious sloping lawn that he named Elysian Fields, and added a hotel patronized by the "best" people. An advertisement boasted that the improvements had turned Hoboken into "one of the most delightful places in the known world." New York's high society picnicked, strolled, and rode horses along Stevens's well-groomed pathways. They praised Hoboken's willow-lined promenades ("the finest walks conceiveable"), its pleasant fusion of sociability and solitude, and its picturesque views of the river full of sailboats, with the city on the opposite shore, "glittering like a heap of toys in the sunny distance." A gentleman poet was pleased: "Good taste and enterprise have done for Hoboken precisely what they ought to have done, without violating the propriety of nature."[47]

Visitors to Hoboken paid no admission. The Stevens family

owned the steam ferries that plied between Manhattan and their little resort, and made their money by encouraging New Yorkers to ride the boats. Steam ferry service began in 1822. By 1828 four large steamboats (complete with women's lounges and fruit, candy, and liquor stores) left either shore on the half hour at a cost of 12.5 cents per passenger. Wealthy strollers and equestrians soon shared Hoboken with swarms of working- and middle-class Manhattanites who came to enjoy the boat ride, the fresh air and river breezes, the open spaces, and each other. As early as 1823 a Scots tourist found Hoboken filled with "idlers of every disposition and capacity": "Here the gallant ogles his beloved, the aged his feeble spouse, the nurse and mother the tender offspring. Whilst [prostitutes], displaying their spangled forms, delude many of the simple sons of Adam." On Sundays (the one full day when most New Yorkers were off work) as many as twenty thousand visitors crowded the lawn and walkways. Most of the new visitors wore their Sunday best and behaved themselves. Some did not. The Scotsman's prostitutes misbehaved, and so did the unknown persons who smashed an obelisk that marked the dueling ground on which Aaron Burr had killed Alexander Hamilton in 1804. The vandals carried off the pieces as relics. (Years later, a man walked into a low groggery in Manhattan carrying the fragment of the obelisk bearing the identifying inscription, and traded it for whiskey.) Rich Manhattanites knew that Hoboken was attracting a new and lower sort of people. Many of them stopped going there.[48]

John Cox Stevens, on the other hand, encouraged his new clientele. Stevens was a jovial, fun-loving gentleman and the leading sportsman of New York. In 1823 he put up the northern bet (an astounding twenty thousand dollars) for the great horse race between Eclipse and the southern champion, Henry. In 1825 he bought the victorious Eclipse and advertised him at stud at Hoboken. Stevens was a rich man who moved comfortably in democratic crowds, and he staged a variety of shows and sporting contests at Hoboken. He brought a circus to the lawn in 1823—complete with equestrians, balancing acts, comic sketches by a Mr. Shinotti, and songs by eight-year-old Miss Blanchard, sung while performing her "pleasing equilibriums" on the slack wire. After the circus, there was a horse race. The next year Stevens sponsored running races at Hoboken. He also established Fourth of July boat races and oratory contests, along with an occasional pigeon shoot. In 1829 he completed a steam railway and offered rides to visitors. Before long there was a merry-go-round, a ten-pin alley, wax figures, a shooting range, and a camera obscura. Stevens completed Hoboken's transition from a retreat for the wealthy to a place for popular and gentlemanly recreation in 1834, when he opened the Beacon Course for horse racing. Twelve years later America's first organized baseball game was played on Stevens's Hoboken lawn.[49]

On the morning of August 6, 1828, readers of the *New York Enquirer* learned that Mr. Stevens had taken another step in the wrong direction:

> Hoboken—this day, 6th instant—Mr. Patch, whose wonderful and intrepid leaps from the Peake of Paterson Falls, to the abyss below, (having been gracefully repeated), announces his intention of making a similar experiment for the gratification of the citizens of New York, THIS DAY, from an elevation of about 90 to 100 feet, now erecting within a few rods of the ferry-house. From the Hoboken shaded green, will be afforded a comfortable and delightful view of this eccentric novelty.

Some New Yorkers thought the jump was a bad idea: it was dangerous, and it would set a bad example for the gullible and unrefined. Two days earlier the editor of the *Enquirer* had written disapprovingly of Sam's last leap at Paterson: "This is in bad taste, for although there is some tact and management in the feat, it is still unnecessarily sporting with human existence, and all such bravadoes should be discountenanced. Rational, scientific, and even daring exploits for rational objects, may be encouraged, but what is there in a leap over a cataract of 90 feet? Danger and desperation." The *Enquirer* then likened Patch to a showman who shot himself dead before an appalled audience. The *New York Statesman* agreed: "If there be any philosophical principles upon which a leap of 100 feet is divested of the hazard usually attached to it, no objection to the attempt can be raised— though the circumstance would soon create 'competition,' and would, moreover, diminish the zest which the supposed danger (to our *credit* be it spoken!) presents to the spectators. But if there be actual peril in the undertaking, we recommend Patch to abandon it." That controversy persisted for the remainder of Sam's earthly and remembered life: popular interest in Sam's "astonishing leaps" versus editorial concerns about the physical danger and public corruption that attended them.[50]

Many wealthy New Yorkers stayed away from Patch's exhibition at Hoboken. Among those who attended the show was the artist Walter M. Oddie. Oddie was a young man in 1828, and he was learning to enjoy the highs and some of the lows of New York City. His social rounds included visits with the wealthy, but he also made time for evenings at the Bowery Theater and the city's pleasure gardens. On August 6, 1828, Oddie went horseback riding in the city. In the afternoon he ferried to Hoboken to view the leap of "the much talked of individual" Sam Patch. Oddie stood on the lawn near the ferry landing, surrounded by four or five hundred New Yorkers who had come to see the show. The sloop from which Sam would jump was anchored close to shore, directly in front of the lawn. A great crowd of boats surrounded the sloop, each of them filled with spectators. No one estimated the full size of the onshore and waterborne audience, but Oddie assures us that "a large concourse of gaping spectators" witnessed the leap. Near four o'clock Sam Patch climbed to a platform at the masthead and viewed the crowd in the boats and on the lawn. The surface of the river, less aerated and more unforgiving

than the pools below waterfalls, waited ninety dizzying feet below. Walter Oddie wrote that Sam "leaped off without hesitation.
He did not descend as erectly as I anticipated but loosely, and
before he had got halfway turned and fell on his back made the
water roar and splash with confusion—he appeared thus when
within 40 feet of the water," and here Oddie sketched the only
surviving eyewitness picture of one of Sam's leaps:

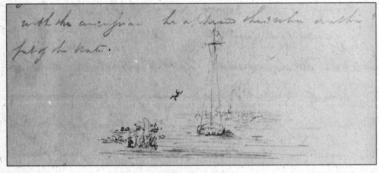

Sam Patch leaps at Hoboken, by Walter Oddie (Walter M. Oddie diary, courtesy
of the Winterthur Library: Joseph Downs Collection of Manuscripts and Printer Ephemera)

Some feared that Sam had hurt himself, but he bobbed up with
nothing worse than a bruise near one of his eyes.[51]

The leap at Hoboken was a turning point: it was there that
Sam Patch left the factory towns and entered the new world of
show business. His leaps at Pawtucket and Paterson had been local events, witnessed by workmates and neighbors who understood the art of falls jumping and knew the situations in which
Sam's leaps were performed. At Hoboken (and at all of his subsequent leaps) Sam leaped for strangers who merely wanted to see
a man jump from high places, and whose enjoyment of Sam's
leaps had nothing to do with labor disputes, fights over local
playgrounds, or the games of factory boys. Sam's new exhibitions
and his new audiences (along with the widening public that read
or heard about Sam's leaps in the newpapers and in barbershop

conversations) transformed Sam Patch into a primitive conqueror of nature, a solitary daredevil who performed "wonderful
and intrepid leaps" for fame and money. After July 1828 Sam
Patch was no longer a local working-class hero. He was on his
way to being a showman and a celebrity.

It was probably not a smooth transition. After the leap at
Hoboken, Sam Patch dropped out of sight. He did not return to
Paterson. There is some evidence that he worked in a mill near
Philadelphia. His one appearance during the next year was a
little-noted Fourth of July leap at Little Falls, well above Paterson on the Passaic River. Beyond that, we know only that gentlemen in Buffalo, through friends in New York City, invited Sam to
leap at Niagara Falls in October 1829. We know also that when
Sam set out on his journey to Niagara, he was drunk nearly all
the time.[52]

III

NIAGARA

In 1829 the innkeepers at Niagara Falls announced an off-season exhibition: they would explode huge rocks into the Niagara gorge, they would decorate a sailing ship and send it over the Falls, and they would ask Sam Patch to perform one of his leaps. They contacted Sam through friends in New York. Sam accepted the invitation and set out to become the first Niagara Falls daredevil.

On the morning of October 6, 1829, Colonel William Leete Stone, editor and part owner of the *New-York Commercial Advertiser*, stepped onto the veranda of William Forsyth's Niagara Falls Pavilion, the grand hotel at British Niagara. Just out of sight, at the base of the island that separated the Canadian and American Falls, was the spot from which Sam Patch would make his leap. Up and to the right, a low pier led out from the island to rocks at the brink of the Falls; a closer look revealed workmen planting charges for the afternoon's explosions. Downriver, on the Canadian side, more workmen packed gunpowder into an overhanging rock shelf. Hawkers of food and drink were setting up their booths. A corps of circus riders had arrived on the

American side. The beginnings of a crowd of country people watched the preparations and gawked at the Falls.

Colonel Stone witnessed the various events of the day and wrote about them. But early in the day and at intermissions he studied Niagara Falls. His travel journal reveals the utter seriousness with which he undertook that study. Stone was a country boy who had made good in New York City. He had power, wealth, and influential friends, and he was an acknowledged spokesman for a mercantile elite that claimed more than money and connections. Stone and his friends were a self-conscious community of sensibility and taste: they knew the best books and plays, they mastered an elaborate system of manners, they followed London fashions, and they spoke an upper-crust English that distanced them from ordinary Americans. In Colonel Stone's social circle aesthetic taste—not money, heredity, or social connections, though all of these were tied to taste—was deemed the principal sign of one's inner worth. They cultivated good taste in themselves and sought it in others, and they were trained to recognize poseurs and pretenders.[1]

In the 1820s this genteel elite began to cultivate an appreciation of natural beauty and a consuming interest in scenic tourism, as their English models had done decades earlier. The wealthy had always traveled for pleasure, but now Americans made long and expensive journeys for the sole purpose of looking at scenery. A pilgrimage to Niagara Falls, which was accessible by Hudson River steamboat and the Erie Canal (completed in 1825), was the high point in what became known as the "Fashionable Tour." People of means came to Niagara to live for a few days or weeks in perfect beauty—an experience that gave them profound and authentic pleasure, and that asserted their membership in an emerging cultural elite.[2]

The journey to Niagara was an important cultural task, and William Leete Stone prepared himself. In New York he read travel books and texts on aesthetics, notably those of Basil Hall

William Leete Stone (*Appleton's Cyclopaedia of American Biography*, New York, 1888)

(whose *Travels in North America* was a popular, if controversial, guide to Niagara) and Edmund Burke, and studied the scale model of Niagara that the rising artist George Catlin was exhibiting in the city. Stone almost certainly attended William Dunlap's drama *A Trip to Niagara*, a popular farce played before a moving diorama of the scenic route from New York to the Falls. Along with the lesson in landscape, Dunlap's play showed audiences how (and how not) to think and act on the journey to Niagara. Colonel Stone was also a regular at Niblo's and the other summer gardens of New York, where the evening often ended with Niagara displayed in fireworks. (The fireworks were a lesson in the sublime: "[The Falls] will be seen in the first instance of great extent and beautiful appearance, but gradually become more and more violent, until they assume the character of 'the Tremendous Cataract,' bursting from its confined and precipitous bed, with the noise of thunder.") Most important, he traveled in the highest circles of New York society, where beauty and taste, the Fashionable Tour, and the proper experience of Niagara Falls were the common coin of polite conversation.[3]

Stone and his wife, Susannah (she was the sister of Francis Wayland, president of Brown University), took three weeks to reach Niagara, taking side trips to Stone's childhood haunts at Cooperstown and his parents' home at Sodus, and surveying the new world that was being made by the Erie Canal. Stone's preparations for Niagara continued throughout those three weeks. His travel journal (a private diary, unpublished in his lifetime) routinely sorted landscapes and people into aesthetic categories. There was the majesty and beauty of the Hudson Highlands seen from the steamboat; the pleasing farmscapes of the Mohawk Valley on the way to Cooperstown (farmscapes that became beautiful when seen from high ground); the grandeur of an old-growth forest in autumn colors (again seen from above, west of Lockport); the mean, unpicturesque aspect of poor towns and uneven country. At times Stone, following the rules of picturesque travel, corrected imperfections: in Rochester, where developers had mowed down a whole forest to make room for a new city, his mind's eye saved some of the prettier trees for shade and ornamentation; later, Stone moved the village of Skaneateles to place it in a more tasteful relationship to its lake. Stone sorted people in the same taste-driven ways: the best of them (judged by their clothes, houses, gardens, manners, and eloquence in conversation) were elegant and genteel, others were respectable and agreeable, the worst were unpleasant. It was a relentlessly aesthetic sensibility that William Leete Stone brought to Niagara Falls.[4]

Twice on the journey Stone's meditations were interrupted by moments of astonishment and fear that he had learned to call sublime. In Cooperstown he stood below a flaming hillside at night, reveling in the red glow of the fire, the ghostly obscurity provided by darkness and smoke, and the dreadful sounds of falling trees. Later Stone felt the same ennobling terror when he turned off a road and suddenly confronted a storm on Lake Ontario. In both instances Stone experienced Edmund Burke's "delightful horror" without fear. The fire near Cooperstown had been started and controlled by woodsmen. It was thus safe, and Stone enjoyed a sublime experience "unalloyed with painful or unpleasant emotions." The storm on Lake Ontario was foregrounded by a "picturesque and beautiful" shoreline of calm inlets and stately forests, "while the view of the mighty expanse of heaving waters beyond, was full of majesty and grandeur." (The older heroic sublime had required danger and physicality; Colonel Stone's new mercantile elite gave up the horrific sublime just as they gave up fencing lessons, mistresses, and physical risks—all of which entailed danger and a breach of genteel spectatorship.) This fusion of beauty and awe, seen from a point that was both pleasing and safe, was what Stone was seeking at Niagara Falls.[5]

In the 1820s William Forsyth and the other hotelkeepers had shaped the land surrounding Niagara Falls with people like Colonel Stone in mind. Before 1815 access to the grand viewpoint at Table Rock on the Canadian side was down a steep, slippery path into the brush. Most visitors made that hike, but few descended to the river below the falls. Goat Island, which afforded the best viewpoints in the United States, was inaccessible. With the end of war between Great Britain and the United States in 1815, and with the completion of the Erie Canal in 1825, the Falls opened to scenic tourism. By 1829 Stone and other tourists found hotels, landscaped paths, planked walkways, bridges, piers, ferryboats, and staircases that transformed the rigors and dangers of Niagara into an ordered and comfortable succession of scenic views. Some viewpoints placed them at brink level or on high ground, affording vast, reassuring horizontal panoramas of the Falls and the surrounding countryside. Safe stairs descended to the banks below the Falls, and Stone experienced the vertical sublimities of the Falls chasm without effort or danger.

Niagara in 1829 presented an aesthetic rather than a physical challenge. It was grand beyond literary description, too vast and varied to be captured by even the most skilled and inspired painter. But the well-prepared tourist could view Niagara from a variety of safe points, framing scenes of natural beauty, the well-balanced picturesque, and the stunning sublime. The most accomplished aesthetes joined the beauties of horizontal vistas with the vertical terrors of Niagara into a spiritual experience of overwhelming beauty surrounding a muffled shudder of fear—an experience that was the unique creation (and then the treasured memory and conversation piece) of every successful tourist. That perfect moment gave the journey to Niagara the transcendent qualities of a work of art, and it made an artist of every good tourist. The opportunity to make that moment was the principal commodity on sale at Niagara Falls.[6]

Colonel Stone and his wife reached Forsyth's Pavilion in Canada on the night of October 5, 1829, at about the time that Sam Patch checked into a hotel on the American side. The Stones ate supper and retired to an upstairs apartment that overlooked the rapids and Falls. Colonel Stone, knowing that astute travelers considered this view banal, fought off his curiosity and kept the curtains drawn—"being resolved," he tells us, "not to dissolve the charm of a first look upon the mighty, glorious whole!" He prepared for bed and lay down in the dark. As the bustle of a busy hotel quieted for the night (on this night before the planned shipwreck and explosions, Forsyth's may have been a bit noisier than usual), Stone heard the roar of the Falls and felt the shudder that they sent through the building, and he slipped into fitful dreams of waterfalls and whirlpools and towering, jagged rocks. In the morning he and his wife rose, ate breakfast, and began composing their experience of Niagara Falls.[7]

Colonel Stone walked to the first-floor veranda, passing up not only the higher view from his room but the great panorama afforded from the roof of the Pavilion. (Forsyth advertised that his hotel sat on "commanding ground," with a rooftop view "unequalled for . . . grandeur & diversity," i.e., for its combination of the grand and the civilized picturesque.) At other points in his journey, Stone had sought high ground—particularly when it afforded him broad vistas of cultivated land. From the roof of a museum in Utica he had enjoyed a "glorious view" of the town and the surrounding countryside; from atop a hotel in Buffalo he had looked at a similar townscape set within a pastoral country, this time with a busy Lake Erie harbor thrown in, and pronounced it "a fine view." At Niagara, however, he did not seek "commanding" ground from which he could subject the scene to a satisfied "Magisterial Gaze." He wanted to be overwhelmed by beauty and sublimity, and he knew that such things were best accomplished at eye level and from below.[8]

The view from Forsyth's veranda disappointed knowledgeable aesthetes. To the right was the distant, mile-long explosion of the rapids, quieting and turning emerald green as the river rolled over the precipice. It was impressive enough, but the veranda afforded only a partial view of the Canadian Falls and no view at all of the chasm. One visitor dismissed the view as "superficial." Another complained that "the prospect there gave me but an indifferent idea of Niagara. . . . I could see only part of the Horse-shoe Fall, and consequently had no idea of the sublime part of the precipice below the Fall." Others pronounced the partial view from Forsyth's a mere appetizer for what was next. According to a visitor in 1828, it "only increased our desire to have the whole scene unfolded"; a Philadelphia merchant dismissed it as a mere "preparation of soul for what was to come." Colonel Stone agreed: he was glad that clouds of spray shrouded Forsyth's broken view of the Horseshoe, though he granted that the beauty and violence of the rapids "afforded a prospect sufficiently interesting to render the senses keenly alive to the more sublime and glorious spectacle that was to come."[9]

Eager for his first full view of Niagara, Stone followed a pathway from the Pavilion to the fabled viewpoint at Table Rock. Forsyth had cleared the path as a pleasant promenade that descended in easy switchbacks, but he ensured that shrubbery obstructed the view. Table Rock would burst properly and suddenly upon the senses at the end, and not before. Colonel Stone, like thousands before and after him, stepped onto Table Rock and was "struck silent and breathless for some moments, with wonder and dread admiration of this stupendous monument of almighty power."[10]

Discerning tourists agreed that Table Rock afforded, as one of them put it in 1823, "one of the grandest and most romantic views in nature": an unobstructed brink-level panorama of the Canadian and American Falls. In 1831 Frances Trollope stood still as "wonder, terror, and delight completely overwhelmed me. I wept with a strange mixture of pleasure and of pain." An Englishman visited Table Rock at night and—like Trollope, Colonel Stone, and many others—waited for astonishment to subside and contemplation to begin. The experience, he concluded, "seemed to complete in absolute perfection the rare union of the beautiful with the sublime." The Englishman Basil Hall was interestingly candid about the place of Table Rock in cultural history: "At one moment I looked upon myself as utterly insignificant in the presence of such a gigantic, moving, thundering body,—and in the next, was puffed up with a sort of pride and arrogant satisfaction, to think that I was admitted into such company, and that I was not wasting the opportunity."[11]

Stone stood on Table Rock and allowed himself a long moment of astonishment and an acknowledgment of God's wonders. He slowly collected himself, looked closely at each portion of the panorama, and recalled the paintings, poetry, and travel books that had shaped his ability to perceive. At last he was prepared to write his account of the view from Table Rock. There were those, he knew, who could be unaffected by such scenes (indeed, on this morning of Forsyth's shipwreck and explosions, Stone may have been surrounded by such persons).

But to one who has an eye alive to the glorious works of the Creator, as manifested in this beautiful world; who has a heart to feel his power and goodness; and perceptions to admire and appreciate their vastness and magnificence, I can think of no other spectacle in nature more calculated to thrill the bosom, and call all those faculties and perceptions into elevated and delightful action, and to lead the mind from the contemplation of Nature up to Nature's God, than this wonderful cataract.[12]

William Leete Stone and Niagara Falls had begun their conquest of each other.

Along with its horizontal beauties, Table Rock afforded a vertical gaze into Niagara's horrible abyss. In 1827 an American had crept on his belly to the edge and looked down. He "recoiled in-

In 1827 a merchant from Philadelphia sketched Niagara Falls from above and below. The panorama from Table Rock is bright, expansive, and reassuring. The view from below is dark and tumultuous, and it is accompanied by sublime poetry (John Fanning Watson Travel Diary, 1827, courtesy of the Winterthur Library: Joseph Downs Collection of Manuscripts and Printed Ephemera)

stinctively, and in horror," explaining that "all distinctness of vision was lost—annihilated by the boiling, bounding, bursting hell beneath me. . . ." Another visitor "glanced in giddy fear on the phrenzied, foaming agitation of the gulph below," while yet another (a man who had just pronounced the horizontal view from Table Rock as Niagara's finest composition) looked down to see only "the wildest confusion." Colonel Stone stared down into the chasm and pronounced the view "overpowerful." He then descended William Forsyth's staircase for a closer look at the base of the Falls.[13]

Forsyth had built the staircase in 1818 as one of his first improvements. It was a spiral staircase covered with wooden siding (a guard against vertigo and a premature view of the Falls) and it gave a comfortable experience of sublime terror. At the entrance Stone paid a toll and signed a guest album. Then he passed down the stairs and through a guide's shack and stepped toward the chasm, a few feet from the stupendous violence at the base of the Falls.

A guidebook pronounced this Niagara's "most sublime scene." Here the visitor stood beneath Table Rock, immediately beside the overwhelming movement and within the deafening roar of the Falls as they exploded into the abyss. The debris of great rockfalls cluttered the way, worrying tourists who looked up at overhanging cliffs. One overwrought English gentleman averred that "the dark firmament of rock which threatened destruction to the intruder, the terrors of the descending torrent, the deep thunder of its roar, and the fearful convulsion of the waters into which it falls, constitute the features of a scene, the sublimity of which undoubtedly extends to the very verge of horror." Another, overwhelmed in precisely the same way, found snakes on the ground: "These, when combined with the other terrors of the place,—the frightful roar of the cataract, and the troubled aspect of the river,—tend powerfully to augment the fearful propensities of the astonished visitor." Yet another English visitor insisted that under Table Rock

Beneath Table Rock, by
W. H. Bartlett (W. P. Willis,
American Scenery, 1840,
author's collection)

"the soul can be susceptible only of one emotion, viz., that of un-controllable terror." The American explorer and ethnographer Henry Schoolcraft, who like the others knew his artistic conventions, explained: it was beneath Table Rock

> that the mind becomes fully impressed, with the appalling majesty
> of the Fall. Other views . . . are more beautiful and picturesque;
> but it is here that the tremulous motion of the earth, the clouds of
> iridescent spray, the broken column of falling water, the stunning
> sound, the lofty banks of the river, and the wide spreading ruin of
> rocks, imprint a character of wonder and terror upon the scene,
> which no other point of view is capable of producing.[14]

Colonel Stone had studied these lessons. Stunned by spray and thunder, he wrote that "he who can unmoved look up from the dreadful gulph, and gaze upon hanging rocks and rushing waters above, and the dizzying whirlpools beneath—upon the clouds of ascending vapour, now dense and humid and now light and fleecy, and reflecting the melting and beautiful tints of the rainbow, must be made of sterner stuff than I." He concluded that the vertical terrors of the chasm (even when softened by a redeeming rainbow) were "intensely and awfully sublime." Then he reminded himself, in proper fashion, that "no passion contributes more to the sublime than terror."[15]

"But I am becoming too prolix," wrote the Colonel at this point, "and must draw this imperfect outline to a close." Little mobs of farmers and laborers now crowded the viewpoints. Forsyth's men would set off their first explosion after lunch, and the wreck of the *Superior* was scheduled for three o'clock in the afternoon. Stone interrupted his tour to watch the show. The next day he crossed to the American side to witness the leap of Sam Patch. He assures us that he "spent the day in studying the cataract," "viewing this wonderful curiosity from different points of observation . . . and [that] each moment . . . was of still more thrilling interest—of more special wonder—of higher and more elevated enjoyment." His journal, however, provides details only for the morning of October 6. At noon that day, apparently, Stone put his travel journal away and picked up his reporter's notebook.[16]

Colonel Stone spent two days at Niagara—the days of Forsyth's explosions, the wreck of the *Superior*, and the leap of Sam Patch. For much of the time he put the exhibitions and the crowds out of mind, and collected sublime spiritual moments for his travel journal. He recorded those moments in the high authoritative language of Anglo-American genteel aestheticism. But in the same two days Stone watched the shows and reported on them for the *Commercial Advertiser.* For that he needed a different voice. The United States, as Colonel Stone frequently complained, was becoming a democratic society that made its own heroes, its own entertainments, and its own political movements. Stone and other genteel conservatives paid as little attention to the emerging democracy as they could. But the mob was everywhere and could not be ignored—certainly not by a daily journalist like William Leete Stone. In the 1820s Colonel Stone experimented with cultivated ways of talking about democracy. He worked a surprising number of those experiments on the exploits of Sam Patch.

In these days before the penny press, New York journalists wrote for the monied elite—an elite that knew Stone's *Commercial Advertiser* as a source of useful news, sound politics, and gentlemanly wit. When Sam Patch first won notoriety, Stone and his colleagues looked for ways to dismiss him. The more self-conscious aesthetes wrote him off as nameless and insane—"a half crazy fellow," in the words of an Albany paper. The *New England Palladium* published an excruciatingly genteel account of a carriage ride from New York to the falls of the Passaic, and concluded with a dismissive scrambling of the single utterance Patch was known to have made. He claimed his jumps were undertaken, said the *Palladium*, to demonstrate that "somebody besides other folks can do something." The *New York Journal of Commerce* (founded by the evangelical Lewis Tappan to provide business news without advertisements for liquor or the theater) described Patch as "a hair-brained fellow in Patterson [*sic*], whose name we do not recollect," and followed with an account of Patch's July 4, 1828, leap couched in the conventions of the sublime: "The universal anxiety of the multitude was manifest in their countenances . . . a cloud had come over the spot, adding to the sublimity of the cataract," and so on. William Leete Stone's first stories about Sam Patch also denied the jumper his name.

An anonymous madman—a "crazy chap" and an "insane gentle-man"—had made these jumps, and "the writ of *de lunatico inquirendo* should be issued before he performs."[17]

Stone soon found better uses for Sam Patch. He had already learned to identify Patch with the followers of Andrew Jackson, who were upending the founders' republic and replacing it with a noisy, plebeian mass democracy. On his journey to Niagara, Stone recounts his discomfort on a canal boat with passengers who were "very good for *universal suffrage folks*—all Jackson men, as the color of their shirt collars abundantly attested." He ran into another "boisterous gang of Universal Suffrage Jackson men" heading for the show at Niagara Falls. At the end of that day he crossed to King George IV's Canada and "seemed to breathe a purer air." "I am as decidedly a *Republican* in *principle*, as any man, but I am no Jacobin—no democrat. I hate the mob."[18]

A year earlier the Paterson strike had broken out during Jackson's triumphant contest for the presidency in 1828. Stone, countering a Democratic journalist's story about the strike, branded it a Jackson riot. The rioters wore hickory sprigs in their hats as homage to their hero, "Old Hickory." Worse, they threatened to throw supporters of President John Quincy Adams into Patch's chasm. "We did not learn to what party [Patch] belongs," wrote Stone, "but take it for granted he is a Jackson man." The easy association of Sam Patch, Andrew Jackson, and anything low became a staple of Stone's journalistic repertoire.[19]

Throughout 1828 the *Commercial Advertiser* argued against Jacksonian suspicions that President Adams had bought the electoral votes cast for Henry Clay in the 1824 contest, in which Andrew Jackson had won the popular vote but not a majority of the Electoral College; Clay had thrown his decisive support to Adams, and had then been appointed Secretary of State. Stone thought the rumors of a "corrupt bargain" between Clay and Adams were political humbug. Immediately after Sam Patch's leap at Hoboken, he constructed "a regular-built Jackson article" documenting a bargain between Henry Clay and Sam Patch—a parody of the missing, misconstrued, and forged evidence on which, Stone claimed, Democrats based their accusations. The fictional Sam Patch of the piece is illiterate and gullible, and his language is the mangled opposite of genteel. "Sur—I got yure note," he writes Clay, "but most haaf on't was tore off. I shall jump accordin to yure wishes, and transackt the bizziness I trust, to your taste. All I complane's of is yure not being suffishently konphidenshall." The letter misrepresents vernacular speech and plebeian-phonetic spelling, but that is not the point. The article was a feast of parodied ignorance and bad taste served up for the Adams supporters who read the *Commercial Advertiser.* The "insane gentleman" of Stone's first Patch article was transformed into a low and ignorant fool.[20]

At Niagara, Stone wrote about Sam's leap under the name and in the character of Hiram Doolittle, Jun. He had invented Doolittle two weeks earlier for a piece he composed for the Cooperstown *Freeman's Journal*, the Federalist weekly on which he had served his journalistic apprenticeship.[21]

Stone's readers knew what to expect from Hiram Doolittle, Jun. The original Hiram Doolittle was the antagonist in James Fenimore Cooper's *The Pioneers* (1823), a novel of politics and social disintegration in early Cooperstown. Hiram Doolittle is a dissembling, cowardly politician who undermines the fortunes of Judge Temple (modeled on the novelist's father, William Cooper), the noble woodsman Natty Bumppo, and the social harmony of Temple's town. Wielding a formidable shrewdness and a rural New England dialect ("heerd" for "heard," and so on) he intrigues after power, money, and respect that he cannot earn. At the conclusion of *The Pioneers*, a defeated and humiliated Hiram Doolittle leaves town, and good order under the Temple family returns.[22]

Cooper's Hiram Doolittle was among the first of the Yankee

characters who invaded American drama and literature in the 1820s. By the 1830s their rustic mistakes and rustic insights were elbowing the wit of English drawing-room ladies and gentlemen off the American stage and out of popular literature. Some Yankee characters were depicted as simple and virtuous, some were simple and dishonest, some were populist democrats, and others found folksy, commonsense ways to uphold the power of the elite. Without exception, however, Yankees named Doolittle were talkative and empty exemplars of what was wrong with democracy.

Stone's Hiram Doolittle, Jun., was one of a growing Yankee clan. The earliest Doolittle character, another verbose and ignorant fellow, appeared in *The Yankee in England*, written in 1814 by the prominent Federalist David Humphreys and performed (once) in the author's factory village of Humphreysville, Connecticut. Cooper introduced Hiram Doolittle in 1823, and in 1828 one Jonathan Doolittle appeared on stage, as impersonated by the Englishman John Bull (both characters played by a young George "Yankee" Hill), in Dunlap's *A Trip to Niagara*. Dunlap's Doolittle is a comic-vernacular braggart who tells exaggerated stories and pretends knowledge of things of which he knows nothing. James Hackett, the first of the great Yankee character actors, brought one Industrious Doolittle to the New York stage in 1829. Industrious was, the playbill says, "A Busy, Talkative Native of one of the Eastern States—Speculator in every thing—Auctioneer, Bank and Insurance Director, and Stump Candidate for Assembly, with a sneaking notion for Caroline, or more 'specially' her rich inheritance in Rice and Cotton Plantations." Like Cooper's original Hiram, these Doolittle characters were neither the sturdy yeomen who formed the ideal base of conservative society nor the gentlemen at its top. They were demagogues and small-time businessmen who cheated and manipulated the yeomanry for their own selfish purposes—purposes often driven by low resentment of their social and cultural betters.] When not in politics, the Doolittles found devious and insubstantial ways to make a living. Dunlap's Jonathan Doolittle manufactured wooden nutmegs. Hackett's Industrious Doolittle talked, among other things, of speculating in feathers.[23]

The Doolittle characters sprang from the imaginations of gentlemen—Cooper, Dunlap, Hackett, Stone—who had been hurt, or believed they had been hurt, by populist democracy. With Hiram Doolittle, Cooper took literary revenge on Jedediah Peck, a real-life evangelical preacher and politician who had in fact undermined the fortunes of the Coopers. William Dunlap spent his life trying to establish an English-style national theater in America, with himself as a principal arbiter of popular taste in drama. Democratic America paid little attention to him. *A Trip to Niagara*, a rare popular success for him, was a light farce intended as an afterpiece. Dunlap acknowledged that it attracted audiences more for its unique scenic apparatus than for the play itself. James Hackett, who after his father's death had been raised among his mother's relatives in the Beekman, Roosevelt, DePeyster, and Duane families, and who continued to benefit from his connections to the old New York aristocracy, was the husband of a classical actress and a friend of William Dunlap's. He developed his Yankee and other vernacular characters in an effort to civilize Americans through comic bad examples. He played successfully to his wealthy friends in the East; western audiences sometimes chased him off the stage.[24]

All these New York gentlemen knew each other. Dunlap and the English comedian Charles Mathews (who is often given credit for developing the first stage Yankee) enjoyed a long evening with Cooper on a Hudson River steamer in 1823. Dunlap also knew and liked Hackett (and may have been on his way to join Hackett in Utica when he ran into Cooper on the steamboat). Stone was a boyhood friend of Cooper's and wrote an early and important review of *The Pioneers*. In New York he lived at the center of the social circle in which Dunlap and Hackett operated.[25]

And he certainly knew the story of *The Pioneers* and Hiram Doolittle as family history. Stone spent his boyhood near Cooperstown in the hardscrabble village of Burlington, where his father was a Presbyterian minister, a Yale-trained descendant of the Puritans who struggled for right religion and tutored his son in Greek, Latin, and Hebrew. Among the Stones' neighbors was Jedediah Peck. Peck, an unaffiliated evangelical exhorter, built a successful politics by asserting the worthiness and political capacity of the poor farmers of Otsego County, and he launched his democratic revolt from Burlington. While his chief target was the proprietor William Cooper at the county seat, he and other evangelical democrats doubtless assaulted outposts of gentility in Burlington—outposts that included the home and church of the Reverend Stone. William Stone hinted as much. "My father," he wrote during a visit to Burlington, "had been cruelly displaced as a minister here."[26]

In 1808, when William was sixteen, the family retreated to Sodus, near Lake Ontario. Stone visited them on his way to Niagara twenty years later. The town was, he wrote, "not a place of much business," and he reached his parents' "humble residence" over "a rough, ragged road." He stayed three or four days, but he recorded no details about his mother or father and did not describe their house or garden, though his diary included long passages about other houses, families, and gardens. The Colonel kept himself busy taking tea with ministers and village dignitaries, surveying the economic prospects of Sodus, surrendering himself to the stormy sublime of Lake Ontario. The only bit of family business was a visit to the graves of his two brothers. Before leaving he paid (as his father apparently could not pay) to have proper headstones erected for them. Between the lines of Stone's record of this brief, uncomfortable visit we glimpse a family living in poverty and obscurity—the squalid result of a disaster that seems to have come at the hands of Burlington's populist democrats, perhaps at the hands of Jedediah Peck (Hiram Doolittle) himself.[27]

Colonel Stone's Hiram Doolittle, Jun., is a worthy offspring of Cooper's original. He is a braggart, a tasteless poseur, and a Jacksonian Democrat. Worse, he is a murderer of genteel English. He tells us that Hiram, Sr., had moved west from Cooperstown to become "the principal architect of all the successive villages which sprung up with the onward march of emigration"; he is now building the capitol at Indianapolis, "the seat of government of the state which furnishes the first four syllables of this name, at once so classical and beautiful." The younger Doolittle has met the Jacksonian journalists Amos Kendall and Duff Green, and recounts a conversation between them conducted in "the pure English of your own country"—talk filled with "a sprinkle of bears," "a heap of Indians," and an occasional "Well, I reckon." But Green, Kendall, and young Doolittle (not to mention whoever thought up the name Indianapolis) are guilty less of speaking in the vernacular than of using big words without the cultivation to back them up. Doolittle expands his vocabulary by reading Green's newspaper, then speaks thus to the hostler at a livery stable: "here—just be so good as to refrigerate my quadruped, by circumambulating him two or three times about this fountain; then permit him to imbibe a moderate quantity of aqueous particles; after which, administer to him proper vegetable nutriment, and inform me what will be considered competent pecuniary satisfaction." The hostler thinks that Doolittle is speaking German. Readers of the *Commercial Advertiser* would recognize him as a tasteless and spiritually empty Jacksonian upstart.[28]

Colonel Stone's report of Forsyth's spectacle and Patch's leap at Niagara used Doolittle's graceless, trumped-up erudition to buttress the real thing. Doolittle begins by divulging that William

Forsyth and his co-promoters were businessmen and the exhibition had profit as its motive. These "benevolent gentlemen," he says, "not the least interested, and in the most liberal manner possible," got up the show as a "treat" for local townspeople and farmers—a "treat" for which they would have to pay if they wanted to eat or drink or stand at the favored viewpoints. Doolittle further commodifies the place with his excuse for attending Forsyth's low entertainment: "But do not suppose . . . because I happen to be here just at this time, that I came from an idle curiosity to see the exhibition. Like a good many other gentlemen . . . I was called here upon pressing business; and being here, I must either shut my eyes, or see the show."[29]

Enlightened readers could recognize this talk about business as a horrible gaffe. If one ignored the hotels and tollbooths, as scenic tourists tried to do, Niagara was a pristine wonder of nature protected from development, a divine gallery of views for fashionable people who were too wealthy to think about business—particularly while they were at the Falls. Doolittle's talk subverted the timeless spiritual moment that was supposedly the one legitimate reason for traveling to Niagara Falls. Doolittle corrupted Niagara simply by being there and noticing, in his vulgar way, that Niagara Falls was a business.] — industry

That is about all that Stone's Doolittle notices about Niagara Falls. The exhibition, he tells us, has been gotten up "to embellish a very tame spot in the map, formerly an object of some interest to the curious, and the lovers of the sublime and beautiful, known as the cataract of Niagara." The crowd shares his aesthetic deadness. Doolittle is joined by a number of gentlemen who, like himself, had come not to see the show but on "special business." On the morning of October 6 "the universal suffrage folks of both nations" converge on the Falls, crowding around the shanties selling food and drink. They watch with great interest as workmen—"brave fellows, who like insects seemed to hang upon the beetling cliffs"—plant charges at the rocks that are to be blown up. They watch the circus men and what Doolittle calls "a ragged company of strolling players," and they keep a lookout for Sam Patch, who had arrived on the American side the previous night. "But few of the crowd, if any, as it is supposed, were foolish enough to lose their time by gaping and gazing at the falls themselves. These they could see at any time; and all that they cared about them now, arose from the fear that the confounded roaring they made, would prevent the hearing of the gunpowder."

Hiram Doolittle, Jun., pronounces the show a failure. The governor of Upper Canada, "fearing perhaps that the whole cataract would be blown up," had banned the explosion at Table Rock. Forsyth had moved his gunpowder to a small island above the Falls and an overhanging ledge below them, and the Americans promised to blast the outer Terrapin Rocks at the end of their bridge. "The explosions took place, and the rocks went off—to the infinite delight of the multitude," but "the sublime effects of these displays" were like "a volley of popguns interfering with the thunder of Jupiter," as if "Gulliver's Lilliputians had been seated upon the loftiest cliffs firing off pocket pistols, and dropping pebbles into the valley below." Doolittle likens the smoke of the blasts to a few Germans blowing pipe smoke into Niagara's immense and eternal spray. Men had done something silly, small, and pointlessly physical in the grand temple of cultured spirituality. Doolittle tells us that "the good people, the sovereigns of our country, and the subjects of the other, were marvellously delighted."

Following the explosions there was an intermission—more eating, drinking, and circus tricks—then the wreck of the *Superior* at three o'clock. The ship appeared far upstream, drifting calmly on the mirror-like river above the rapids. "How deceitful the calm!" gushes the mock-literary Doolittle. "And here I might moralize, if I had time." The crowd gaped with "breathless interest" as the schooner entered the rapids, "plunged gallantly among the successive breakers, like a noble war-steed in battle," then spun broadside to the current, rode up onto a flat rock, and stayed there.

At this point, Doolittle tells us, the crowd grew unruly. The explosion at Table Rock had not taken place. The substitutes were disappointing, the shipwreck had gone wrong, and Sam Patch had not made his leap. He promised to jump the next day, but most people had to go home, and some suspected a hoax. "The people on both sides," Doolittle reports, "went home heavy and displeased." On the Canadian side, "His Majesty's colored and Killarney subjects" ended the day with fistfights.

Sam Patch rescheduled his leap for noon on October 7. It rained hard that day, but Doolittle saw that "Sam was determined to have his jump. His reputation was at stake. True, the people were gone, but Sam was to jump for glory, not filthy lucre." (Even after Sam had died, Stone insisted that his motive had not been money but a celebrity that he did not merit, a breach of propriety that was at least as bad as mere greed and that he shared with Hiram Doolittle.) The plan was for Sam to leap from a platform atop an eighty-foot ladder that leaned from the base of Goat Island out over the pool beneath the Falls. It was an unwieldy apparatus, and workmen dropped it while raising it in the rain and broke off its end. Doolittle tells us that Sam "was visibly and very sensibly affected, insomuch that the big tears did roll down his manly cheeks in pearly drops." But Doolittle assures us that Sam's sentimental repertoire is as limited as his own, and that his disappointments and hopes are imprisoned in the ordinary and the squalid. Doolittle retells the story of the tailor who saw Niagara and declared it "a fine place to sponge a coat! In like manner did Mr. Patch, after a solemn pause when he first beheld this tremendous cataract, exclaim in an ecstacy of delight: 'What a darned fine place to jump!'"

Sam surveyed the weather and the broken ladder and rescheduled his leap for four o'clock. At that hour the storm returned. For an hour the little crowd stood in the rain; Sam sat beneath a rock ledge. The storm finally let up, and Sam Patch walked to the ladder "amidst cheers so loud that they would have been heard far abroad," said Doolittle, "had it not been for the roaring of the turbulent Niagara." He climbed the ladder, bowed to the men and blew a kiss to the ladies, then stepped off into the abyss.

"What a fall was that, my countrymen," wrote Doolittle. "He sank down genteely" and disappeared. Then a play on the emotional limits of ordinary men: " 'He has made an everlasting leap,' said an old man, wiping away a tear"; " 'I wonder if he was told to look for the bones of Morgan,' inquired a little old man who looked as though he wanted to go to the Assembly." (This was a gibe at the populist Antimasons, who were building a political movement on the belief that members of the lodge had murdered a man named William Morgan at Niagara.) Finally there was Doolittle himself, rustic and overblown, mouthing a classical reference and getting it wrong: "It was indeed a wonderful, a prodigious jump, such as mortal man had never made before; and the fishes must have stared some, I reckon, when he popped in so suddenly upon their unvisited kingdom—a province which even Neptune himself, nor any of his tritons, had ever yet dared to visit."

As a boat crossed the pool looking for him, Sam bobbed up, swam to shore, and "was discovered clambering up the rocks, like a soaked muskrat!" (Doolittle also tells us that the crowd in the rain looked like "drowned rats." We are left to wonder how he would describe wet fashionables; probably not as rodents.) "He was received with hearty cheers, and the people all scampered home to dry their clothes and talk grandiloquently of the hero of the day. At our house it was voted that . . . *Sam Patch* is but a scurvy name for the hero . . . and that henceforward he shall be known by the more appropriate cognomen of SAMUEL O'CATARACT, ESQ."

Stone gave his dispatch an anti-Jacksonian finale. The steamboats *Pioneer* and *Henry Clay* had ferried passengers between Buffalo and the Falls for the shipwreck and explosions on October 6. Returning to Black Rock, the *Pioneer* struck an ice break and sank. Doolittle moves this accident to October 7, putting it at the conclusion of Sam Patch's day at Niagara, and concocts a race between the two boats: "Being a Jackson man," he writes, "I don't like the *sign* at all. I fear that it is the sign of an omen, or the fore-end of a runner. I don't know which. It is plaguey hard that Henry Clay should always run ahead thus."

Niagara Falls in 1829 was exclusive and expensive. The four hotels kept by Parkhurst Whitney and William Forsyth could accommodate only a few hundred guests—visitors who stalked the sublime with parasols and spyglasses by day, then retired for educated conversation over hotel dinner tables. Forsyth advertised a good library and wine cellar, a pianoforte, a billiard table, and other accommodations for "noblemen and gentlemen of the highest rank with their families." The hotels published lists of their famous and highborn guests. An upstate editor looked at these lists and claimed that "in the grand piazzas may be seen at times, exiled Monarchs, Republican Generals, European Ambassadors, Whigs, Tories, Radicals, and Royalists, and Naval and Military officers of almost every nation in Europe. . . ." Others journeyed to Niagara only if they had money and were (or wanted to be) at ease in a place where aristocrats, rich merchants, and those who served them set the tone.[30]

The plain people of Upper Canada and western New York knew that Niagara was not for them. On the British side, only housemaids, ferrymen, guides, and others who served the tourist trade lived at the Falls. On the New York side the village of Manchester (its name betraying the early water-power ambitions of its proprietor) housed paper and woolen mills, but the village remained tiny, and was devoted almost solely to tourism after completion of the Erie Canal in 1825. Villagers and farmers in the surrounding countryside welcomed the annual invasion of wealthy sentimentalists who bought food, rented horses, and gave them seasonal work. ("It is well known," a village newsman confided, "that the people of 'rank, of fortune, of fashion, and of flash' which yearly crowd this frontier . . . all 'pay out like princes' when they travel.") But few locals traveled to the Falls, particularly when the fashionables were in residence. Of the thousands who lived nearby, wrote a local editor, "not one in one hundred have ever taken the trouble to visit the Falls."[31]

Yet visitors to Niagara in the 1820s encountered plenty of evidence that others had been there: hundreds of names were carved into rocks and trees—they covered the surface of Table Rock, and few of the trees on Goat Island were untouched— recording the visits of soldiers, traders, watermen, hunters and fishermen, and off-season gazers at the Falls. (The earliest carved inscription was dated 1769, which suggests that this was an English and American practice; French and Indian passersby surely saw the Falls before that time, but did not record their visits on rocks and trees.) Genteel tourists, who put their names only in albums at the hotels, viewed these carvings as relics of unworthy persons "anxious for immortality." A Philadelphia businessman recorded that on Goat Island "all the beech trees here are cut & carved with *names*—forming quite an *album*," and dismissed them with a bit of poetry: "Their names, their years, as spelt / The place of Fame or elegy supply!" Yet the names and dates inscribed on Niagara were tied to stories about the Falls—stories that were remembered and rehearsed in hundreds of places beyond the parlors of Philadelphia or the printing houses of London.[32]

Many of the Niagara stories were about war. Prior to completion of the Erie Canal, Niagara Falls had formed the one break to continuous water travel between the Great Lakes and the Atlantic Ocean. For a century and a half, Huron, Iroquois, French,

British, and American armies fought battle after bloody battle for control of the choke point at the Falls. In the War of 1812, fighting between British and American forces was almost continuous along the Niagara frontier. The American debacle at Queenston Heights, the exchange of bloody and inconclusive victories at Chippewa and Lundy's Lane, and the long siege of Fort Erie all took place near the Falls. In between the big engagements, raiders burned both Buffalo and York (now Toronto) and pillaged farms up and down the Niagara frontier. Well-heeled tourists in the 1820s passed near the ruins of Fort Erie and the bullet-pocked barns and cottages on the fields of battle. Some bought souvenir musket balls from Canadian children and a few rooted around for soldiers' bones. They could read battle accounts in their guidebooks and imagine sublime, ennobling contests fought within hearing of Niagara's glorious roar. But to the farmers and villagers who had fought in the militias of New York and Upper Canada or who had been burned out of their homes, as well as those who heard the stories from their elders and neighbors or saw the memories on their faces, the horrors of border war lived on, unsoftened by the divine wonders that refined outsiders came to see.

Along with the war stories, scores of smaller tales reinforced local knowledge of the immense, indifferent violence of Niagara Falls. There was a particular interest in the fate of animals, boats, and men caught in the rapids and swept over the Falls, the worst of Niagara's vertical terrors. "The inhabitants of the neighborhood," said one early guidebook, "regard it as certain death to get once involved in [the rapids]." Ravens picking at the fragments of birds, fish, and deer (along with an occasional human limb) below the Falls were ghoulish testimony to Niagara's malevolent power. (Birds and carrion, interestingly enough, disappear from travelers' accounts in the 1820s.) The soldiers who were among Niagara's first European residents experimented with the destructive force of the Falls. In 1750 Peter Kalm had watched when French soldiers pushed whole trees into the rapids; they tumbled over the brink and disappeared forever. In 1787 British soldiers launched a damaged boat over the Falls and watched it break up and disappear. In 1815 a British officer offered a reward for the largest fragment of three old gunboats sent over the Falls. The winning entry was a foot long.[33]

As settlement on the banks and commerce on the Niagara River increased, a growing tribe of journalists recorded disasters. In 1810 a salt boat fell "into the jaws of this tremendous cataract." The boat and its crew were "dashed to atoms" as the men's families and friends watched from shore. In the following spring the rapids devoured a canoe and three men. In 1820 two American whiskey smugglers went over the Falls. An unhappy trio rowed a boatload of furniture too near the rapids in 1821 and suffered "one of the most aweful deaths which it is possible to conceive." Only two weeks later, guests on Forsyth's veranda watched as two boats carried four men over the Falls. In 1824 two men ferrying apples and cider across the river entered the rapids and were "hurried into the awful gulf below!" A barrel of cider survived the plunge intact, and a ferryman downriver saw apples floating toward him. But the men had disappeared forever. Three boatmen capsized in the rapids in 1826; one struggled to the banks above the Falls, the bodies of the others were never found. Another boat with two men ran afoul of ice in the river in 1828 and plunged over the Falls; searchers found only fragments of clothing. There were hunting accidents as well. In 1828 a hunter fell from the cliffs trying to retrieve an eagle that he had shot. The following spring men drove a deer over the Falls, then nearly died trying to get it out of the icy chasm.[34]

Tourism itself created a full share of dangerous work, and the odd tourist who stopped to witness or imagine working at Niagara experienced a shudder of the old sublime. Workmen building the bridge to Goat Island, said an English visitor, "must have been in full possession of Horace's *aes triplex*, for a more perilous situation could scarcely be imagined. A slip of a workman's foot would precipitate him into the Rapids, whence he would pass with the rapidity of lightning over the Falls." Frances Trollope felt "sick and giddy" as she watched men building a spiral staircase while suspended from ropes. "I had never seen life perilled so wantonly," she said. Few tourists, however, recorded these terrors. Most of the construction and all of the boating and hunting disasters took place during the off-season. (The most dangerous month for watermen was November, when blustery weather coincided with the seasonal obligation to move harvested and processed farm goods before the winter freeze set in.)[35]

Tourists who visited during the sunny months also recognized Niagara's power to kill. But they buried their fear in vastness and beauty, and in an airy knowledge of cosmic order that removed physicality, pain, and fear even from the contemplation of violent death. In 1834 a young Harriet Beecher Stowe stared into the brink at Table Rock. "Oh, it is lovelier than it is great," she wrote, "it is like the Mind that made it: great, but so veiled in beauty that we gaze without terror. I felt as if I could have *gone over* with the waters; it would be so beautiful a death; there would be no fear in it." To those who lived near Niagara year-round, who knew the rigor and danger of the Niagara frontier, and who shared neither Stowe's immersion in perfect beauty nor her sentimentalized God, Niagara Falls still threatened, as the newsman put it, "one of the most aweful deaths which it is possible to conceive." There was more than one way to think about Niagara's power.[36]

Twice during the 1820s the hotelkeepers arranged off-season festivals for local crowds. Both were staged in the autumn, when fashionable visitors were gone and people from the countryside felt welcome at Niagara Falls. Both offered rustic audiences feats of human skill and daring, and both demonstrated the killing power and the vertical horrors of Niagara Falls.

In September 1827 the innkeepers dressed up the old lake schooner *Michigan* as a pirate vessel. They loaded the ship with live animals: a buffalo, two bears, a dog, a cat, a raccoon, a fox, a small flock of geese, and a tethered eagle—along with effigies of buccaneers, politicians, and the stage villain Blue Beard. Before a crowd estimated at somewhere between ten thousand and fifty thousand persons, they sent the ship over the Horseshoe Fall. Some in the crowd were late-season tourists, but most were local farm families. They witnessed the catastrophe of the *Michigan* and her doomed animals and patronized sideshows which included three brass bands, fiddlers and dancers, the educated dog Apollo, a menagerie with a caged African lion, and a ventriloquist from New York City. Pickpockets, gamblers, and women hawking beer and gingerbread worked the crowd.

Promoters advertised the "*Michigan* Descent" as an exercise in "INFERNAL NAVIGATION, OR A TOUCH OF THE SUB-LIME!" Deploying a mix of Burkean terror and Bowery Theater melodrama, they told people what to expect: "*The condemned vessel, with her strange cargo*, will pass away to her destiny, swift as the bosom of destruction." Captain James Rough ("the oldest navigator on the lakes," they tell us) would command the scow that towed the *Michigan* into the channel. His boat would pass near the rapids, and only experience and courage would keep its crew from being killed. The overpowering current would speed the *Michigan* and her cargo of trembling beasts into the rapids. "The cascades passed—if pass them she can without damage, she moves swiftly to the green glancing curve of the horse-shoe . . . where there as she lifts her bow, she will *seem* to pause ere she rides furiously down the feathery sheet, down, down, below! What can more enwrap the imagination—what can more freeze the senses—than such a scene. . . ." It was a treat, said the promoters, "to the lovers of novelty, and more especially of grandeur and sublimity. . . ." The best points for viewing the spectacle were on Goat Island and the British shore, "or (for those who wish to add to the scene a little more of the terrifick,) in the basin below the Falls." The *Michigan* Descent was, if nothing else, an exercise in the vertical sublime.[37]

The second autumn entertainment at Niagara was, of course, "the Blowing up of the Falls," and the "Earthquake, Sam. Patch, and the Superior Shipwreck!" in October 1829. Hotelkeepers advertised the show as a sequel to the *Michigan* Descent. The *Superior*, they said, was "a stout, staunch vessel," which drew less water than the old *Michigan*. She would be guided into the rapids by Captain Weissoon of Chippewa, who had been an oarsman in Captain Rough's boat. Promoters asserted that the *Superior* would reach the brink of the Falls in one piece, and that "her descent would be most splendid and imposing"—"a grand spectacle in going down the great falls: such a one as may ne'er be seen again." The explosion at Table Rock would be deafening ("a greater concussion is not in the power of human means to create"), and it would make for vertical thrills: the blastoff would dislodge ten million tons of rock, "a great part of it furiously precipitated into the bosom of Niagara." Finally, the leaper Sam Patch, a matchless performer of vertical excitement, would "give a specimen of his unique skill and daring."[38] The show took place long after the regular summer tourists had gone home. Promoters invited the plain people of the neighborhood to make Niagara Falls their own on October 6. "This is to be a frolick, it is true," went the final advertisement,

> and it will be a very proper day of relaxation for the farmers of the neighboring counties, to harness up old dobbin and give their wives and daughters (heaven bless them) a good snug ride to the falls, all for to see the thousands of ladies, dandies, wizzards, witches, fops, clodhoppers, macaronis, a few terrible, dry, particular old bachelors, and sundry ready-to-go-the-first-load old maids: all rushing to and fro, to see and be seen.—The country girls, though not dressed in the extremes of fashion, will be the toast at

the falls on the 6th of October: blooming cheeks, light buoyant step: oh; for the Sunday days of youth: we must all go to see the grand review!

A village editor helped out, noting that "there are to be 'pretty particular' doings of an amusing nature at Niagara Falls . . . and the lovers of novel exhibitions, we think, would be well repaid for a visit to our great natural curiosity—leaving all other attractions of a graver nature out of the question." (A less friendly editor noted that the Niagara tavernkeepers "have a wonderful desire and art for making money." He predicted a large crowd, "and we shall then again learn that the 'fools are not all dead yet.' ")[39]

Farmers and villagers accepted the invitation, but they went to Niagara knowing that the show would be flawed. Rumors that Sam Patch would not leap on schedule were hardening into official announcements. Two weeks earlier the governor of Upper Canada had forbidden William Forsyth's planned explosion at Table Rock, and while journalists repeated the governor's official explanation for the prohibition, the locals knew better: the royal governor spoiled the festivities because he hated Forsyth. After a checkered career as a farmer and militiaman, Forsyth had tried to monopolize tourism at British Niagara, and he had run afoul of the authorities. He had been accused of engrossing stage travel to and from Niagara through deals with out-of-town hotels, and many suspected that he had set a rival's hotel on fire. Then, in 1827, he built plank fences from his Pavilion to the banks above and below Table Rock. Henceforth, the only way to that favored viewpoint would be through his hotel. (That year two young men in a story by Nathaniel P. Willis raced their horses down the Canadian road toward the column of mist and were brought up short—not by Niagara Falls but by Forsyth's hotel and fence. Forsyth stood holding his hat at the door, asking, "Will you visit the Falls before dinner, gentlemen?") The government reminded Forsyth that a sixty-six-foot ribbon of land at the edge of the cliffs was reserved for the Crown, and was not a part of the Forsyth properties. The governor sent soldiers to tear down the fence. Forsyth rebuilt the fence, the soldiers tore it down again, and Forsyth sued the government. The case was still in court when Forsyth announced his plans to blow up a part of Table Rock—an explosion that would have asserted his ownership of what the government insisted was the King's rock. Forsyth made plans for substitute explosions, but the spectators were disappointed before they arrived.[40]

On October 6 a Buffalo journalist noted that "there appears to be a general movement in the direction of the falls." The steamboats *Henry Clay* and *Pioneer* ferried well-dressed spectators to Niagara, but most of the crowd arrived on foot and in farmers' wagons. A reporter claimed that "a great crowd of people, of all sorts, sizes, and conditions, flocked in from all quarters . . . 'all for to see the show,' and be seen themselves in turn." One visitor estimated the crowd at five thousand. More cautious locals guessed three thousand. In either case, the crowd was no more than a fourth or a fifth the number that had witnessed the *Michigan* Descent two years earlier. Vendors sold food and liquor from shanties on both sides of the river, but there were no brass bands, no caged lions, no learned dogs or New York ventriloquists. Hiram Doolittle, Jun., reported only "a forlorn corps of equestrians and a ragged company of strolling players" as sideshows. (The equestrians were from the company of Bernard and Page, a shoestring circus troupe that played the Erie Canal and Great Lakes circuit. We are left to guess about the strolling players.) A New Yorker reported that promoters promised fireworks, and that "for the gratification of the agricultural visitors, 'Mr. Tompkins will exhibit two fine pigs' of extraordinary size."[41]

Sam Patch was in the crowd. He had reached Buffalo on October 4 and taken a room at Whitney's hotel on the American side the night before the show—too late to test the wind and currents or to oversee the raising of his platform. Sam called off the jump for October 6, promising to leap the following day. There were rumors that he would not jump at all. The reporter who spotted Sam tells us he was drunk.[42]

On the morning of October 6, with both Table Rock and Sam Patch eliminated from the show, promoters announced a different schedule of events: the ledge downriver from Table Rock would be blown off at half past noon; the explosion on the island above the Canadian Falls would go off at one o'clock; and the Americans would blow up the Terrapin Rocks at the end of the footbridge from Goat Island a half hour later. There would be an intermission, and the *Superior* would begin her final voyage at three o'clock precisely.[43]

Newspapers did not comment on the sites of the substitute explosions. But the promoters and their rustic patrons knew them well. The ledge on the Canadian side was near the old Indian Ladder, a precarious system of notched logs that carried the bravest of early visitors down the cliffs to the river's edge below the Falls. Few tourists mentioned the Indian Ladder after Forsyth built his stairs, but it remained in place at least as late as 1823. It was away from the tourist haunts and it did not require a toll. Doubtless many locals had shinnied down the logs to explore the chasm and to try their luck in one of North America's great freshwater fishing grounds. A crowd of people walked to the Indian Ladder on October 6. The few tourists among them saw an unremarkable rock ledge, while the minds of the locals filled with stories of the danger of the descent and the pleasures and adventures awaiting those who made it.[44]

The Terrapin Rocks, so close to the brink of the Falls, offered a giddy, terrifying vertical gaze into the abyss. Some fashionables shuddered at the view, but others despised it as giving cheap thrills for the unrefined. "The prevailing feeling is that of horror," said an English gentleman, "and a spectator partial to inordinate excitement, may get enough of it. But his eye can rest only on a small portion of the Fall, and the position is decidedly unfavourable for pictorial effect." The locals had other ideas. The Terrapin Bridge had opened only in August 1827; some assumed that it had been built to provide the best view of the *Michigan* Descent. The proprietor sold reserved tickets to the bridge on that day, but the crowd overran the tollkeeper and took their stations near the brink. A few left the bridge and cavorted on the Terrapin Rocks themselves, enjoying a full measure of the "inordinate excitement" that the Englishman had found so unpleasant. At the end of the show they staged a small riot against the tollkeepers and went home. Journalists made no special mention of the Indian Ladder and the Terrapin Rocks. But local people knew they were not random spots on the map of Niagara. They were special places with histories of danger and fun.[45]

The crowd on the Canadian side walked downriver and stood at a safe distance as Forsyth's men touched off the first explosion. The blast, according to one witness, "deposited an immense mass of rock into the gulf." It was the one successful explosion. The second blast on the little island "took effect," but caused no special comment. Finally, the blow-up of the Terrapin Rocks failed: the blast went off, bits of debris ("to the amount of *several cart bodies full!*" said one disdainful reporter) dropped into the chasm, but the rocks stayed where they were. A Canadian, borrowing a line from Hiram Doolittle, Jun., said the gunpowder explosions at the Terrapin Rocks "sounded like pop-guns to those on the opposite shore." An American denounced it as "an abortion—'a mere flash, scarcely audible ten rods.'" (Promoters had promised blasts that would be heard forty miles away.)[46]

Only a perfect shipwreck could save the day. At three o'clock spectators on Goat Island spied the *Superior* and Weissoon's towboat far upriver. For fifteen minutes the ship floated easily toward them. Having pointed her into the channel, Captain Weissoon cast off and reached the Canadian bank above the rapids. The *Superior* drifted closer, and spectators could clearly make out her masts and the stripes painted on her side. With the audience (including, apparently, even the scoffing journalists) staring in silent anticipation, the doomed ship passed from green into white water. In the first rapid she struck a rock and rolled onto her side. The masts snapped off, and the ship righted itself and plunged on. "At this moment," said an enthralled reporter, "every eye was rivetted to the spot, with looks and feelings of the keenest and most thrilling anxiety." The battered ship rode over the first great shelf of rapids and fought its way through the second. But in the next rapid—about one third of the distance to the brink—she spun up onto a large smooth rock and keeled over, her decks facing the Falls. The crowd waited for the *Superior* to ride off the rock and plunge on. But the wait stretched on and on; at the end of the day journalists guessed that the ruined ship would remain part of the landscape of Niagara for a long time. They salvaged the shreds of their sublime expectations by pronouncing the wreck "an interesting spectacle," a relic of the terrific sublime lodged among the emerging beauties of Niagara Falls. One suggested that those who "have a taste for witnessing such scenes . . . go and view . . . this devoted vessel, in her present singularly melancholy and teriffick situation."[47]

Most journalists—like Hiram Doolittle, Jun.—declared the exhibition a failure. "Nothing but *Patch* work," wrote a wag from Ohio, while the Cooperstown paper declared the show "altogether a failure"—though the editor (Colonel Stone's old boss) went on to hope that "the natural beauties of the scene . . . repaid the curiosity of the throng." Another recognized the show as a botched repetition of the *Michigan* Descent. "*Grand Farce at the Falls*," he began, and went on: "The second part of the '*Grand Show and Farce*,' at Niagara Falls, which was begun two years ago" took place, and "*all was abortion and failure.*" A somewhat stuffier newsman in Providence opined, "We should hope that the failure of the attempt to send an empty vessel over the falls of Niagara, which was made a few days since, would put an end to that species of boyish amusement. It would seem to be a small concern, to draw together the inhabitants of *two nations* to witness a feat that had neither ingenuity, wit, nor talent to recommend it."[48]

Avoiding the fistfights and steamboat disasters, the crowd and most of the reporters went home. Yet Sam Patch was determined to jump on October 7. In the rainy afternoon he performed a perfect leap of more than eighty feet into what William Lyon Mackenzie's *Colonial Advocate* called "the vast abyss below." The Canadian (he may have been Mackenzie himself, who had written a sprightly firsthand account of the *Michigan* Descent) was more attentive to what Sam did than Colonel Stone's Doolittle had been:

> Sam walked out clad in white, and with great deliberation put his hands close to his sides and jumped from the platform into the midst of that vast gulf of foaming waters from which none of human kind had ever before emerged in life. . . . [Sam] furnished in his own person an extraordinary proof of the power which self-possession joined with determined resolution gives to man.

Sam also possessed the rustic nonchalance of a true American hero. He swam to shore without help "and was heard on the beach, singing as merrily as if altogether unconscious of having performed an act so extraordinary as almost to appear an incredible fable." (No talk of rodents here.) "Sam Patch," concluded the Canadian, "has immortalised himself."[49]

Sam Patch advertised a second leap at Niagara for October 17 and spent the intervening days in Buffalo. "He is now the paragon, the lion," said a Buffalo editor. He "attends the parties of ladies—everyone desires to pry into his countenance, to see if something extraordinary cannot be discovered—they discover nothing, however, but a careless, good humored phiz, fond of conviviality and good cheer." There was another way of putting that: both friends and enemies agreed that Sam was drunk most of the time. One village critic described him as a "drunken loathsome object," and even the friendliest of journalists admitted that Sam, "like many other great geniuses is a greater friend to the bottle than the bottle is to him." Indeed, it may have been Sam's ongoing retreat into alcohol that had delayed his arrival at Niagara. Sam's journalistic friend noted that he was dark and morose, perhaps suicidal. (The drinking stories suggest that Sam's attendance at the "parties of ladies" was either apocryphal or disastrous.)[50]

Sam passed his days in Buffalo in taverns. In the evenings he exhibited himself at Jonathan McCleary's Buffalo Museum. There is no detailed account of what he did there. It seems that he simply sat and talked with visitors. One unfriendly journalist reported that during the week the price of admission was cut in half, largely because Sam was known to be drunk. In any event, he became a staple of McCleary's Museum. In the weeks after Sam's departure McCleary delivered a comic recitation entitled "Sam Patch in all his Glory!" and exhibited a portrait of the "celebrated aero-nautical performer," painted from life.[51]

McCleary's Museum, only three months old in October 1829, was an eccentric establishment even by the standards of provincial museums. While museum keepers in other towns sometimes presented theatrical acts, they cloaked them in the rhetoric of rational (respectable, educational) amusements: stuffed birds, aboriginal artifacts from around the world, panoramas, cosmoramas, phantasmagoria, electrical machines, shells, coins, medals, paintings, menageries of live and preserved animals, and galleries of wax figures. McCleary, on the other hand, opened his Buffalo Museum without a collection. He simply asked the citizens of Buffalo to donate curiosities. Within a few weeks he had procured, among other novelties, a mineral collection, paintings through arrangement with a local portrait and miniature artist, eight Indian spears, an Indian pipe with four stems, another Indian pipe garnished with porcupine quills (neither tribes nor localities were mentioned), specimens of cornelian and petrified wood, a Sioux bow, the skin of a Lake Michigan swordfish, a "Splendid Petrifaction of the back bone of a large fish," and a stuffed duck. In his second month McCleary added a half-tamed bear, along with a brace of ravens and some rattlesnakes. "The Museum," he explained, "is yet in its infancy, and requires but the fostering hand of a generous public to make it equal if not surpass any in the United States."[52]

Everyone in Buffalo knew that Jonathan McCleary was not a museum keeper but a theater man. During his first week of full operations he announced an evening of "Recitations and Songs," and before long there were satiric skits, then performances by such "gentlemen of superior histrionick talent" (not "actors," who were, as we shall see, increasingly unwelcome among respectable western New Yorkers) as James Anderson, late manager of a theater in the West Indies, and J. M. Hewitt of Montreal and Charleston. (Both men claimed to have appeared in New York; neither appears to have done so.)

McCleary's performances were eclectic and light. His "interesting and humorous description of the wonderful and extraordinary exploits of the justly celebrated and unique aero-nautical performer, SAM PATCH" was "interspersed with Original Anecdotes—Agitations of the Public Mind—Patriotic Feelings—Laughable Observations, and concluding with an entire new Comic Song." The song went like this:

> Huzza! Huzza! The Dandies cried,
> Sam Patch does beat the Nation!
> The fishes fled, and Quadrupeds
> Crept off on the Occasion!

McCleary preceded this with an impersonation of the great English comedian Charles Mathews (himself an impersonator), and with the "Comic Yorkshire Recitation" of "Richard and Betty at

Hickleton Fair." The evening concluded with McCleary dressed as an Ottawa war chief, "reciting Pontiac's Appeal to His Warriors, written and presented to Mr. M'Cleary, by the Hon. H. R. Schoolcraft."[53]

During the week between his first and second jumps at Niagara—perhaps with the help of Jonathan McCleary—Sam Patch began turning himself into a showman. He now wore a black silk scarf at his neck. At subsequent leaps he would tie it around his waist, in the fashion of prizefighters and circus men. He also began wearing a sailor's jacket. Thus jauntily dressed, he appeared in the streets of Buffalo with a final touch of showmanship: a pet black bear on a chain. (He probably bought the bear from McCleary: Sam took the animal with him when he left Buffalo; at the same time, the bear disappeared from McCleary's advertisements.) The newspapers talked Sam up as a celebrity, and other men—perhaps jokingly, perhaps not—tried to horn in. Back in July, the owner of the Pagoda and Labyrinth Garden in Philadelphia had challenged Sam to jump against his "antedelluvian frog." More seriously, a W. P. Moore challenged Sam to a Niagara jump-off from any height.[54]

While he dressed up, drank, and exhibited himself in Buffalo, Sam Patch advertised a second leap at Niagara Falls. The elaborate handbill presented levels of showmanship that had been absent from Sam's earlier notices:[55]

TO THE LADIES AND GENTLEMEN OF WESTERN NEW YORK, AND OF UPPER CANADA

All I have to say is, that I arrived at the Falls too late to give you a specimen of my Jumping Qualities, on the 6th inst.; but on Wednesday, I thought I would venture a small leap, which I accordingly made, of Eighty Feet, merely to convince those that remained to see me, with what safety and ease I could descend, and that I was the TRUE SAM PATCH and to show that some things could be done as well as others; which was denied before I made the jump.

Having been thus disappointed, the owners of Goat Island have generously granted me the use of it for nothing; so that I may have a chance, from an equally generous public, to obtain some remuneration for my long journey hither, as well as affording me an opportunity of supporting the reputation I have gained, by Aero-Nautical Feats, never before attempted, either in the Old or the New World.

I shall Ladies and Gentlemen, on Saturday next, Oct. 17th, precisely at 3 o'clock p.m. LEAP at the FALLS of NIAGARA, from a height of 120 to 130 feet, (being 40 to 50 feet higher than I leapt before,) into the eddy below. On my way down from Buffalo, on the morning of that day, on the Steamboat Niagara, I shall, for the amusement of the Ladies, doff my coat and spring from the mast head into the Niagara River.

Buffalo, Oct. 12, 1829   SAM PATCH
                                                Of Passaic Falls, New Jersey

The economic arrangements were secure. The proprietors promised Sam the tolls from the Goat Island bridge on the day of the leap—twenty-five cents per spectator. In addition, the jumper doubtless had an arrangement with the steamboat *Niagara*, which would treat its passengers to a private showing of Sam Patch and a leap from the masthead into the Niagara River. It would be a good payday for Sam Patch.[56]

Sam Patch boarded the steamer for Niagara Falls on the morning of October 17. The price of passage limited the audience for Sam's promised leap from the boat to the more well-heeled among the local sporting crowd, and Sam steamed downriver in that company. At noon the boat anchored in the river and crewmen raised the foreyard to about fifty feet above the water. Sam climbed up and dropped gracefully into the river. He surfaced and the passengers greeted him with three cheers. Some on the boat thought the jumper had hurt his back. But he climbed on board uninjured and in good spirits. "A beautiful leap it was," stated one account. Another agreed that Patch had "performed the leap with dexterity and ease." The boat steamed on to Niagara Falls.[57]

It was another cloudy and rainy day, but Sam was determined to leap. He passed over the bridge and joined three hundred spectators who had paid the toll to watch him jump from Goat Island—a guaranteed $75 for Sam Patch. Nonpaying spectators stood atop the cliffs on both sides of the river. In Canada a smaller crowd stood beneath Table Rock, looking at eye level across the basin at Sam Patch. Journalists estimated the total crowd at two thousand.

Sam Patch walked to the head of the island and to the entrance to the Biddle Stairs—built at the private expense of Nicholas Biddle, president of the Bank of the United States, and completed only weeks before Sam's arrival. He entered a sloping tunnel and stepped into the dimness of covered circular stairs. Eighty feet down he stepped into light and noise, walked down Biddle's tastefully rustic stone steps, and stood in the chasm of Niagara Falls.

It was a perfect place to jump. The advertisement for the Biddle Stairs claimed that before September 1829 only "an occasional and daring adventurer" had descended into the gorge from Goat Island. The stairway "enables the visitor to place himself at the bottom of the abyss, midway between the two descending sheets, where, surrounded by rushing waters and impending rocks, the spectacle is magnificently sublime and electrifying." ("Here," gasped Harriet Martineau, "every successive pulse of the cataract was like a cannon shot a few yards off. . . .") Upward and to Sam's left, the stupendous Horseshoe Fall curved toward Canada, with an unending and impenetrable explosion all along its base. To his right, violent crosscurrents troubled the river as it gathered itself for the journey to Lake Ontario. Straight ahead, however, swelled a huge eddy pushed up by the Falls—an aerated, calm spot into which Sam would jump. Sam's leaping apparatus was ready. It was the ladder that workmen had used to erect the Biddle Stairs, held up by four trees spliced together and steadied by ropes leading back to the island. The platform from which Sam would leap leaned about 40 feet out over the water at a height of 120 feet, and from its top flew an American flag.

Sam Patch had promised to leap from more than forty feet higher than any of his previous jumps, and the jerry-built ladder of October 17 kept that promise. Inevitably, the audience and the reporters experimented with viewpoints. From the little windows in the Biddle Stairs, revealed a newsman, the height "did not appear so grand . . . but to descend to the margin of the water, in the gulf beneath, and then look up at the perpendicular ladder, made you imagine that it would require superhuman powers to accomplish such an enterprise." Later in the day, a daring gentleman scaled the ladder and mounted the platform from which Sam had leaped. He insisted that "few could imagine or appreciate the sublimity of the scene" who had not done the same.[58]

(We might comment on Sam's American flag. The Niagara innkeepers, as well as governments on both sides of the Falls, had a strong interest in stabilizing Niagara as a friendly border after 1815. So did British tourists and their genteel counterparts from the United States—most of whom, like William Leete Stone, were dedicated cultural Anglophiles who disliked democracy and who knew that Niagara could be properly apprehended only outside of nationality and historical time. The off-season spectacles, on the other hand, invited British Canadians and upstate New Yorkers who held historical grudges against each other. Impresarios carefully kept nationalism out of the shows. National symbols tied to the *Michigan* Descent suggested that it was an episode of cooperation between British Canada and the United States: the Stars and Stripes flew from the *Michigan's* stern while the Union Jack was attached to the bow; two of Captain Rough's oarsmen were Canadians, the other two were Americans; one of the bears was from Canada, the other from the

United States. At the shipwreck and explosions of 1829, as well as the first leap of Sam Patch on October 7, there were no national symbols at all—aside from flags flown from some of the refreshment stands. Yet Sam Patch made his second leap at Niagara facing Canada, with "the banner of his country above his head!" Jonathan McCleary noted that Sam's visit stirred "Patriotic Feelings." Northeastern workingmen were notorious Anglophobes, and they co-opted emblems of American nationality when attacking targets such as blacks, English actors, or wealthy and Anglophilic Americans who questioned the worth of ordinary white men. Sam's flag was probably not an affront to all that was British: his mentors in Pawtucket and his workmates in Paterson had been English workmen, and he made good friends in Canada. The flag did, however, recall Niagara's angry history, and it assaulted the Anglophilic gentility with which William Leete Stone and others of his social class approached Niagara Falls.)[59]

Sam Patch stood at the foot of his dizzying ladder. He wore his spinner's uniform under a black vest and the sailor's jacket, and he wore the scarf at his neck—touches of celebrity dandyism he had acquired since his first Niagara leap. As he took off his coat and shoes men stepped forward to shake his hand. Some had tears in their eyes, and a few tried to talk him out of jumping. Sam brushed them aside and scaled the ladder. For ten minutes he stood on the little platform. The ladder veered in the wind and under his weight; the flag snapped above him. Sam took the scarf from his neck and tied it around his waist. He scanned the audience, bowing to his left and right. (Sam was learning how to work a crowd.) Far below him, a boat passed upriver and waited near where Sam would leap. Sam turned and took a corner of the flag in his hand, and kissed it. Then he stepped to the edge and stood still, and the crowd fell silent. Sam jumped outward and dropped into the abyss. A Buffalo reporter who watched from the foot of the ladder saw Sam fall "like an arrow into the flood below," and pronounced it a "matchless and tremendous leap."

From his viewpoint below Table Rock, a Canadian reported that the ladder wobbled as Sam leaped and that he made a sickening half-turn in the air and entered the water with one leg cocked and with a terrifying splash. For endless seconds the crowd stared at the point where Sam had disappeared; a third newsman reported that "a general burst of 'he's dead, he's lost,' ran through the crowd." In about half a minute Sam bobbed to the surface, waved the boat off, and sculled on his back toward shore. "Then it was," wrote the Buffalo newsman, "that a painful and unpleasant, yet indescribable sensation was driven from each breast, by the flood of joy which succeeded, on seeing that he was safe. —Then it was that the benumbing spell which had reigned a minute or two, from the moment he arose on the platform, was broke by the burst of the voice of congratulation. . . ." Sam stepped onto the American shore amid cheers and a little storm of white handkerchiefs. To the first man who offered his hand he said, "There's no mistake in Sam Patch!" It was a near-perfect exercise in the workingman's sublime.[60]

While at Niagara, Sam Patch talked at length with two journalists: William Lyon Mackenzie, the firebrand editor of the York (Toronto) *Colonial Advocate*, and the editor of the *Buffalo Republican*. The *Republican* was the mouthpiece for Jacksonian democracy in Buffalo. Mackenzie was the loudest voice for anti-Tory reform in Upper Canada and an admirer of the republican institutions of the United States.

William Lyon Mackenzie witnessed Sam's leap from below Table Rock and greeted the jumper that evening, when Sam ferried to Canada. Mackenzie was an educated man with a taste for popular entertainments (he had brought his family to witness the *Michigan* Descent two years earlier). He described Sam Patch as "slight, but well made . . . and of a temperament as indicated by his dark countenance, rather inclining to melancholy," and too fond of drink. Sam revealed a few of his secrets: he inhaled as he leaped (again, the Pawtucket form), and entering the water had never hurt a bit. Armed with his eyewitness experience of the leap, and with a firm grounding in the literary sublime, Mackenzie wrote his story. It helped that the weather was gray and rainy, and that the mist from the Falls was particularly thick on that day. The ruin of the *Superior*, still stranded in the rapids, contributed its own dark note to the proceedings. Mackenzie added to all this by viewing the leap at water level, directly across the river from Sam's ladder. It was a "dangerous spot" below threatening, overhanging cliffs. Sam himself provided Mackenzie with more thrills and a horrifying allusion:

> When he swung round and placed his elbows close to his back . . . he was an exact representation of a man being hanged, and I felt for the moment a sensation of terror which scarcely subsided till I saw him re-appear on the water. . . . To a mind fond of romance, and desirous to realize now and then a sufficient share of the marvellous, Sam's 118 foot jump, the cataract above him and the cataract below him, the seemingly bottomless pit at his feet, the 200 feet of perpendicular rock behind him, the apparatus from which he sprang, so like the fatal ladder of the state, added to the horrid din of the Horse Shoe Cauldron continually sending forth thick clouds of smoke, presented a scene seldom equalled by the most splendid and gloomy descriptions of our modern dealers in magic.

The immense power and the old vertical horrors of Niagara provided the backdrop. The skill, daredevil courage, and plucky nonchalance (with its touch of the morose and suicidal) of Sam Patch provided the action. Mackenzie—unlike Hiram Doolittle, Jun.—fused Sam Patch and Niagara Falls in an unsettling and deeply satisfying moment. But he could do so only by affirming the terrors of Niagara and the worth of Sam Patch.[61]

The *Buffalo Republican* shared Mackenzie's taste for the more melodramatic forms of the sublime. The editor of this paper talked of the unimpressive view from the Biddle Stairs, the awful look upward from the base of the ladder, the dizzying horror of Sam's view from his perch, of Sam's plunge "into the depths of the abyss," of the "painful and unpleasant, yet indescribable sensation" and the "benumbing spell" endured and enjoyed by the audience; "what a dreadful moment! There was not perhaps ten who saw him, that believed he would come down safe."

Even more than Mackenzie, this editor took the trouble to understand what Sam Patch was doing. He knew that Sam did not merely throw himself into space and hope for the best. Sam's survival depended on practiced physical skills and absolute concentration during the leap. "This celebrated and unique aeronautical performer," he wrote, "seems to control the dangerous effects of rapid specific gravitation in the atmosphere. . . . Sam possesses, what few have arrived at, contempt of danger." He went on with a full description of Sam's jumping technique: "He seems to have perfect command of his motions during his swift transitions through the air, because, when near the water, he brings his hands suddenly from above his head to below his hips, and strikes the water in such a position as guards his back, his breast and his face, from injury." Along with these skills and beneath his cheerful nonchalance (this is the editor who identified Sam as a "good humored phiz"), Sam knew that a bad leap would kill him. ("Had he entered the flood in any other way than the way his skill enabled him to do so many times with entire safety," the journalist recalled in a later article, "his life, he knew, was the forfeit.") He practiced his skills, he made experiments with wind currents and water depths, and he focused into spiritual stillness and practiced movements in his leaps. "This jump of Sam Patch," concluded the *Republican*, "is the greatest fete of the kind ever effected by man. He may now challenge the universe for a competitor."

Sam admitted to the *Republican* that "his system of jumping"

was dangerous. The platform for his second Niagara leap swayed under his weight, making him feel "like a bug on a blade of grass" and nearly causing him to fall. But "he only feared, as he said, the disgrace of falling off the trembling platform. . . . *'Disgrace'* indeed!—The fall would have been his destruction." Where genteel journalists found only mindless, suicidal bravado in Sam's leaps, and where Hiram Doolittle, Jun., found only the butt of stage Yankee jokes, the Buffalo editor recognized skills and concentration honed over years, joined with physical courage and a firm sense of personal honor. It was praise grounded in personal knowledge of Sam Patch—praise that the boys in Pawtucket would have understood.[62]

[handwritten: ↳ praise of the working class]

IV

ROCHESTER

Fresh from his triumph at Niagara, Sam Patch rolled into Rochester—half drunk, wearing his sailor's jacket, leading his pet bear on a chain. He paraded down Exchange Street and took up residence at a bar and confectionery called the Rochester Recess. He would stay at the Recess for the next two weeks, lionized and entertained by Rochester's sporting crowd. As he drank, talked, and strolled between his barroom and his waterfall, Sam may have noted that Rochester was a lot like Pawtucket and Paterson: another mill town set beside a waterfall. He probably did not know that Rochester was a landmark on the Fashionable Tour. While Niagara revealed God's grand design and the Erie Canal demonstrated the vastness of the entrepreneurial imagination, Rochester was known far and wide as the town where civilization had replaced wilderness overnight.

Rochester," remarked an Englishwoman in 1827, "is the best place we have yet seen for giving strangers an idea of the newness of this country." She might have read that in her guidebook, for Rochester was a high point in the portion of the Fashionable Tour that was about progress. The banks of Genesee Falls had been wilderness in 1812. Then the end of the British-American war in 1815, the rush of settlement into western New York, and the completion of the Erie Canal, which crossed the Genesee River at Rochester, transformed the Genesee Valley into thickly settled wheat country, and Rochester, the perfect millsite at the junction of the river and the Canal, became a city. In 1829 Rochester numbered nine thousand persons, with thousands more in the shacks and houses that sprawled beyond the village limits. An easterner gaped at Rochester and pronounced it "standing proof that the wilderness may be made to vanish almost at a stroke, and give place in as little time to a city."[1]

Guidebooks and other travelers encouraged tourists on their way to Niagara to stay a day or two in this "Young Lion of the West," and the fashionable stopover at Rochester was scripted at an early date. The town was all movement and growth, said the tourists—piles of scrap lumber and broken bricks, fresh tree stumps in the streets and in the basements of fine homes, the clatter of hammers everywhere, mills and factories rising out of nothing. Visitors stood at the Four Corners (the central intersection of Buffalo and Carroll—soon to be renamed State—Streets) and dodged wagon traffic as they looked down solid lines of brick and glass storefronts, set out on paved streets with flagstone sidewalks. On a spacious square on Buffalo Street stood a courthouse and stone Presbyterian and Episcopal churches. Behind the square stretched Fitzhugh and Troup Streets, where tourists were invited to view brand-new Greek Revival mansions. And there was, of course, the Erie Canal, which passed through downtown Rochester.

Near the Canal, on the west bank of the Genesee River, stood a row of the famed Rochester flour mills. Another row of factories and mills lined the east bank, backed by a jumble of new houses and topped by the ambitious spire of St. Paul's Episcopal Church. The downtown buildings were of brick and neatly painted white wood. The city boasted eleven churches, seven

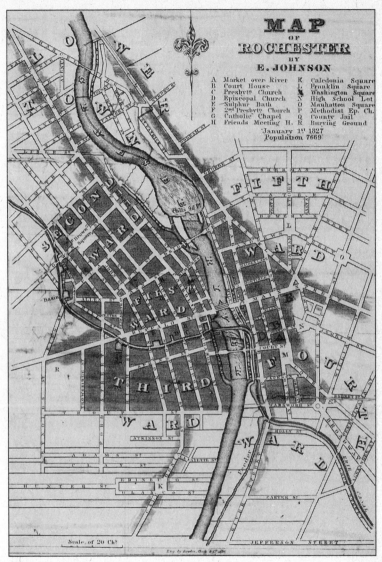

Rochester in 1827 (Directory of the Village of Rochester, 1827, courtesy of the Local History Division, Rochester Public Library)

newspapers, eleven hotels, two libraries, a glass-ceilinged business arcade, a museum, an atheneum, a high school, and a bank. Rochester in 1829, sprung from nothing in fifteen years, was a sparkling model of American progress.[2]

Along the corridor of factories and mills in downtown Rochester flowed the Genesee River—one of the most thoroughly conquered of the great streams of North America. The river began in the Alleghenies in Pennsylvania and flowed north out of the hills and through the broad and fertile Genesee Valley. South of Rochester it supplied a feeder for the central section of the Erie Canal. The river crossed the village limits and encountered a mill dam that diverted more water into raceways on both banks, then rolled over the dam and crashed through shallow rapids with water-powered mills and workshops on both sides. In downtown Rochester the river passed under a footbridge, then

Erie Canal Aqueduct at Rochester (Cadwallader Colden, *Memoir . . . of the New York Canals*, New York, 1825, courtesy of the Local History Division, Rochester Public Library)

under the graceful stone aqueduct that carried the Erie Canal over the Genesee. For many tourists, the aqueduct was the aesthetic high point of a stopover at Rochester. Travelers on the Canal passed between tall stone buildings at either end of the aqueduct, then suddenly found themselves in the open and high above the rapids. "The river dashes rapidly along beneath," said a guidebook, "while boats, with goods and passengers, glide safely above." Visitors called the scene "splendid," "magic," a work of "inconceivable boldness" at which "we are lost in wonder." The Marquis de Lafayette, the French hero of the American Revolution, spoke from a platform on the aqueduct during his triumphant return to America in 1825, and he said it best: "The grand objects of nature, which threatened to impede, have been made only to adorn, as we see in the striking spectacle which is at this moment presented to our enchanted eye."[3]

The Genesee ran under the aqueduct and beneath a wide market bridge that connected Buffalo Street on the west side and Main Street on the east. It rolled on, surrounded but unhindered, for a quarter mile. Then it encountered a final bridge and another mill dam and dropped, almost by surprise, ninety-six feet into a vast, high-walled chasm. Viewed from the built landscape above the falls, the river simply ended.

Tourists agreed that Rochester was the best place to view the rapid and ongoing domestication of the American wilderness. They differed only in what they thought of the results. On his way home from Niagara, William Leete Stone stayed in a fine hotel, lounged at the Atheneum, toured two flour mills ("as full of machinery as the case of a watch"), and attended Presbyterian and Episcopal church services. Stone loved progress as much as sublimity, and he pronounced Rochester a stunning monument to utility and commerce, "with its two thousand houses, its elegant ranges of stores, its numerous churches and public buildings, its boats and bridges, quays, wharves, mills, manufactories, arcades, museums, everything—all standing where stood a frowning forest in 1812! Sure the march of improvement can never outstrip this herculean feat." British aesthetes, on the other hand, while they marveled at Rochester's mushroom growth, re-coiled at the results of a great, half-planned collision between democratic capitalism and the American forest. It was in Rochester that Basil Hall "began to learn that in America the word improvement, which, in England, means making things better, signifies in that country an augmentation in the number of houses and people, and, above all, in the amount of area of cleared land." Hall asserted that Rochester looked as though "a great boxful of new houses had been sent by steam from New York, and tumbled out on the half-cleared land." An equally of-fended Englishman viewed Rochester from high ground and swore that "nothing can be more miserable than its appearance from a distance. An open space has been merely burnt in the for-est."[4]

Rochester's leading families never tired of showing their town to visitors. The downtown, with its mills and stores and elegant residential blocks, was a monument to their own labors and spec-ulations. But unlike the tourists, they did not experience their city as a gallery of aesthetic opportunities. They were making lives in the Genesee boomtown, and in the process they were making a new American middle-class culture. Most in Roches-ter's elite were natives of the interior of New England—small-town descendants of the Puritans who had moved on and made good in the new market economy of the West. Their busy streets and pleasant homes told them—as Pawtucket's mills, Abigail's house, and Greenleaf's disappearance had told Sam Patch—that the agrarian world of stern fathers and inherited land was dead. They had moved west believing, despite the family money that most carried in their pockets, that they could build lives out of commerce, ambition, and the disciplined self. In making their new lives they borrowed from the old gentility: they learned good manners, they developed the rudiments of taste, and they bought a lot of nice furniture. But at bottom they were middle-class, evangelical, and hostile to much that gentility held dear. They valued domestic comfort over public display, work over idleness and leisure, sincerity over affectation, prayerful contemplation over gay sociability. They dismissed the genteel as thoughtless people who wore fashionable clothes, read novels, drank brandy, went to the theater—and spent God's money on trips to Niagara Falls. This way of living and presenting oneself to the world was coming to be called "respectable." It was new in the 1820s, and Rochester's business-owning families knew that it worked: Rochester and their own places within it were ample proof of that.[5]

The respectables, however, shared Rochester with others. Some in the business community continued to enjoy a glass of wine and a night at the theater, thus serving as bad examples for others. Worse, the Erie Canal had filled the town with boatmen, laborers, and other undesirables. Their own building sites, mills, and workshops employed thousands of day laborers and journeyman craftsmen—young men who had fallen through the disintegrating grid of inheritance and into wage labor, and who saw only dimly and imperfectly that Rochester offered boundless opportunities. Workingmen and transients, who outnumbered the respectables, were engaged in their own forms of self-fashioning. Poor neighborhoods—peppered with dramshops, gambling dens, groceries, billiard rooms, and low boardinghouses—surrounded the well-to-do neighborhoods, providing them with wage labor by day and worrisome levels of noise and disorder at night. The Canal also brought in people who made their living on the road: gamblers, pickpockets, prostitutes, confidence men, and a parade of show people ranging from circus riders and strolling actors to the drunken falls-jumper Sam Patch.

In the late 1820s pious improvers organized to impose respectability on the town as a whole. They formed societies to combat sabbath-breaking and drunkenness. They outlawed gambling. And they did what they could to keep low showmen out of Rochester. The reform movements failed. Most Rochester workingmen—and more than a few in the new middle class—continued to drink and go to shows, and to elect local officials who would not try to prevent them from doing such things. To the deep discomfort of pious respectables, Sam Patch entered Rochester unopposed, took up residence at a bar, and advertised his leaps at Genesee Falls.[6]

Sam Patch passed up the farmers' hotels and low boardinghouses at which he might have stayed. He also avoided the fine hotels, a few of which surely would have welcomed him. Instead, Sam Patch settled into the Rochester Recess on Exchange Street near the Erie Canal bridge. The Recess was a bar, confectionery, and soda fountain. A journalist called it "a saloon." The Recess promised "gentlemen" (the advertisements did not mention ladies) a place "fitted up in style corresponding to the taste of the day." Along with pickled oysters and soda waters, the Recess provided hot meals, and the bar was fully stocked. William Cochrane, the proprietor, invited Sam and his bear to lodge at the Recess.[7]

Later, people in Rochester remembered that Sam Patch had enjoyed the hospitality and support of the town's "sportsmen"— men who favored hunting and fishing, drinking, gambling, and male jocularity over respectability. Sam did not put himself into the hands of impresarios, as he had at Hoboken and Niagara. He simply left subscription papers at Rochester taverns, where "gentlemen who feel disposed to witness the spectacle" were encouraged to leave money with the landlords. Insofar as Sam Patch had a sponsor in Rochester, it was the town's sporting crowd. More particularly, it was the loose fraternity of men who drank alcohol.[8]

The Recess was a hangout for sportsmen, and given its downtown location and its genial host it surely was a busy place. Rochester people knew it best, however, as headquarters of the Rochester Town Band—one of the first institutions of sporting Rochester. J. C. Bond, a fiddler who played at balls and parties, had been the original proprietor of the Recess. In 1825 he took on the artist and restauranteur J. L. D. Mathies as a partner. Both Bond and Mathies played in the band. The Recess carried, along with its confections and liquors, a line of musical instruments, and Bond and Mathies let the band practice upstairs. When Bond moved to Pittsburgh and Mathies took up hotel-keeping, the bass drummer William Cochrane took over the Recess in partnership with Orson Weed (the younger and less successful brother of the journalist Thurlow). In 1829 the band was still practicing above the Recess, the Recess was still selling musical instruments, and William Cochrane was secretary of the band. Sam's first associates in Rochester were the town's amateur musicians.[9]

The Rochester Band (their formal name was the Clinton Band, but they seldom used it) formed in 1817, and was tied to a male social life that preceded the cant of domesticity and respectability and then persisted alongside it. Membership was open to any white man who could play an instrument, and there were cymbals, drums, and triangles for many who could not. The Rochester Band played at all public festivities: notoriously drunken militia musters; Fourth of July festivities that were about the same; and celebrations of the completion of the Canal aqueduct in 1823, and of Lafayette's visit and the opening of the Erie Canal in 1825. The band played an occasional indoor concert, made appearances at the town's commercial pleasure garden, and on warm nights sometimes took their stations under the trees and serenaded their neighbors.[10]

In the early years the band included many of Rochester's leading men: the tannery owner Jacob Graves, the merchant

L. W. Sibley, the landowner Bradford King, and Nathaniel T. Rochester, son of the town's proprietor, to name only a few. The band also enlisted housepainters, shopkeepers, tailors, grocers, and apprentices. Among these were men known as jokers. A shoemaker-clarinetist named Thompson was (according to the journalist Edwin Scrantom, a bassoonist who became the band's historian) "inclined to be fast, was of a genial make, and cracked a great many jokes." George Cameron, a flute-playing tailor, was "full of frolic and anecdote and fun." Another fun-lover was the flautist Alfred Judson, inventor of a patented fishing rod, who attracted playful nonmusicians who wanted to hang out with the band. The trumpeter Alpheus Bingham enjoyed the company of show people, and he had sold a respectable business to become proprietor of the barroom in the theater on State Street. And Sam Patch's host, William Cochrane, "greatly esteemed as a good social clever fellow," beat the bass drum, managed the band's affairs, and tended bar. Old and young, rich and poor, family men and bachelors—the Rochester Band marched and played with their differences disguised by their white uniforms, by a common enthusiasm for music, and by a playfulness that had a lot to do with informal male democracy and very little to do with piety and progress.[11]

Only once in the early days did the demands of respectability invade the Rochester Band. At a practice session in 1818, the clarinetist Thompson sent downstairs for a round of drinks. Myron Strong, another clarinetist, objected. Strong was a shopkeeper who went on to become a leading layman at the First Baptist Church and secretary of the Monroe County Sunday School Union. "He was a prompt, efficient man," recalled Edwin Scrantom, "always counselling temperance and good hours." Thompson, on the other hand, was the shoemaker who was "inclined to be fast." The band, by a narrow majority, voted against drinking that evening, but Strong's victory was short-lived. The barkeeper William Cochrane became secretary of the band, and the band played on summer nights at an outdoor pleasure ground and drinking establishment called the Monroe Garden. In their most blatant breach of respectability, they continued to practice above the Recess barroom on Saturday evenings—in direct violation of the New England Sabbath and of the aural sensibilities of pious Rochesterians. The band also began to take pleasure trips. In 1827 they journeyed to Niagara Falls for the *Michigan* Descent, playing in front of Whitney's hotel early in the day, joining the crowd to watch the grand catastrophe of the ship and its animals in the afternoon. In 1830 they would again travel to Buffalo and Niagara.[12]

In the course of the 1820s the band's wealthier members— pushed by business and the demands of respectability and domestic life (and perhaps repelled by the barroom headquarters, the pleasure garden concerts, and the trip to the *Michigan* Descent) dropped out of the band. Six weeks before Sam Patch came to Rochester, the band took another trip—serenading passengers on a packet boat making its maiden run to Utica, and staying over to enjoy the hospitality of that town's band. (It was "emphatically a jaunt of pleasure," they said.) The fifteen players who made that trip suggest the makeup of the band in autumn 1829. No merchant, miller, land speculator, or lawyer made the trip to Utica. (Neither, of course, did the pious Myron Strong.) The traveling band included six mechanics—both journeymen and masters—four short-term residents who did not appear in Rochester records, two barkeepers (Cochrane and the man from the theater), a printer's apprentice, a deserter from a British army band, and the genial publisher of the *Rochester Gem*. These were the men who greeted Sam Patch at the Rochester Recess in November 1829.[13]

William Cochrane introduced Sam Patch to others who would be his friends in Rochester. First in line was Cochrane's younger brother, Joe (he played the cymbals), who became Sam's guide and companion and the keeper of Sam's bear. There was the Irishman John O'Donohue, whose auction store stood next door to the Recess. And then there was a bookbinder named Sam Drake.[14]

Sam Drake was foreman in the bindery attached to the printing establishment of Everard Peck on State Street. Peck was a Connecticut Yankee, a wealthy publisher, a leading member of the First Presbyterian Church, and a prominent temperance man and Sabbath reformer—one of the most active respectables in town. As an employer, he took a fatherly interest in the morals of the men and boys who worked for him. Drake, on the other hand, was a charter member of Rochester's sporting crowd, a legendary hunter and fisherman and a captain of militia who was known far and wide as the town cutup. He was also a homespun infidel who took great pleasure in offending people who went to church. In 1823 one of his friends killed a large rattlesnake and gave Drake the hide. Drake tanned the skin and made purses and wallets. Then he used a leftover swatch to bind a copy of the New Testament, and went into the streets, waving it under the noses of horrified churchgoers. "I wanted to see," Drake explained, "how the word of the Lord would look, bound up in the hide of the devil."[15]

There are a lot of stories about Sam Drake, but one suggests the kind of man he was and the sporting world in which he lived. In 1826 a white owl flew into Rochester and perched atop a dry-goods emporium on State Street, across the street from Peck's printing offices and bindery. Sam Drake sent an apprentice to get his gun. Word spread that there would be a shooting exhibition on State Street, and what a witness described as "the whole community" stopped work and gathered around Sam Drake, placing bets on whether he could hit the owl. When the bets were down, Drake aimed and fired. There was a cloud of dust where the owl had been, white feathers floating at its edges. But there was no sign of the owl. The gamblers began to argue: some said the owl had flown off unharmed, others insisted that it had been blown to bits. The argument turned ugly, and a dozen men began shoving and fighting in the street. Sam Drake ordered one of his apprentices onto the roof. The boy reached into a false chimney and came out with the bloodied corpse of the owl. The gamblers stopped fighting and settled their bets, and Sam Drake climaxed the episode by leading the crowd across the street for a round of drinks at the Mansion House Hotel.[16]

Everard Peck may have said something when Drake and the boys got back to the bindery. For in one episode Drake had combined most of what Peck and other pious respectables disliked: offered an opportunity to play outdoors, he had walked out of work, taking his apprentices and journeymen along with him; he had stood with his gun and drawn a motley crowd that gambled and fought in the street; he had blasted away at the owl within a few steps of the Four Corners; and he had finished the day in a barroom. Most troubling of all, he had seduced young men into another thoughtless and disorderly afternoon.

Sam Drake did similar things in his capacity as an elected captain of militia. In the 1820s there were complaints about the militia law from all sides. Workingmen and many others resented the legal obligation to present themselves, armed and uniformed at their own expense, for training days that occurred at the busiest time of the year. Even more, they disliked the fines levied against those who avoided militia training. The respectables saw training days as an occasion for drunkenness and riot. While they petitioned and editorialized for order-inducing reforms, Sam Drake and like-minded militiamen took steps to laugh training days out of existence. Their model in this was the Eighty-fourth Regiment of Pennsylvania militia, recruited in the working-class Northern Liberties of Philadelphia. In 1825 the men of the Northern Liberties, sharing widespread hostility toward militia service, elected one John Pluck as their colonel. Pluck, a short, hunchbacked, bowlegged, and perhaps feebleminded man, worked as a hostler, mucking out stalls in a livery stable. As colonel, he marched in a grand parody of an officer's uniform (it featured a large lady's bonnet and outlandishly large spurs), leading a regiment dressed in silly clothes and carrying broomsticks and cornstalks. The performance was repeated, and Philadelphia training days were transformed into popular and well-attended farces. The following year Colonel Pluck, in full "uniform," exhibited himself in New York (where he rode an elephant at the Lafayette Amphitheatre), Providence, Albany, and other cities, and announced plans for appearances among the fashionables at Saratoga Springs and Niagara Falls. Before long, antimilitia forces in a number of northern cities and towns had organized their own "Fantastical" militia farces.[17]

According to local historians, the Fantastical maneuvers in New York State began in Rochester and spread from there to other towns. The original Rochester Fantastical was John Robinson, proprietor of a downtown barbershop employing at least three barbers. He offered an assortment of gentlemen's hairpieces and toiletries, and he sold playing cards, suggesting strongly that his "Tonsorial Emporium," like Cochrane's Recess, was a hangout for Rochester's sporting fraternity. Robinson was a militia officer, and he began the Fantastical tradition in Rochester by leading his unit onto the parade ground wearing a German cap with a huge leather bill, yellow pants with ribbons at the knees, a hunting jacket, a ridiculously high collar, and a pair of green goggles. A few days later hundreds of Fantasticals paraded through Rochester. One officer led his men riding a bull and waving a handsaw, others wore tall black hats and carried conductor pipes as weapons, and a particularly waggish officer arrived with a live goose strapped to his head. They fought mock battles with brooms and rolling pins, and they attracted huge and boisterous crowds. A local historian recalled that some opposed the levity, but "popular sentiment was with the frolickers, and Training Day was looked for as our Southern friends count on Mardi Gras." Along with the fancy haircutter John Robinson, the leaders of the Fantasticals included a druggist, a stage agent, and six mechanics—including the infidel bookbinder Captain Sam Drake.[18]

Sam Patch's sporting friends in Rochester were not the low vagabonds, sneak thieves, and drunkards who haunted respectable imaginations. They were long-term town residents—skilled craftsmen and small businessmen, many of them family men, none of them associated with criminality or violence. They were simply men who enjoyed the company of other men, sipping alcohol, telling stories, planning hunting and fishing trips, and concocting broad practical jokes. Neighbors often remembered them with affection. Merchants retold Sam Drake's hunting and fishing stories for decades, and of the three reminiscences that are our only sources on the militia Fantasticals, two were written by socially prominent women who as girls had looked forward to the performances. Even the self-consciously genteel William Leete Stone, when he met the traveling members of the Rochester Band near Utica, pronounced them "very respectable young men."[19]

Still, these men were playful and irreverent, and they sometimes openly opposed piety and respectability. Only one of the band members or militia Fantasticals belonged to an evangelical church in 1829: the Presbyterian housepainter Jerry Selkrig, who played the French horn; the one other church member (a Fantastical saddlemaker) was an Episcopalian. Others were openly irreligious. Sam Drake's snakeskin Bible was not his only attack on the evangelicals. In 1831 temperance reformers, encouraged by a huge revival of religion, organized a separate, alcohol-free celebration of the Fourth of July, hoping to avoid "that noise and disorderly conduct among the lower class" which usually accompanied such celebrations. Sam Drake attended the official civic celebration and offered this volunteer toast: "*Short shoes* and *long corns* to those who refuse to celebrate with us." In the 1830s two anti-evangelical, free-thought editors established newspapers in Rochester. It was by then an evangelical town; most business-men opposed the free-thought press and most of the others were afraid to advertise there. Sam Patch's old acquaintances were prominent among the few who dared to buy space in the infidel press. The Irish auctioneer John O'Donohue (who helped to pre-pare Sam Patch for his final leap), the gunsmith Joseph Medbury, and the druggist Reuben Bunnell (both of the latter leaders of the Fantasticals) were among the advertisers. So was J. L. D. Mathies, the former owner of the Recess. So, of course, was Sam Drake, and so was Sam Patch's young friend Joe Cochrane, now the proprietor of a grocery and provisions store that featured "Pure Wines and Liquors."[20]

Now and then Sam Patch took a morning off from drinking at the Recess and walked through town to survey Genesee Falls. The trip took him north on Exchange Street, over the bridge that spanned the Erie Canal, across the Four Corners, and onto State Street. It was the heart of Rochester's landscape of progress: broad streets, substantial buildings, the lacework of millraces, foot and wagon bridges, and the stone aqueduct visible down the streets to his right. But in the company of his friends from the Recess, Sam passed through another Rochester—a place that tourists did not see, a place that respectables saw and heard only from a safe and disdainful distance. The corridor between the Recess and the falls was part of a city that sportsmen and work-ing people constructed and carried in their heads, and for those who did not wholly believe in the rhetoric of progress and re-spectability, a walk through Rochester was a play of story and memory that constituted another city—a city that had become a battleground between the respectables and the people who be-friended Sam Patch.[21]

South of the Rochester Recess, near the beginnings of a poor neighborhood known as Cornhill, stood a circus amphitheater. It had been built for equestrian exhibitions in 1825. In the next few years Bernard and Page (the "forlorn corps of equestrians" that Hiram Doolittle, Jun., had spotted at Niagara Falls) repeatedly brought their horses and riders, trick ponies, and wire-walking clown to the circus on Exchange Street. Circus crowds were notoriously unruly, and Rochester's churchgoing elite, spearheaded by the evangelical *Rochester Observer*, had tried to stop the shows. The village trustees licensed circus riders with the stipulation that they not perform on Saturday night or Sunday. Bernard and Page made reassuring gestures of their own: they banned smoking in the audience, they refused admittance to unaccompanied women (a guard against prostitution), and they hired men to police the audience. Such precautions had no effect on the *Observer*. No circus, said the editor, could claim respectability. As for the circusgoers, they were thoughtless young men who shirked work and study, stayed out late, and too often stole the price of admission from their parents and employers. Circusgoers, concluded the *Observer*, were nothing more than ill-behaved boys "ready to pay money for the gratification of a depraved taste."[22]

North of the Recess on Exchange Street, Sam crossed a wooden bridge over the Erie Canal, overlooking the boat harbor at Child's Basin. Boosters praised the Canal as a wondrous feat of engineering and as the source of their prosperity, and they were right. But the Canal was also a river of noise and disorder running through the heart of Rochester. It employed thousands of young, unskilled boatmen and laborers, many of them immigrants, all of them living outside of families and settled communities. There were fights and occasional murders among the canawlers, and there had been two fatal riots west of Rochester at Lockport (site of a grand staircase of locks that was much admired by tourists) and another at Black Rock, near Buffalo. In Rochester, grogshops and boatmen's boardinghouses dotted the Canal's towpath, widening into rough shanty neighborhoods east and west of the town. Child's Basin was busy, and the narrow channel on the aqueduct permitted only one-way traffic. As boats lined up and jockeyed for position, the crews sometimes misbehaved. There were numerous fights between boat crews, and in 1826 a steersman named Erastus Bearcup went to jail for shouting obscenities at ladies on a passing boat. Peddlers sold ice, flowers, crackers, and whiskey to passengers and workmen on the boats; porters and boatmen shouted and sometimes fought as they worked. Boat captains, many of them Irishmen and Scots, announced their comings and goings with bugles—serenading the village with "The Yellow-Haired Laddie," "Paddy Carey," and other badly played Celtic airs. Child's Basin and the Canal, the heart and the central artery of Rochester's prosperity, were also the source of incessant shouting, profanity, and horn blasts, and too frequently they were the site of violence.[23]

The canal bridge on which Sam Patch stood had played a part in that. Joe Cochrane may have pointed out that the bridge was new in November 1829. A month earlier two soldiers had fought on Exchange Street, and a crowd had rushed out to watch. The fight careened up the street and onto the bridge and the old bridge collapsed, plunging about fifty persons "of all ages and sizes, of all colours and characters," into the Canal. The newsman Thurlow Weed described "the ludicrous appearance of the motly crew, crawling out of the canal, wet and dirty, [presenting] a spectacle worthy the pencil of a Hogarth." (Excepting accounts of Sam Patch's leaps, Weed's article on the fight on Exchange Street was reprinted in more out-of-town newspapers than any other Rochester story of the 1820s.)[24]

Across Buffalo Street, the first block of State Street boasted pavement and sidewalks, brick stores, Peck's printing establishment and bookstore, and two good hotels. But standing among them was a theater. The theater had gone up in 1826, with a resident company and the backing of prominent local citizens. Immediately and continually, outraged evangelicals branded it "a noisesome sink of immorality" and the "chief of Satan's engines," a place that bred "poverty, ill health, intemperance, false feelings of honour, insubordination in youth, temptation to pilfer, and finally, loss of character"—clearly, the wrong kind of self-fashioning. In the summer of 1826 the village government ran the theater company out of town, along with a smaller competitor on Exchange Street.[25]

But to the dismay of Rochester respectables, strolling entertainers (the comic actor "Yankee" Hill, the master ropedancer Vilallave, and a parade of itinerant acting companies) obtained licenses and played short runs at the theater in the late 1820s. The village government banned Saturday night and Sunday performances, ruled that the shows must end before ten-thirty in the evening, and demanded that the managers hire officers to prevent disturbances. Still, pious citizens complained about the noise. A particularly objectionable troupe took up residence early in 1828. The trouble, as with the circus, was with the young men who made up the audience—shouting at the actors, getting drunk in the barroom that William Cochrane's band mate kept in the basement, gathering on State Street to laugh and make noise. "For several weeks past," wrote one paper, "the inhabitants who are so unfortunate as to reside within gun-shot of the Theatre, have been compelled to hear, till midnight or after, reiterated peals of *hooting, howling, shouting, shrieking* and almost every other unseemly noise, that it is possible for the human gullet to send forth, insomuch that it is next to impossible to obtain repose till the theatrical audience have retired to *their* homes or hovels." A few weeks later, Rochester heard that the troupe had moved on to Batavia, where their advance man greeted that town's authorities in a very drunken state.[26]

State Street had also witnessed daytime scenes of disorder. Militia parades—both the half-drunken "official" processions and the Fantasticals'—wove up the street repeatedly, and it was on State Street, remember, that Sam Drake had shot his owl. Worse,

State Street commerce had given way to a number of political fistfights, all of them tied to the Antimasonic controversy of the late 1820s. When the murderers of William Morgan (a Mason who had threatened to reveal the secrets of Masonry) were not punished, thousands in western New York and elsewhere began to suspect a Masonic conspiracy. Politicians, with Rochester's Thurlow Weed at their head, seized the opportunity to turn populist Antimasonry against Martin Van Buren's nascent Democratic machine in Albany, and politics in Rochester and the surrounding territory became personal and ugly. In 1828 Democrats chased Weed up State Street brandishing a pair of shears, and innkeepers pulled another Antimason into the Mansion House Hotel to rescue him from a mob. In 1829 the Antimason Frederick Whittlesey beat up a fellow lawyer in the bar at the Eagle Tavern, at the northwest corner of Buffalo and State. (Whittlesey was an interesting character: a wealthy and respectable man—Yale graduate, lawyer, Episcopal vestryman, husband of the treasurer of the Female Charitable Society—who was competent and at ease in the sporting world. In 1829 he was elected to Congress. Whittlesey was also a theatergoer who wrote the prize poem read at the opening performance of the State Street theater, and he got into a surprising number of fights. A few months before the bout at the Eagle Tavern, he had been assaulted by "unknown persons." And a month after his barroom victory—and a few weeks before Sam Patch came to Rochester—a Democratic blacksmith named Patrick Cavanaugh broke Whittlesey's nose in another brawl.)[27]

At the end of the first block of State Street the sidewalks stopped, the street bent to the left, and the brick stores gave way to workshops and frame houses. Here Sam Patch stepped out of the world of commerce and into a neighborhood known as Frankfort. Promoters had envisioned Frankfort as the center of Rochester, but through the political tricks of rival businessmen their speculations failed. While the old proprietors maintained big houses in Frankfort, a working-class neighborhood had grown up around them; their projected town square had become a dirt field used as the militia training ground. The men of Rochester knew Frankfort well, for most of them had spent training days on the square—as participants or spectators at militia drills that were getting out of hand. In the afternoon, the citizen soldiers retired to McCracken's Tavern at the corner of State and Mumford. Some of the men went there regularly, for the tavern was another favored haunt of Rochester's sporting crowd. There were dances at McCracken's. There would have been horse races as well, but county officials had banned them. In 1834 the barkeeper McCracken still complained that his prize trotter was kept out of competition by the "superstition and hypocrisy" of the respectables and their laws.[28]

To the right, entering Frankfort, stood frame houses, then the falls-side Brown's Race, lined with foundries, factories, and mills. Separated from the commercial bustle and the engineering marvels that surrounded their downtown counterparts, the mills of Frankfort stood as what they were: big buildings full of machinery and sweating workers. On one of his visits to the falls, Sam Patch went into an iron foundry on the raceway and introduced himself to a boy named Andrew Jackson Langworthy, the son of one of the owners. Sam wanted to take soundings in the falls basin, and young A.J. gave Sam the key to his boat. Patch stepped to the back of the foundry and looked out on the hundred-foot chasm of Genesee Falls.[29]

Across a dizzying gorge frowned the wooded island precipice from which he planned to leap. A mill dam crossed the river from the island to the east side; mills and church spires formed the backdrop. But on the east side of the falls the landscape thinned as it had on State Street. There was a cluster of mills above the falls; below them the banks sloped into brushy pasture. Behind the pasture sprawled the Irish shantytown known as Dublin. The Irish had come to Rochester as workers on the Erie

Canal and aqueduct, and hundreds of them had stayed on to dig ditches, load boats, and make flour barrels for the mills. Prejudice and the price of housing kept them out of the village center, and in the late 1820s they were colonizing the east side below the falls. A journalist—himself an Irishman—described the romantic view of the falls from the east bank, but warned that "access to it is not very inviting." Like Frankfort on the west side, Dublin was a neighborhood where improvers found a lot of wage labor and very few friends.[30]

Many elite travelers, not wanting to spoil their memories or anticipation of Niagara, did not visit Genesee Falls. Others took the short walk from downtown and judged the falls worth seeing, though they could not separate the waterfall from the technological landscape that surrounded it. In 1828 a young woman saw the falls at night and pronounced it "not perhaps less beautiful" when illuminated by the furnace fire and showers of sparks coming from the Langworthy foundry. William Leete Stone viewed Genesee Falls from the east side and concluded that the waterfall was "beautifully picturesque" (framed and reassuring). But it was in the mills lining the far side of the river that he found the fusion of nature and art that he had admired downtown: the streams of spent water running from underneath the mills and down the bluffs charmed Stone as the waterfall had not. The silvery man-made streams "present a beautiful spectacle as they tumble in foam into the deep bed of the river."[31]

Genteel foreigners and American romantics worshiped American progress less devoutly than did Stone, and they did not see beauty in waste canals. They could only lament the man-made ugliness that had defaced Genesee Falls. The British actress Fanny Kemble had this to say about Stone's "beautiful spectacle":

> From a thousand dingy-looking mills and manufactories the poor little rivulets of labouring water come rushing through narrow dirty channels, all stained and foaming, and hot from their work,

to throw themselves into the thin bosom of their parent stream. Truly, mills and steam-engines are wonderful things, and I know that men must live, but I wish it were not expedient to destroy what God had made so very beautiful, in order to make it useful.

Nathaniel Hawthorne was another who guessed that Genesee Falls had been grand before the people of Rochester diverted its "unprofitable sublimity" into canals and millraces. N. P. Willis saw the falls framed by factories and church steeples, listened as Rochesterians bragged about water power and progress, shook his head, and pronounced Genesee Falls "the only instance in the known world of a cataract turned, without the loss of a drop, through the pockets of speculators." Like Kemble and Hawthorne, Willis did not like what he saw at Genesee Falls. And like the others he experienced the falls only as an unlovable extension of the built environment above the drop and along the banks. Among educated aesthetes, differing experiences of Genesee Falls stemmed very largely from differing attachments to American canals and factories.[32]

Sam Patch surveyed Genesee Falls, untroubled by wealthy aesthetes and their arguments about utility and beauty. He had spent his life beside mill-town waterfalls. A cataract surrounded by factories was his home landscape, and he had his own uses for it and his own ways of seeing it. He saw Genesee Falls not as a ruined and conquered stream but as a broad, one-hundred-foot drop full of wonder and danger.

Many of Rochester's men and boys experienced Genesee Falls in the same way. They often took chances at the falls and chasm, and there had been accidents. In January 1826 constables arrested a visiting country boy for getting drunk and picking fights in downtown Rochester. As they led him across the bridge, the drunk broke free and leaped into the river, and would have gone over the falls if citizens had not rescued him. Two months later, an unlucky boy fell while retrieving driftwood from the

Genesee Falls, by W. H. Bartlett (author's collection)

lower bridge; he swam mightily but was swept over the falls and killed. A workman clearing ice from Brown's Race in January 1827 fell into the channel and was swept ninety feet down the man-made fall that Colonel Stone had so admired. His workmates found him in the chasm with nothing worse than a few bruises. The following year a seven-year-old boy fell through the bridge near the brink, and was saved by a day laborer who jumped in after him. A Mr. Livings fell through the same bridge in November 1827; his body was found amid floodwood below the falls seven months later. People knew that the brink of Genesee Falls was dangerous. Yet one of the favorite games of boys in the 1820s was to walk across the river on the narrow, submerged mill dam that ran a few feet from the fatal drop.[33]

From the back of the foundry Sam Patch descended a steep path to the falls chasm. This was a place that Rochester's men and boys knew well. The gorge twisted seven miles up to Lake Ontario, with high bluffs on both sides, interrupted by a second fall of water. Out of sight and sound of the village, they could swim and hike the banks. The fishing was good, particularly below the lower falls, and the forested banks were full of animals. It was here that the sportsman Reuben Bunnell, one of the militia Fantasticals, had killed the rattlesnake that bound Sam Drake's Bible. There were parties as well: a man named Joab Britton kept a yawl in the chasm and conducted pleasure outings for sporting men and their ladies.[34]

The banks along the gorge could be a hazardous place, full of snakes, impenetrable brush, sheer drops, and, now and then, dangerous men. That had been dramatized powerfully in September 1828. Downtown, Presbyterian and Episcopal ministers, along with assorted businessmen and master mechanics, had founded the Franklin Institute in rooms at the courthouse in 1826. The institute maintained an apprentice's library, chemistry sets, and models of machines, and it provided free Friday-night lectures on scientific and mechanical subjects—all of it intended, as the Presbyterian put it, to educate young workingmen and "to furnish a *public amusement*, safe for the young and worthy of a people whose boast and pride is and ought to be *common sense*, *useful knowledge* and *cultivated intellect*, rather than tinselled theatricals, dissipated revelry, idle parade, or sickly sentiment." In 1828 the Franklin Institute engaged George Catlin to paint a full-length portrait of (who else?) De Witt Clinton, to be hung in the hall of the institute. Julius Catlin, the artist's brother, delivered the painting and collected the fee in September 1828. With his downtown business completed, Catlin hiked the bluffs to below the lower falls and descended into the chasm. He sketched the falls, then apparently decided to go swimming. There was a cry, and Catlin disappeared. His body was found a few days later. A man who made a living as a fisherman in the chasm—the only witness to the drowning—was found gathering up Catlin's clothes on the bank, and it was discovered that Catlin's money and a gold watch were missing. Officials questioned the fisherman closely, then let him go. But many in Rochester continued to believe that Julius Catlin had been murdered. The episode reinforced what Rochester already knew: downtown was a good place to do business and hang pictures of De Witt Clinton. In the chasm, young men took their chances.[35]

Sam found young Langworthy's boat and pushed off. He spent hours in the chasm, taking soundings and picking his spot. The busyness of Rochester—the aqueduct, the churches, the brick stores of the Four Corners—was above the falls and out of sight. High above Sam on the Dublin side, the cliffs climbed straight up and ended in wild greenery, and the sky began without a break. The factories on Brown's Race were up and to Sam's right. Towering in front of him was the face of the falls—broad sheets of falling water separated by the island, revealing the broken and seemingly unstable stack of limestone shelves that lay beneath the town. (Said Mrs. Trollope: "The fall of the Genesee is close to the town, and in the course of a few months will, perhaps, be in the middle of it.") Upriver, the world was right angles, bricks, and white paint. Here the world was green: the stunning green violence of the falls, the mossed-over rocks, the heaving emerald of the basin, the verdant disorder of the trees and bushes that clothed the banks. It was a place that improvers had not touched. It would form a fine amphitheater for what Sam Patch would do.[36]

Sam Patch advertised his leap for Friday, November 6, at two o'clock. Spectators began moving toward the falls at midday. A visitor from Albany reached the scene and found "not less than 10,000 persons" waiting for Sam Patch. A reporter from Auburn agreed on that number. A local editor guessed a more modest six to eight thousand, but was certain that the crowd was "greater than ever before witnessed in Rochester." Whatever the number, the crowd came close to equaling the population of Rochester. Insistent on seeing Sam Patch, they had left their stores, workshops, and farms in the middle of a working day, walked north through Frankfort and Dublin, and turned around to look at Rochester from below Genesee Falls—a view that sportsmen and playful boys knew well, and that improvers seldom saw. The landscape of work was transformed into the landscape of danger and play.[37]

The men and women in the crowd lived in Rochester or on nearby farms, and they knew the town. Most of them stood on the west bank, but across the chasm on the Dublin side stood another solid phalanx of spectators, "like an army drawn up in battle array," according to the man from Albany. "If the intense feeling which pervaded that vast assembly is taken into view, the scene could not have been much unlike the 'moment before the battle.'" They stood jostling and talking, letting the tension build, and took a long look at Sam Patch's amphitheater. Above and behind the falls stood Rochester's familiar landscape of progress: a broad green river spanned by bridges and dams, the banks lined with factories and mills, church spires reaching out of the townscape and into the sky. It was a peaceful and impressive sight—a new city living in harmony with its conquered river. But to people standing below the falls (and awaiting Sam Patch) the triumph of art over nature may have seemed less permanent and complete. From where Sam's audience stood, with Frankfort and Dublin at their backs, with the cracked limestone shelves on which the city stood clearly visible, and with the giddy disorder of the chasm at their feet, it was the landscape of progress that seemed somehow thoughtless and dangerously out of place.[38]

The show, according to one account, began with a joke. Two o'clock came and went without Sam Patch, and at two-fifteen a man strode out of the crowd and walked to the spot from which Sam was to leap. He bowed to the audience, stared gravely into the abyss, then crouched and braced himself for the jump. At the end he leaped—backwards—and turned and ran off the island. (This may not have happened, for the same newspaper also in-

Sam Patch at Genesee Falls, from the *Rochester Gem* (courtesy of the Local History Division, Rochester Public Library)

sisted that Sam's bear was included in the day's proceedings. The correspondent tells us that after his leap Sam returned to the island and threw the bear over the falls, "to show that 'some things can be done as well as others.'" Sam's advertisement had not mentioned this part of his show, and the other three newspaper accounts made no mention of the bear. Seventy years later, however, Sam's friend A. J. Langworthy remembered seeing the bear leap the falls on November 6:

> The performance was not yet concluded, however, as he returned from below, having a good-sized black bear with him, who seemed unwilling to go over where Sam did. After much wrestling Sam finally forced him to do so. The bear made several promiscuous turns, then sat bolt upright in mid-air until he struck the water stern first, from which he soon struck for shore.

In later years, other old people who had witnessed the leap as children swore they had seen the bear go over the falls. The folklore and celebrity status surrounding Sam Patch, apparently, were well under way in November 1829.)[39]

A little before three o'clock the real Sam Patch stepped before the crowd, white in his spinner's shirt and pants. He stepped to the edge and scanned the crowd, bowed to them and waved his arms. People on the bluffs cheered him, then grew quiet. Sam stood still for a long moment. Rochester stood primly behind him. Beneath his feet the layers of timeless and indifferent limestone frowned from behind broken sheets of falling water. The only sound was the primordial roar of the falls. The crowd on the banks stared at Sam and knew what he would do: he would leap out of the landscape of progress and into deep green chaos.

The jump was perfect. Sam sat back on his haunches and leaped out, white against the dark chasm wall, and entered the basin with his body erect, almost without a splash. ("Beautiful," gasped the man from Albany; "frightful," said the Rochester editor; and they meant the same thing.) For long seconds the audience stared at the spot where Sam had gone under; in what was becoming a ritual that followed Sam's jumps, some murmured, "He's dead." At last Sam bobbed to the surface, sported in the waves, and paddled to shore. The crowd on the banks roared with one voice as Sam's friends greeted him. To the first he said, "This is the real Sam Patch—no mistake." The crowd on the cliffs gave three cheers. They looked down and saw a man hand Sam his sailor's jacket. Another handed him a bottle of rum.[40]

Sam Patch determined to jump again at Rochester before returning east. He went back to the Recess and—probably with some combination of sportsmen and journalists—designed the fanciest handbill he could think up. Sam's love of applause was up, and so was his contempt of danger. He would jump from a staging that raised the height to 125 feet—matching his greatest leap at Niagara. An hour after jumping, he would return to throw his bear over the waterfall. (The erroneous story about his first

Rochester leap may have encouraged him to make it true in his second.) And he would "fearlessly" do these things not on an ordinary day but on Friday the thirteenth—the day that Christ died on the cross, believed by millions to be a lethally unlucky date.[41]

Handbills were posted throughout western New York and Upper Canada. Schooners from Canada and Oswego headed across Lake Ontario, and on the morning of the leap country people and other out-of-towners thronged the streets of Rochester. The groceries conducted a brisk Friday-morning business in whiskey, and the hotel bars were filled with better-dressed spectators—many of whom placed bets on whether Sam Patch would leap. (A later rumor would have it that Sam borrowed money to bet on himself.)[42]

Two hours before the advertised leap, the crowd moved toward the falls. The papers agreed that Sam's second leap drew more people than the first; one estimate put the crowd at twelve

Last-leap handbill
(courtesy of the Local History Division, Rochester Public Library)

thousand persons. Hundreds stood directly at the brink of 125-foot cliffs, some of them kicking loose pebbles into the chasm and watching them drop. Behind them stood rank upon rank of more cautious spectators. The roofs of all the factories and houses on Brown's Race were alive with onlookers. Those who knew the right people peered from the windows of factories and mills. William Haywood—one of the village trustees who were empowered to stop objectionable entertainments—left his wife and five-year-old son at a fourth-story window and joined a long, single-file parade down the path into the chasm. Some brave men left the path and climbed perpendicular rocks to perch on ledges jutting from the cliffs themselves. At the bottom, the crowd filled every space on the flats; scores of boys climbed trees for a better look. Those in the chasm looked nearly straight up at the point from which Sam Patch would leap. A journalist who understood such things approved of the "romantic station" taken by the boys in the trees.[43]

The crowd was in place by one o'clock. They talked and shivered in the November chill for more than an hour. Men passed hats through the crowd, collecting coins for Sam Patch. (Later, no one could say what happened to the money.) Latecomers walked along the bluffs almost to where the river twisted out of sight and took places half a mile from Sam's platform.[44]

Sam Patch spent the morning at the Rochester Recess, talking and sipping brandy. As the hour approached he rose and donned his white spinner's pants and shirt, and then his friends began to decorate him. The Irishman John O'Donohue produced a large handkerchief of black silk, and Sam tied it jauntily around his waist. It was a cold day, and the cotton pants were thin. William Cochrane offered the white trousers of his band uniform, and Sam slipped them on over the spinner's pants. The seaman's jacket and a woolen skullcap, and Sam and his entourage stepped out onto Exchange Street.[45]

A crowd was waiting in the street, and Sam walked, in a procession led by what a witness called "the fancy" of the town, up State Street to the falls. The paraders were "cheering as they went," remembered the witness. "It created a mixed sensation, between a horse race and an execution." The parade crossed the Four Corners—deserted on the afternoon of a business day—and headed up State Street. Near the falls, Sam crossed Brown's Race and waded the shallows onto the island. The crowd on the island (many of the journalists were here) applauded. Sam stepped out of the trees and pushed through the spectators. When the crowd along the bluffs saw him, a resounding cheer echoed up and down the gorge. Sam ignored the applause and outstretched hands and within seconds stood beside the scaffold at the brink of Genesee Falls.[46]

Sam scanned the thousands standing on the Frankfort and Dublin cliffs and the mass of men and boys who stood far below him in the chasm. The workshops and mills at his left were thronged with anxious spectators. From one fourth-story window Mrs. Haywood stared at Sam, her little boy at her side. Another young mother stood in the crowd with an infant of six weeks in her arms. Amid the onlookers a prominent citizen stood transfixed, his thumb in his mouth. When Sam leaped, the man would clench his jaws and bite it off. In yet another part of the audience an old woman broke the silence: "If there's anything in dreams, that man is dead."[47]

Sam stared into the crowd for minutes, and some saw his eyes go blank. His body went slack, and for a second he swayed absentmindedly at the edge. Some thought he was losing his nerve. But others, seeing Sam's body sag, looked into his eyes and knew that he was drunk. Joe Cochrane had been ordered to keep an eye on Sam, and for years afterward he swore that the jumper had taken no more than a single glass of brandy at the Recess to cut the November chill. (As the decades passed, this drink transformed into a single shot of gin taken a minute or two before the leap.) But others knew better. Assessments of Sam's condition ranged from "partially intoxicated" and "apparently under the influence," through "considerably intoxicated" and "quite tipsy," to the flat assertion that Patch could not stand up straight because he had "a skin full of whiskey."[48]

Sam snapped himself alert and stepped to the rear of the platform, and at this point he delivered a little speech. One witness remembered "a half hour's speechifying and monkey capers." Thurlow Weed, who stood beneath the platform, wrote that Sam "harangued the multitude" with a "short, incoherent speech," while Henry Stanton simply recalled the oration as "ridiculous." Joe Cochrane was the one witness who claims to tell us what Sam said, and it was another sample of Sam's new showman's mix of grandiosity and comic nonchalance. "Napoleon," said Sam, "was a great man and a great general. He conquered armies and he conquered nations. But he couldn't jump the Genesee Falls. Wellington was a great man and a great soldier. He conquered armies and he conquered Napoleon, but he couldn't jump the Genesee Falls. That was left for me to do, and I can do it and will!"[49]

The men near Sam puzzled over what that meant, and tradition has it that they tried to talk him out of the jump. Sam would hear none of it. He turned and faced the crowd once more, took off his cap and sailor's jacket and laid them aside. He stood at the edge in Cochrane's band trousers, his cotton spinner's shirt, and the Irishman's black scarf, the town at his back, the basin at his feet. Then he crouched and leaped into the abyss.

The leap began as gracefully as the others. Sam arched his torso and threw his head back and his arms out and sailed outward and down. But a third of the way down things went wrong. Sam's head dropped to his chest and his body veered sideways, and the crowd watched in horror as he fell with his arms flailing in the air. He hit the water out of control and was dead in that instant.[50]

The crowd stared into the spot where Sam had disappeared.

There were no exclamations, no talk at all. Seconds and then minutes passed, and the curiosity and anticipation that had brought them to the falls curdled into horror and shame. Thousands, unable to talk or look each other in the eyes, turned and walked silently away. Within minutes, nearly everyone was gone. That night, while haunted spectators played the scene over and over in their minds, and while journalists and preachers worked on what they would say, Joab Britton's pleasure yawl, lined with burning torches, scoured the chasm for the corpse of Sam Patch.[51]

CELEBRITY

They did not find the body. Days and then months passed, and many believed that Sam Patch was alive. Sam, the story went, had swum behind the waterfall to a rock ledge where he had hidden dry clothes and a bottle of rum. He waited until dark, climbed out of the chasm, and headed east. A few days after the last leap a letter signed by Sam Patch appeared at the entrance to the Arcade Building. Sam promised to deliver a speech at the Eagle Tavern a few days later. Some placed bets on whether he would appear (the tannery owner Jacob Graves, a former player in the town band, wagered one hundred dollars that Sam would keep his promise) and a crowd showed up on the appointed day. Sam was spotted in upstate villages, and a New Yorker claimed to have met and spoken with him in Manhattan. In late November a Boston paper printed a long letter from Sam Patch. The leap at Rochester had been a "capital hoax," wrote Sam. The Sam Patch who made the leap was a man of straw and paint, weighted with rocks to ensure that it would sink. The real Sam Patch stood in the crowd, enjoyed the grief and elegies, and walked out of Rochester. The stories persisted for years. When Nathaniel Hawthorne passed through Rochester in 1832, locals told him that Sam Patch had hidden behind the waterfall, and that he was still alive.[1]

Two weeks after the leap an upstate newspaper reported that Sam's body had been found in the chasm. Surgeons, said the paper, had discovered that both shoulders were dislocated and, worse, that Sam had suffered "the rupture of a blood-vessel, caused by the sudden chill of the atmosphere through which he passed to the water." Newspapers all over the Northeast picked up the story, but the Rochester papers remained silent. There had been no body. A similar bogus story surfaced in February.[2]

In March 1830 a laborer named Silas Hudson found the body of Sam Patch. Hudson was working at the Latta House in Charlotte, where the Genesee River empties into Lake Ontario. On a cold March morning he walked the hotel's horses to the river to water them. He kicked through the spring ice, and up bobbed Sam Patch. Hudson ran to the Latta House and fetched the owner and some others, and they pulled the body from the river, laid it out on a stoneboat, and hauled it to the hotel. There was a school nearby. Some of the boys and girls, though they knew they would get a licking, ran out of the schoolyard and joined the little crowd around the stoneboat.[3]

The dead man was indeed Sam Patch. The body had been in the water for four months and had been dragged down seven miles of riverbed and over the lower falls, but it was in remarkably good shape—proof, said an unkind editor, of the preservative effects of alcohol. Most of the hair was gone, the face was battered, and there was a deep gash over one of the eyes. But there were no broken bones, and Cochrane's band pants and the Irishman's black scarf were still in place. The doctors had their look, then Sam was buried in a little graveyard near the mouth of the Genesee. Someone put up a rough wooden board with an epitaph:

> Sam Patch
> Such is Fame

The epitaph was mistaken: Sam Patch was famous not only in the last months of his life but for decades after his death. Americans heard about Sam Patch in newspapers, sentimental poetry, and parlor magazines. He showed up in comic annuals, farmers' almanacs, dream books, and minstrel shows, and Sam Patch stage plays were mainstays of democratic theater for the rest of the nineteenth century. Sam's name and sayings entered popular speech and stayed there. "Some things can be done as well as others" became a popular saying—both a throwaway line and a sign of calm determination. Angry people were "as cross as Sam Patch." "What the Sam Patch" and "Where in Sam Patch" were common ways of swearing without swearing, and Americans pinned the name Sam Patch on anything or anyone that jumped or dropped or fell. In 1853 Commodore Matthew Perry's expedition to Japan adopted a castaway Japanese sailor named Sentoro, took him on as a servant and mascot, and named him Sam Patch. There have been four children's books and two modern novels about Sam Patch. A President of the United States owned a horse named Sam Patch. There was a Sam Patch brand of cigar.[4]

This was modern celebrity, and Sam Patch was one of its American pioneers. Sam had been born into the unstable margins of a world governed by inheritance, fixed social rank, and ordained life courses—a world where people like Sam Patch did not become famous. Public renown had followed the classical forms of the Romans: it was the unsought result of civic, religious, or military accomplishment, enjoyed only by disinterested, civic-minded gentlemen. The founders of the American republic were such gentlemen. They were deeply concerned with fame, but they knew that ambition and fame-seeking must be grounded in disinterested service. Trangressions of that rule led—as in the notorious case of Aaron Burr—to infamy. Americans during the lifetime of Sam Patch knew classical fame in the person of George Washington, the planter-patriot who led the Revolution, established the new republic, and then retired to his farm with his dignity and integrity intact. They had seen classical fame most recently in the national tour of the "Old Republican" Lafayette—another gentleman who served humanity without looking for applause.[5]

Sam Patch won a new kind of fame. He was born into obscurity, and he did nothing that classicists considered worthy of renown. Yet he *wanted* to be famous and he succeeded: he made a name that everyone knew, deeds that everyone had heard of, virtues and peculiarities that were the stuff of boyhood fantasies and barroom jokes. There were other, similar new celebrities in the 1820s. Sam shared the spotlight with the half-mythical western heroes Mike Fink and Davy Crockett, and with the actor Edwin Forrest, who was emerging as the workingman's tragedian. Even the comic Philadelphian Colonel Pluck competed for attention. Newspapers in the fall of 1829 talked about Fanny Wright, the notorious British feminist and socialist who traveled about the country preaching against marriage and religion. There were the Siamese Twins, who arrived in America that fall and were drawing crowds and a lot of discussion. There was, of course, President Andrew Jackson, who won his fame in the old military way, then became the first President with a "personality" and some of the trappings of modern celebrity. And there was Sam Patch, who rose from low beginnings to make a name known throughout the republic—simply by leaping waterfalls.[6]

Americans who read the newspapers in the late 1820s (whether they liked what they read or not) learned that anyone could be famous. Democracy, commerce, and new kinds of popular imagination were rising all at once. Cut loose from their pasts and picking their way through uncharted territory, Americans crafted themselves as their ancestors had crafted chairs and farm fields. Celebrities played a part in that: they dramatized the possibilities of individual self-making in the nineteenth century. At the same time, celebrities were *commodified* individuals—imagined and sold by a new apparatus of publicity (newspapers, popular theater, democratic literature) that shaped stories for an emerging mass audience. The

Sam Patch who reached the public was seldom, to borrow Sam's phrase, the Real Sam Patch. The celebrity Sam Patch existed first in newspaper stories that gave few details about him, then in talk about those stories, then in the work of actors, poets, preachers, newsmen, and writers who had their own uses for Sam Patch, then in talk about all of that. (Here the distinction between "authentic" folklore and commercial "fakelore" misses the point. Celebrity is one of the materials from which people in democratic, capitalist America make their folklore and themselves.)[7]

Sam's posthumous notoriety was strongest in the 1830s and 1840s, when living memory of his leaps was fresh. These were also the years of Jacksonian democracy and the invention of a two-party politics that, along with celebrity and the newspapers and much more, marked the rise of a mass democratic public in the United States. Whigs and Democrats reduced public debate to two choices. Those alternatives shaped politics decisively, and they went a long way toward organizing individual personalities. The man who identified himself as a Democrat or Whig disclosed his position on big questions on nationality, economic development, and the proper nature of government. At the same time, he dropped powerful hints about his cultural loyalties: the church that he attended, the entertainments that he patronized or avoided, the newspapers that he read and believed, the women whom he found attractive, the notions of manhood that he adopted or rejected—and what popped into his head when he heard the name Sam Patch. Most of the writers, actors, and others who invented the celebrity Sam Patch were openly Whigs or Democrats. The same was true of people who read the newspapers and went to shows. There are countless ways of talking about the posthumous Sam Patch, but it makes historical sense to note that Americans remembered Sam Patch in distinctively Whiggish and Democratic ways.

↳ class and political tendencies help shape what people think

The literati of the old seaport cities (an emerging cluster of New York critics and writers in particular) were almost unanimously supporters of the Whig Party. They were few in number and out of step with much that was becoming American, but they were wealthy and educated, they viewed themselves as the makers of American taste, and they controlled important printing presses. These gentlemen upheld the old society of rank and classical notions of fame. They disliked Sam Patch because he was vulgar, and because he transgressed the order of renown. In tones ranging from genteel wit to outright disgust, the Whig literati confronted the unsettling fact that Sam Patch was famous.

"Celebrity of character gives every republican a title," bemoaned the Philadelphia *Saturday Evening Post*'s account of Sam's first Rochester leap. Sam was determined to escape "the gloomy shades of obscurity" and to "immortalize his name among the great men of the age," and the paper suggested that Sam affix "Some things can be done as well as others" to his family crest (it was better than "that wishy-washy stuff, which composes the arms of other great men"), that he call himself "Samuel Patch, Esq.," and that he leap from Paterson to Washington to address Congress. A New York City editor, similarly upset by the disorderly implications of modern celebrity, pronounced Sam Patch "indisputably the most distinguished man of his day, with the exception of Miss Fanny Wright."[8]

Two weeks after Sam's death, William Leete Stone's *New-York Commercial Advertiser* published "A Monody, made on the late Mr. Samuel Patch, by an admirer of the Bathos." The admirer was Robert Sands, "a clever and learned Columbia man" who was a gentleman poet of New York City. Between his mock admiration for Patch's bravery and his contempt for Sam's low ambition ("drunk, with rum and with renown") Sands managed to fit in references to Pope, Longinus, and Byron, and to make comparisons between Sam Patch and Leander, Sappho, Empedocles, Icarus, Helle, Vulcan, Apollo, Phaeton, Alexander the Great, and the offspring of Maia: they all reached for too much, and they all fell. Sam would join them on the roll of failed classical heroes;

> His name shall be a portion in the batch
>   Of the heroic dough, which baking Time
>   Kneads for consuming ages—and the chime
> Of Fame's old bells, long as they truly ring,
>   Shall tell of him; he dived for the sublime,
> And found it.

One of Colonel Stone's rival editors condemned Sands's "Monody" as "*a hundred and seventy one lines* of vulgarisms" and a sustained crime "against rhyme, reason, the king's English, and common sense." Sands continued to live and write among the New York literati.[9]

In 1840 the *Knickerbocker Magazine* published a long poem on Sam Patch. The *Knickerbocker* spoke for a circle of New York Whigs who practiced writing as a leisured avocation and who aspired to make their city, their magazine, and themselves the arbiters of American cosmopolitanism and taste. The author of "The Great Descender" was a gentleman physician named Thomas Ward who wrote under the pseudonym "Flaccus." "The Great Descender" was a mock epic in the dark modes of the literary sublime. The Sam Patch of the piece is solitary, half-crazed, obsessed with fame. ("His care-worn features, wild and fever-tinged / Bespoke a soul ambition's fire had singed.") Sam cannot think of a way to become famous. He asks the stars for help, and spies a meteor crossing the sky: "Renown is mine!—the heavens have marked the way: / Yon meteor whispers: wherefor climb at all, / Since fame as well irradiates things that fall?" and he is off and jumping. The poem lumbers through twenty-four pages of epic heroism, sublime and philosophical asides, science lessons, and the odd genteel joke (Sam's death: "He yielded, vanquished by a drop too much"), and ends with what the modestly anonymous Flaccus really had in mind:

Oh! Happy chance that gave thee for my theme!
Now, linked together, will we sail the stream;
Thou shalt be called the **Patch** whom Flaccus sang,
Or I the bard who **Patch's** praises rang:
Yes! I shall buoy thee on th' immortal sea,
Or, failing that, thyself shalt carry me!

Flaccus's unembarrassed cupidity, not to mention the *Knick-erbocker*'s readiness to put it into print, was possible only because the notion that an American could become famous either by leaping waterfalls or writing about people who did such things was new. (In the case of Flaccus, it didn't work. The *North American Review* praised the effort to make literature out of Sam's "strange notoriety," but pronounced the story's mix of "the mean and sublime" too difficult a task for even the best of genteel poets. Edgar Allan Poe was less friendly. Poe roundly disliked the *Knickerbocker*'s attempt to stake out an emerging American literature as the province of New York gentlemen. He lambasted "The Great Descender" as "twattle," "elaborate doggerel," and an "atrocity" that proved the Knickerbocker Circle's incompetence in literary matters. As for Flaccus, he was simply "the very worst of all the wretched poets that ever existed on the earth.")[10]

After 1840 the parlor magazines and New York poets moved away from Sam Patch, but they returned to him whenever they encountered instances of low fame, low ambition, and the mindless bravado that went with both. A balloonist who got drunk before ascending was "like Sam Patch, so famous for a similar absurdity." The celebrated French novelist and critic Madame de Staël might travel openly and in sin with an English lover, but, a magazine warned, while one woman might get away with such indiscretions, "it would be just as safe for others to follow her example, as it would have been for a man to have jumped down Niagara after Sam Patch." A young Civil War lieutenant told his mother, "I shall rival Sam Patch at a leap, and jump to the head at once. Three months is enough to make a colonel of me." (He was, of course, killed.) When President Andrew Johnson, against the very public advice of General Ulysses Grant, removed Philip Sheridan from his post as military reconstructor of Louisiana and Texas, one commentator noted that the removal "shows [Johnson] to be a bold man, but of the kind of boldness that led Sam Patch to leap upon the Genesee Falls—to his destruction." King Louis Philippe built a regime upon demagoguery and facade, and was doomed to fall like Sam Patch. Ralph Waldo Emerson lowered himself to deliver half-coherent public lectures for money, wrote one critic: "his readers, at least, if not his hearers, are fully justified in looking upon him only as a sort of intellectual Sam Patch, who makes it his profession to go about the world, leaping down precipices, plunging into abysses, in every deep seeking a still lower [sic] in which to expose himself for the sake of the applause and the pay, which men are always willing to bestow on any one who is fool-hardy enough to entertain them with such extravagances."[11]

Sam also survived as a target of polite wit, usually by being put into learned company in which he was comically out of place. Harvard's Hasty Pudding Club entertained itself with a poem about Sam Patch, and the medical faculty at that school included him (along with the Sea Serpent and the Siamese Twins) as a doctor in its Latin parody of the Quinquennial. When a book on prominent men of the nineteenth century included such unworthies as the sensational journalist James Gordon Bennett, the camp-meeting preacher Peter Cartwright, and the duplicitous showman P. T. Barnum (all of them Democrats), a reviewer wondered why such a silly list of "noticeables" could not be expanded to include, among other undeserving Americans, Sam Patch. Whigs recognized the problem: a new kind of popularity was overrunning good sense. "A cheap method of notoriety, the world over, is this rearing and plunging," preached Mark Hopkins to the young men of Williams College. "Sam Patch, leaping over Genesee Falls, could gather a greater crowd than Daniel Webster."[12]

The genteel circles that included Flaccus and the Hasty Pudding were a minority within the Whig Party. Northern Whiggery found its core constituency among an emerging middle class that called itself "respectable." Middle-class Whigs embraced democratic ambition and the self-made man. But they knew that the free individual could be dangerous, and they insisted that ambition be acted out within a disciplined and domestic bourgeois universe. In distinguishing laudable aspiration from destructive self-seeking they found their bad examples among gamblers, confidence men, speculators, merchants who sold slaves or whiskey, and—to a remarkable degree—entertainers. The daredevil Sam Patch provided a near-perfect example of self-fashioning gone wrong: he was an itinerant showman who had no home, he avoided useful work, he was reckless, he drank, he sought fame for its own sake, and he corrupted the young.

In the late 1820s Rochester's respectable preachers and journalists railed against military parades, the theater, the circus, shooting matches, patriotic celebrations, public hangings—anything that drew citizens away from home and work and put them into pleasure-seeking crowds. The leaps of Sam Patch were among the worst of these. Patch roamed the country seeking fame and money. He seduced young men into his exhibitions of reckless daring, filled their heads with overheated fantasy and wild, impossible dreams, and left their spirits dissipated and ready for more. After Sam's last leap, preachers and editorial writers blamed the public that had paid money and provided an audience for Sam's audacious stunt. One told a Sunday school class that any of them who had witnessed the jump would be judged guilty of murder by God. Another spoke of "strange and savage curiosity."[13]

Sam Patch himself demonstrated what happened when a young man shunned work and morality for a life of itinerant fame-seeking. Following Sam's death a Providence paper disclosed that he had worked in Pawtucket, but "gave up mule spinning for his idle employment, until his vaulting ambition o'r leapt itself and the loss of his life has been the consequence." An English visitor to Rochester learned that Sam was "given to drinking, and led a sort of vagabond life, such as one may well imagine a young fellow would fall into, who got his living through the summer by diving into various gulfs and rapids for the amusement of the fun-hunting ladies and gemmen." Later, a local newspaper recalled Sam Patch as "an unmitigated 'Loafer,' stolid, besotted, ignorant; it was impossible, almost, to conclude that he could be ambitious [and here the respectable distinction between right and wrong ambition], and yet a love of notoriety was his ruling passion." Those who would be prosperous and respectable were warned to stay away from shows. In 1836 the editor of Boston's *Farmer's Almanack* quoted Farmer Cautious: "Confound all these idle sharpers, who get their living by making the people stare." The editor agreed: "So I say. If any one has a little money to spare, let him put it into the savings bank, that he may be benefitted by it at some future time, when the Durants and Sam Patches, the fish-gulpers, the tumblers, the fire-eaters and the jockey balancers, and all the wheedling crew will not be worth a last year's bird's nest."[14]

There were funnier uses for Sam Patch, and writers for a middle-class public soon found them. Most obviously, Sam made a fine comic Yankee. William Leete Stone, of course, had concocted the first Yankee Sam Patch. Seba Smith, editor of the *Portland Courier* in Maine, made the second. The *Courier*, a Whig paper labeling itself "The Daily Courier and Family Reader," refused lottery advertisements, and Smith took entertainment ads only from the Portland Museum, assuring his readers that it was a "rational and harmless enjoyment." He hated Jacksonian democracy, and in his war against incompetence and selfish ambition he concocted one of the great Yankee characters: Major Jack Downing of Downingville, a down-easter, a supporter of Andrew Jackson, and a rising politician driven by groundless

ambition that was both cunning and naive. Smith's Major Downing would soon be a member of Jackson's Kitchen Cabinet and an
aspirant to the presidency.[15]

The *Courier*, true to its ethos of family readership and
rational enjoyment, printed no accounts of the Niagara and
Rochester leaps of Sam Patch. But Patch's death was too good to
pass up. Seba Smith's verse "Biography of Sam Patch" appeared
early in 1830. Smith's Sam Patch was a poor man without talent
or connections but with a thirst for fame:

> And if he would become renown'd
> And live in song and story,
> T'was time he should be looking round
> For deeds of fame and glory.
>
> What shall I do? Quoth honest Sam;
> "There is no war a brewing;
> "And duels are but dirty things,
> "Scarce worth a body's doing.
>
> "And if I should be President,
> "I see I'm up a tree.
> "For neither prints or Congress-men,
> "Have nominated me."
>
> But still the maggot in his head
> Told Sam he was a gump,
> For if he could do nothing else,
> Most surely he could jump.

Driven by applause, he went from waterfall to waterfall, winning
fame and, at Niagara, the title "Squire Samuel O'Cataract." (Seba
Smith was evidently a reader and casual plagiarizer of Hiram
Doolittle, Jun.) Then the fatal descent at Rochester:

> And here our hero should have stopt,
> And husbanded his brilliant fame,

But, ah, he took one leap too much,
And most all heroes do the same.

There was, of course, a Whiggish moral to the story: "It will deter others from jumping from the same heights that Sam did; and in these times of political excitement, why may not politicians derive a useful moral from the same, and learn to jump with moderation? They should be cautious of the cheerings and shoutings of warm partizans, for verily in politicks, as perpendicular heights, there are some jumps which are fatal." (A few years later, Smith identified the author as Major Jack Downing, who had recognized a kindred spirit in Sam Patch.)[16]

Hard on the heels of Jack Downing's Patch came "The Last Leap," a mock Yankee-dialect autobiography in Henry Finn's *American Comic Annual* for 1831. Finn's humor—like Seba Smith's—was decidedly Whiggish in tone: didactic, reformist, and worried about the wrong kinds of ambition. Finn's Sam Patch wrote his story on the eve of his last leap, "for the eggsample uv posterity." Patch begins: "The famullee uv the Patches are about as old as Josefs cote uv menny cullers; and by jumpin down as offen as I hav, I hav pruv'd myself a ginuine *desendent*—if they wur properioters of land, it must have ben but a foo Patches." He goes on to his triumphs at Paterson and Niagara, and comments on the allure of cheap celebrity—"Hoo wood n't be a hero? hoo wood n't be proud of the shouts, witch is shouted fur a Ginral what conkers with his swored, and a jugular what swallers it." Finn, like Seba Smith, reassumed his own Whiggish voice when he concluded with a moral on the rights and wrongs of ambition: "Gentle Reader, it *was* his last jump.—The lesson is instructive. It will serve to teach you, that in all the concerns and contentions of our little life, the trials of temper—the propensities of passion—the many temptations that make the sweet music of social combination discordant—, if you would keep yourself and others out of harm's way, adopt and act up to this homely precept: *Look, before you leap.*"[17]

A third Yankee Sam Patch came from Canada. In 1836 William Haliburton, a Tory magistrate in Nova Scotia, imagined a Yankee clockmaker named Sam Slick—yet another rustic and devious upstart. Haliburton was a British subject and a monarchist, and he thought that every republican was a self-serving fool. At one point he has Sam Slick console a preacher who is bewailing the fate of the Liberty Tree—once fenced and protected and pronounced the most beautiful thing in the world, now defiled by mobs until "it looks no better than a gallows tree." Faced with the collapse of republicanism, Sam Slick—like Napoleon and the Americans before him—masks his failures by invading other countries. He casts an imperialistic eye on Nova Scotia, and thinks of enlisting Sam Patch into the cause. For Sam is alive. He entered the water at Niagara with such force that he swam through the earth and came up in the South Sea, where he was picked up by a whaling captain. ("In that are Niagara dive," Sam explained to the captain, "I went so everlasting deep, I thought it was just as short to come up tother side, so out I came in these parts. If I don't take the shine off the Sea Serpent, when I get back to Boston, then my name's not Sam Patch.") Sam Slick proposes hiring Patch to dive deep into the North Atlantic with a torpedo and blow up Nova Scotia to make way for American roads, canals, and republican bombast. (The plot against Nova Scotia was soon forgotten, but Sam's dive to the other side of the world reappeared three years later in *The American Joe Miller*, a popular comic almanac.)[18]

Gentility and respectability were roughly uniform across the North, and Whigs fabricated political culture for a broad and self-conscious constituency. Jacksonian Democrats faced a more complicated task. Democrats ranged from New Hampshire yeomen to Indiana farmers to New York City artisans to Methodist preachers to Rhode Island mule spinners—a motley array of the marginal, the local, and the disaffected. Democrats shared suspicions of the emerging commercial culture and the self-assured moralizers who often carried it. They also shared memories of a Revolution that endowed ordinary lives with dignity and that promised a democratic distribution of respect. But those commonalities were grounded in ways of life that were local and particular, and that often cared little about the wider world. It was the task of the Democratic Party to organize those local hopes and fears into a national democratic culture, and in doing that they turned to the new forms of communications and popular culture. Whigs denounced the rude and often silly democracy that made Sam Patch a celebrity. Democrats embraced it, had fun with it, and made much of their political culture out of it. In the process, Sam Patch became a model American democrat.

The Sam Patch who became most familiar to nineteenth-century Americans was fabricated by an actor named Dan Marble. Marble's political affiliation is not known, but he certainly acted like a Democrat: he made his living as a low comedian at a time and in places in which Whig respectables denounced the theater out of hand; he was a spread-eagle patriot who hated Britain and monarchy (he narrowly avoided fistfights with royalists while touring Canada), and he transformed the stage Yankee—in the person of Sam Patch—into a popular democratic hero.[19]

In 1836 the twenty-six-year-old Marble was playing bit parts and telling Yankee stories with a strolling troupe in Buffalo. A local lawyer liked his Yankee sketches and presented him with an amateur play entitled *Sam Patch, the Yankee Jumper*. Marble played Sam Patch at Buffalo's Eagle Theater in December 1836—acting before elaborate scenery and costumed, according to a boy who saw the performances, "much after the present caricature of Uncle Sam, minus the stars but glorifying in the stripes."[20]

Marble's company moved on to Columbus, Ohio, where they transformed *Sam Patch* into an elaborate stage spectacle. They hired a master scene painter to make a huge Niagara backdrop for the climactic scene, and carpenters and stage machinists built troubled waves in the foreground, with a wide trapdoor hidden behind the waves. Dan Marble, adding danger and physical spectacle to his shuffling, hands-in-pockets Yankeeisms, ended the play by leaping from the flies, forty feet down the painted Niagara, through the trapdoor, and onto bags of shavings, popping up while someone, somehow, created "a bubbling river of spray and foam, amid shouts of the heartiest western applause." It was a perilous leap. Marble injured himself repeatedly, and a machinist who insisted on making the jump at his own benefit performance took a few drinks, leaped in a fit of nerves, and broke his leg.[21]

The Columbus theater filled for every performance. Ohio boys leaped over fences and out of haylofts, and clerks jumped over their counters, all of them trying to be Sam Patch. Dan Marble could have taken his hit play directly to New York. Instead, he toured the western rivers, jumping Sam Patch in Pittsburgh, Cincinnati, St. Louis, Memphis, and Wheeling before heading east. He opened at the Bowery Theater as the first democratic star to emerge from the western theaters, and he had learned a lot in the river towns. The farmers, laborers, and watermen of the Ohio Valley disliked actors (or anyone else) who put on airs. They insisted that players drink and sport with them, and they expected the occasional nod or knowing wink from the stage to the boys in the pit. They got all that from Dan Marble, as well as a jumping hero shaped to their tastes. New York's Bowery audience encountered Sam Patch as a stage Yankee who had gone western. There were "flying leaps among the fancy—through a window by Sam," and someone named Phillip carried Katharine across a river during a terrible storm. Sam Patch shared a scene with Mrs. Trollope, and leaped Niagara Falls in a "union of courage and virtue—proving 'Some things can be done as well as others'—Mr. Marble will leap from the extreme height of the theatre, a feat never attempted by any one but himself [this neglects the wounded machinist back in Columbus], and prove that 'cold water can't drown love.' "[22]

Dan Marble's Sam Patch merged the old Yankee drolleries and the bombast of the western hero into a new and enduring American character—an early and successful attempt to merge regional types (Tennessee frontiersmen, Ohio-river flatboatmen, New York firemen, and Rhode Island mule spinners—heroes whom folklorists call Ring-Tailed Roarers) into a national democratic vernacular. Marble received three more Sam Patch dramas: *Sam Patch at Home*, *Sam Patch in France* (in which Sam cavorted "among the 'Monsieurs'"), and, for Marble's London tour in 1844, *Sam Patch, the Jumper*. The last is the one Sam Patch play for which a script survives. It is a very bad English melodrama that concludes with Sam Patch leaping Niagara Falls to kill three villains, rescue the lead characters, and save their land. The Sam Patch of this play had taken on not only a penchant for righteous violence but a new way of talking. "Well, I reckon I'm as hungry as a sarpent," says Sam. "I can fight like a bullet, dance like a bed bug, sing like a tea kettle, & court the gals just as slick as a time-piece." Somewhere between Buffalo and London, it seems, the Yankee Sam Patch had merged with the western frontiersman to form an all-American democratic hero: steadfastly brave and capable of great mayhem, crudely funny, governed by a born democrat's transcendent knowledge of right and wrong, and prone to begin his sentences with "Well, I reckon."[23]

While Marble acted Sam Patch in Buffalo, young Charles C. Brown was attending Jamestown Academy in nearby Chautauqua County, where he studied the classics. But of course he and the other boys fantasized and made up stories out of school. His composition book included essays on temperance, phrenology, liberty, Andrew Jackson, and Sam Patch. Charles worshiped Andrew Jackson as a model American hero, "one who to protect his country knew no difficulty to great to be encountered and who by his firmness and unconqurable perseverence amid surrounding dangers, had saved her from foreign and intestine foes," even when "thousands were perishing by the victors sword and humanity shuddered at the sight." Jackson saved the republic, "not by the art of intrigue or the jugling tricks of diplomacy," but by doing the right thing and fighting against all odds.

Brown's composition book also included a "Eulogy on Sam Patch," apparently written by one of his schoolmates. The Sam Patch of the piece was like Andrew Jackson, only more so. Sam was a poverty-stricken orphan who hungered for fame, like (here it goes again) Empedocles, Demosthenes, King Henry, "Cesar," and Napoleon. He was, it turns out, a forgotten hero of the Revolution: "He was unfortunate he deserved many honors which others usurped and it is even whispered that many of the Laurels which Washington won ought in justice to have adorned the brow of Pach," who "acted a most conspicuous part in acheiving and defending the liberties we now enjoy." Having been cheated of the renown due to him as the "principal agent" of the American Revolution, Sam Patch put down his arms and sought marital bliss. Unhappily, he became "the victim of a cross and scholding wife." It was at that point that Sam (in a victory of democratic justice over classical form) "resolved to fill the world with his fame," and to "accomplish this purpose without the aid of others"—the chicanery of gentlemen and the perfidy of women, apparently, justifying his descent into ambition. While we cannot re-create schoolboy dreams at Jamestown Academy, they seem to have featured transcendent individuals like Andrew Jackson and Sam Patch who triumphed over misfortune and the dishonest tricks of their enemies through courage and indomitable will. Both on stage and at Jamestown Academy, Sam Patch lived on as a hero of Jacksonian melodrama.[24]

Democrats with education and literary taste came to their own terms with Sam Patch. The editors of *The United States Democratic Review*, which began publication in 1837, sometimes shared their Whig competitors' views of men like Sam Patch. In 1858 they denounced William Walker, a proslavery adventurer who tried to conquer Nicaragua with a ragtag army of American volunteers: "It was a kind of Sam Patch heroism, ludicrous and melancholy." In

1847, however, the *Democratic Review* had sketched Mother Bailey, a Connecticut heroine of both the Revolution and the War of 1812, now eighty-eight years old and a model Democrat. She loved America and Andrew Jackson, and she hated British monarchy. (Her explanation of the potato blight of the 1840s: the British had buried their hireling Benedict Arnold in Nova Scotia, and the disease had spread from his accursed grave.) Mother Bailey was a spry old woman, "and even if she be called to '*trip it on the light fantastic toe*,' she can show you, Sam-Patch-like—'that some things can be done as well as others'—on the sole condition that the tune be 'Yankee-doodle,' or 'Jefferson and Liberty.' "[25]

Nathaniel Hawthorne and Herman Melville were perhaps the most distinguished of the Democrats who found literary uses for Sam Patch. A young Hawthorne stopped over at Rochester in 1832, where, at dusk and alone, he viewed Genesee Falls—less to see the ruined and overdeveloped falls, he tells us, than to imagine Sam Patch. "How stern a moral may be drawn from the story of poor Sam Patch!" he wrote. We wait for another sermon on low ambition and imbecile bravado, but Hawthorne's lesson goes deeper than that: "Why do we call him a madman or a fool, when he has left his memory around the falls of the Genesee, more permanently than if the letters of his name had been hewn into the forehead of the precipice?" Hawthorne nodded to the classical limits upon fame, but he insisted that Sam Patch was not the only man who was transgressing them: "Was the leaper of cataracts more mad or foolish than other men who throw away life, or misspend it in pursuit of empty fame, and seldom so triumphantly as he? That which he won is as invaluable as any except the unsought glory, spreading like the rich perfume of richer fruit from various and useful deeds." "Thus musing," he continued, "I lifted my eyes and beheld the spires, warehouses, and dwellings of Rochester." He went on to compose one of the livelier accounts of the grasping busyness and boomtown growth that other and (to Hawthorne) equally empty ambitions had made be-

side Genesee Falls. Hawthorne was among the few literary de-
fenders of Sam Patch. But only because he knew that democratic
ambition (Sam's, merchants' and millers', and his own) was
breaking up an old world and replacing it with something new
and morally uncertain.[26]

Herman Melville reached conclusions more like those of the
entertainer Dan Marble and the schoolboy Charles Brown. In
Redburn (1849), Melville tells the story of a gentleman's son who
becomes a common seaman. Early on, the boy laments that his
mismatched, ill-fitting used clothes make him look "like a Sam
Patch, shambling round the deck in my rags and the wreck of my
gaff-topsail boots. I often thought what my friends at home
would have said, if they could but get one peep at me." But as his
sailor's education proceeds he drops his self-consciousness and
takes on the dangers of life at sea: "It is surprising," he says," how
soon a boy overcomes his timidity about going aloft. For my own
part, my nerves became as steady as the earth's diameter, and I
felt as fearless on the royal yard, as Sam Patch on the cliff of Niagara." Weeks at sea had turned the ragged, ridiculous boy into a
trained man who approached dangerous work without fear. At
the same time, Melville had moved his literary deployment of
Sam Patch between precisely the same two points.[27]

Finally, there was Andrew Jackson himself. In 1833 the City
of Philadelphia presented President Jackson with a beautiful
white horse. The horse became Jackson's favorite. President
Jackson posed for a painting (not in his presidential black broad-
cloth but in his Old Hero's uniform) astride him, and rode him
every morning in his retirement, through the slave quarters and
cotton fields of the Hermitage, his Tennessee plantation. At its
death, the horse was buried on the grounds of the Hermitage
with full military honors. Jackson, before he became America's
Man on Horseback, had bred, raced, and traded horses. In a
mock apology for his informal education, Jackson claimed, "I do

Andrew Jackson on Sam Patch, by Ralph Earl
(courtesy of the Ladies' Hermitage Association)

not pretend to know much, but I do know men and horses." The name of President Jackson's horse was Sam Patch.[28]

By 1850 (if we ignore the occasional genteel screed on low ambition) Sam Patch had lost the power to raise political and cultural hackles. He disappeared, then resurfaced as a plucky and harmless American folk hero. A children's book entitled *The Wonderful Leaps of Sam Patch* appeared in 1870. It was beautifully illustrated, and it featured a farm boy who loved to jump—from his mother's lap, from haylofts and church steeples, and from the dome of the national Capitol as well as from waterfalls. At about the same time, Sam appeared in a serious novel. In *Their Wedding Journey* (1871) William Dean Howells describes a honeymoon trip to Niagara Falls. At Rochester the groom is surprised to learn that his bride has never heard of Sam Patch, and he tells Sam's story. With his superhuman leaps and his "Some things can be done as well as others," explains the young husband, Sam Patch supported "a great idea—the feasibility of all things"—a line that absorbed Sam Patch into a boundless and optimistic America that had never been his home.[29]

The folklorist Richard Dorson rediscovered Sam Patch in 1945. In a series of articles, Dorson portrayed the leaper as a Ring-Tailed Roarer along the lines of Davy Crockett, Mike Fink, and Mose the Bowery B'hoy. Dorson put Sam's name back in play, and among the results were three more children's books. Two are light and untroubled, but a tale put together by Arna Bontemps (of Harlem Renaissance fame) and the radical Jack Conroy pits the northeastern factory boy in jumping contests against a bullying western Hero. In 1986 there was a novel about Sam Patch, narrated by his bear.[30]

The towns that had known Sam Patch remembered him in their own ways. Sam survived in the official memories of Pawtucket and Paterson only as a romantic oddity, but popular recollection was longer-lived. Paterson boys repeated the leaps of Sam Patch (they charged a quarter to visitors who wanted to watch), and people whittled souvenirs from the pine stump at Sam's jumping spot until the stump disappeared. At Pawtucket, boys jumped from the bridge until authorities put up a steel railing—backed up by a twenty-five-dollar fine—to stop them. In 1891 Pawtucket celebrated its Cotton Centennial with weeklong festivities that included a parade in honor of Samuel Slater. Following the parade, a fifty-year-old carpenter named Patrick Devlin joined the crowd on the bridge, climbed the railing, and jumped off. He told a reporter that he and his friends thought the celebration would be incomplete without a performance of this "ancient custom."[31]

Niagara Falls became a more popular tourist attraction, and its businessmen found small ways to cash in on Sam Patch.

Cover of *The Wonderful Leaps of Sam Patch* (author's collection)

Middle-class honeymooners, day visitors, and the denizens of penny arcades and family hotels stood at "Patch's Point" and read the story of Sam Patch in their guidebooks. They also watched ropewalkers cross the chasm. In the twentieth century, barrel riders invented the most dangerous ways to play with Niagara. Sam was the first to test himself against the Falls, and he is honored in the Niagara Falls Daredevils Hall of Fame—tucked among rose gardens, wax-museum horror shows, money-changing booths, and franchise burger shops on the Canadian side.[32]

Only Rochester nourished a public memory of Sam Patch. While respectables denounced Sam, others tried to have his body dug up and reburied at the Upper Falls—where he would greet visitors to the city. Taverns and canal boats displayed pictures of the Last Leap, and travelers were taken to the spot from which Sam had jumped. Sam's bear (or an animal advertised as such) was on display at a Rochester hotel. Little girls in Charlotte decorated Sam's grave with clamshells, and visitors—the sportsman

Sam Drake among them—showed up to pay their respects. In 1848 a Rochester boy named Hosea Hollenbrook, on the chance that someone might pay him for the performance, repeated Sam's leap at Genesee Falls. Hollenbrook was killed—in part, apparently, because he could not swim. Another jumper was Sam Scott. Scott had begun jumping from yardarms while in the Navy. In 1837 he came to Rochester and worked as a bartender at (coincidence seems unlikely) the Recess, in rooms below a music store. Scott left town to leap from bridges, ships' masts, and the tops of buildings in the late 1830s. Then he went to London, where he accidentally hanged himself performing a stunt before a horrified crowd.[33]

The controversy over Sam Patch quieted down, and Rochester boosters found ways to make Sam a civic asset. Rochester did not remain a model boomtown. Sam Patch was one of its few claims to fame, and he became an adopted citizen. For many years, the predecessor of the New York Central Railroad stopped its trains while conductors pointed out the spot from which Sam had leaped. The town fathers determined to make Sam part of a civic celebration in the 1870s, and took the "Such is Fame" marker downtown and put it into a parade. Someone stole it, and the grave was unmarked until the 1940s, when a Rochester schoolboy launched a campaign that resulted in the erection of a proper headstone. On the west side of the Upper Falls, industrial development absorbed Sam's island late in the nineteenth century, and the area gave way to the abandoned factories and dangerous streets of a postindustrial city late in the twentieth. In recent years things have changed. The old militia ground and much of industrial Frankfort are occupied by a new baseball park, and Brown's Race is restored and lined with restaurants and shops; postcards and souvenir pencils are available at Sam's Gift Patch. Above the falls, the visitor can cruise the Genesee River on the restored canal boat *Sam Patch*, and retire to a local microbrewery for a pitcher of Sam Patch Nitro Porter.[34]

NOTES

I. Pawtucket

1. The date of the Patch family's arrival in Pawtucket is uncertain. They had lived previously in Marblehead, where their last entry in civil records was in February 1805. Sam's mother and sister joined a church in Pawtucket in April 1807. Family memory and subsequent folklore say they came to Pawtucket in 1807.

2. See in particular Alexander Hamilton, "Report on Manufactures, December 5, 1791," in Jacob E. Cooke, ed., *The Reports of Alexander Hamilton* (New York, 1964), esp. 130–31 (quote, 130); Tenche Coxe, *A View of the United States of America, in a Series of Papers, Written at Various Times, Between the Years 1787 and 1794* (New York, 1965; orig. 1794), 14, 55. No Manchesters: George S. White, *Memoir of Samuel Slater, the Father of American Manufactures, Connected with a History of the Rise and Progress of the Cotton Manufacture in England and America* (New York, 1967; orig. 1836), 135. Such reassurances appear frequently in tracts reprinted in Michael Brewster Folsom and Steven D. Lubar, eds., *The Philosophy of Manufactures: Early Debates over Industrialization in the United States* (Cambridge, Mass., 1982).

3. Gary B. Kulik, "Factory Discipline in the New Nation: Almy, Brown & Slater and the First Cotton Mill Workers, 1790–1808," *Massachusetts Review* 28 (Spring 1987), 165–84 (quotes, pp. 172, 173); "poor children": "Account of a Journal of Josiah Quincy," *Proceedings of the Massachusetts Historical Society*, 2nd Series, 4 (1888), 124. Baptist:

David Benedict, *Fifty Years Among the Baptists* (Boston, 1860), 312, and Elizabeth J. Johnson and James Lucas Wheaton IV, comps., *History of Pawtucket, Rhode Island: Reminiscences & New Series of Reverend David Benedict* (Pawtucket, 1986), 121–22. (This is a compilation of the Reverend Benedict's newspaper articles published in 1853–64; cited hereafter as *Benedict Reminiscences*.) Travel guide: [Theodore Dwight], *The Northern Traveller, and Northern Tour* (New York, 1830), 314. On the degradation of mill labor and the increasing roughness of Pawtucket, see Gary B. Kulik, "The Beginnings of the Industrial Revolution in America: Pawtucket, Rhode Island, 1672–1829" (Ph.D. dissertation, Brown University, 1980), 188–251, 284–85; and Brendan F. Gilbane, "A Social History of Samuel Slater's Pawtucket, 1790–1830," (Ph.D. dissertation, Boston University, 1969), 271–83.

4. Patch gave the name Greenleaf to the census taker in 1790, and his great-granddaughter knew him by that name. U.S. Bureau of the Census, *Heads of Families at the First Census of the United States Taken in 1790: Massachusetts* (Washington, D.C., 1908), 152.

5. The declining rural communities of the North Shore and Middlesex County, from which the Patches came, have been well studied by social historians. See especially Philip J. Greven, Jr., *Four Generations: Population, Land, and Family in Colonial Andover, Massachusetts* (Ithaca, N.Y., 1970); Christopher M. Jedrey, *The World of John Cleaveland: Family and Community in Eighteenth-Century New England* (New York, 1979); and Daniel Vickers, *Farmers & Fishermen: Two Centuries of Work in Essex County, Massachusetts, 1630–1850* (Chapel Hill, N.C., 1994). Also very useful is Toby L. Ditz, *Property and Kinship: Inheritance in Early Connecticut, 1750–1820* (Princeton, N.J., 1986).

6. William Richard Cutter, comp., *Genealogical and Personal Memoirs Relating to the Families of Boston and Eastern Massachusetts* (New York, 1908), 1:219; *Wenham Town Records, 1730–1775* (Wenham, 1940), 1:141, 184; 2:3, 5–6, 8, 20; 3:23, 115, 177; *Massachusetts Soldiers and Sailors of the Revolutionary War* (Boston, 1903), 11:1000.

7. Will of Timothy Patch, Administration No. 20744, Essex County Court of Probate, Salem, Mass. Adult brothers shared houses and/or outbuildings with increasing frequency in the late eighteenth century. See Jedrey, *The World of John Cleaveland*, 73–74, and John J. Waters, "Patrimony, Succession, and Social Stability: Guilford, Connecticut, in the Eighteenth Century," *Perspectives in American History* 10 (1976), 150. A more general discussion of the overlapping obligations

attached to inherited property is provided in Ditz, *Property and Kinship*, esp. 82–102.

8. Landholdings computed from the Essex County deeds listed in note 9. *Vital Records of Wenham, Mass. To the End of the Year 1849* (Salem, 1904), 65–66, 152, 214.

9. Court cases: Records of the Essex County Court of Common Pleas (Essex Institute, Salem, Mass.), July 1764 (*Dodge v. Patch*), September 1766 (*Cabot v. Patch, Jones v. Patch, Dodge v. Patch, Brown v. Patch*), March 1767 (*Brimblecom v. Patch*). Land transfers: Essex County Registry of Deeds (Essex County Courthouse, Salem, Mass.), Book 123:103; 120:35; 124:64; 116:96; 123:105; 123:44; 121:132; 120:278. Timothy's land transfers to his sons are recorded in Books 120:273 and 115:210. Family persistence traced in *Vital Records of Wenham*.

10. Essex Court of Common Pleas, July 1770 (*Andrews v. Patch*), July 1779 (*Gerilds v. Patch*), July 1782 (*Prince v. Patch, Putnam v. Patch, Wilkins v. Patch, Patch v. Sawyer, Endicott v. Patch*), September 1782 (*Prince v. Patch*), December 1783 (*Upton v. Patch*).

11. Reading Town Rate Books, 1773–93, Assessor's Office, Reading Town Hall. Available at the Family History Library of the Church of Jesus Christ of Latter-day Saints, microfilm reel #0968004. In 1787 Patch paid a poll tax and the tax on a very small amount of personal property.

12. Marriage: *Vital Records of the Town of Reading, Massachusetts, to the Year 1850* (Boston, 1912), 413, 178. Abigail gave birth seven and one-half months after the wedding.

13. A good recent account of the Battle of Dunbar and its aftermath is Roger Hainsworth, *The Swordsmen in Power: War and Politics under the English Republic, 1649–1660* (Phoenix Mill, England, 1997), 80–106.

14. Cutter, *Genealogical and Personal Memoirs*, 3:1155; Lilley Eaton, comp., *Genealogical History of the Town of Reading, Mass.* (Boston, 1874), 96; Will of Joseph McIntire, Middlesex County Court of Probate (Middlesex County Courthouse, Cambridge, Mass.), Administration No. 14496; Inventory of the Estate of Archelaus McIntire, Middlesex Probate 14481; Reading Town Rate Books, 1792.

15. Daniel Scott Smith and Michael Hindus, "Premarital Pregnancy in America, 1640–1971: An Overview and Interpretation," *Journal of Interdisciplinary History* 5 (Spring 1975), 537–70. McIntire marriages and births are recorded in *Vital Records of Reading*.

16. The house and shoemaker's shop seem to have been substantial. The

record of debt (dated September 1789, and carried on into 1790) includes the boarding of workmen (masons as well as carpenters) for nine weeks. Middlesex Probate 14481.

17. On outwork in New England, see Mary H. Blewett, *Men, Women, and Work: Class, Gender, and Protest in the New England Shoe Industry, 1780–1810* (Urbana, Ill., 1990), 3–96; Thomas Dublin, *Transforming Women's Work: New England Lives in the Industrial Revolution* (Ithaca, N.Y., 1994), 29–75; Alan Dawley, *Class and Community: The Industrial Revolution in Lynn* (Cambridge, Mass., 1976); Paul G. Faler, *Mechanics and Manufacturers in the Early Industrial Revolution: Lynn, Massachusetts, 1780–1860* (Albany, N.Y., 1981); Vickers, *Farmers & Fishermen*, 309–24; John Philip Hall, "The Gentle Craft: A Narrative of Yankee Shoe Makers" (Ph.D. dissertation, Columbia University, 1953).

18. John Philip Hall, comp., "The Journal of James Weston, Cordwainer, of Reading, Massachusetts, 1788–1793," *Essex Institute Historical Collections* 92 (April 1956), 188–202.

19. Reading Town Rate Books: Town and County Tax, December 1790 and November 1792.

20. Bureau of the Census, *Heads of Families . . . Massachusetts*, 152; Reading Town Rate Books, 1792.

21. Middlesex Probate 14481; Middlesex Court of Common Pleas, November 1791, March 1792, and September 1792 (*Patch v. Parker*); Middlesex County Registry of Deeds (Middlesex County Courthouse, Cambridge, Mass.), Book 165:60; Eaton, *Genealogical History of Reading*, 246; Town of Reading: Orders and Receipts, 1773–93 (Assessor's Office, Reading Town Hall), entries for 15 September 1794 and 25 August 1795.

22. Middlesex Probate 14481.

23. References to Deborah McIntire in the Will of Archelaus McIntire (Middlesex Probate 14481) and the Will of Archelaus McIntire, Jr. (Middlesex Probate 14483). Patch's appointment as executor, Archelaus Jr.'s assignment to a guardian, and the widow Abigail McIntire's letter of complaint (in which the sixty-four-year-old Abigail identifies herself as an invalid) are in Middlesex Probate 14481. Patch assets recorded in Reading Town Rate Books, 1791, 1792.

24. Nancy Barker is identified as the half sister of M. G. Patch in the Will of Job Davis, Essex Probate 7278. She had lived in Wenham and had married into some branch of the Patch family; at her marriage to Jonathan Barker of Haverhill (in Wenham) in 1786 she was "Mrs.

Nancy Patch." Jonathan and Nancy Barker moved to Haverhill and appear there as the parents of children with the names of those later brought to North Reading by Nancy. A shoemaker named Jonathan Barker died intestate and nearly propertyless in Haverhill in 1791. The "it seems" in the text is due to the fact that the probate file identifies that man's widow as "Anna." Vital records do not list a marriage or children for a Jonathan and Anna Barker; nor do they list the death of another Jonathan Barker. My guess is that a probate clerk simply misrecorded the name of Jonathan Barker's widow. Marriage of Mrs. Nancy Barker and Jonathan Barker of Haverhill: *Vital Records of Wenham*, 152. Their children and his death: *Vital Records of Haverhill, Massachusetts, to the End of the Year 1849* (Topsfield, Mass., 1910), 2:29, 287. Will and estate inventory of Jonathan Barker: Essex Probate 1682. Marriage of Archelaus McIntire, Jr., and Nancy Barker: *Vital Records of Reading*, 387.

25. Boundary dispute: Records of the Town of Reading, Massachusetts, 1639–1812. Land Grants and Boundaries (typescript, Lucius Beebe Memorial Library, Wakefield, Mass.), 3:148. Tax dispute: Reading Orders and Receipts, 14 November 1797. Patch does not appear in this record as landlord to schoolmistresses after 1795; the teacher stayed with John Swain in 1796. Court cases: Middlesex Court of Common Pleas, December 1798 (*Patch v. Tuttle*); Essex Court of Common Pleas, October 1798 (*Herrick v. Patch*) and March 1804 (*Reid v. Patch*). The last lists the lawyer's bill as outstanding.

26. Records of the Town of Reading, 3:148; Federal Direct Tax of 1798: Massachusetts (New England Historic Genealogical Society, Boston), returns for the town of Reading list Archelaus McIntire, Jr., as the owner of two houses, neither of which was occupied by M. G. Patch.

27. Guardianship papers dated 7 September 1791, Middlesex Probate 14482.

28. The McIntire-Felton transactions are recorded in Essex Deeds, 153:95, 165:60. Suicide of Debbie McIntire: *Vital Records of Danvers, Massachusetts, to the End of the Year 1849. Volume II: Marriages and Deaths* (Salem, Mass., 1910), 405. No one named Deborah or Debbie McIntire was born or married in Danvers.

29. Population Schedules of the Second Census of the United States, 1800: Essex County, Massachusetts, listed a "Mahue" G. Patch in Danvers. The sexes and ages of members of his household match the Patch family exactly. In 1803 the recorder of a deed involving Greenleaf Patch spelled his name "Mayhew." (Essex Deeds, Book 172:252.)

Indexes to Danvers Town Records, Family History Library of the Church of Jesus Christ of Latter-day Saints, Salt Lake City, microfilm reels 0876107 and 0876184. North Parish Valuation, 1799. The valuations for 1800, 1801, and 1804 do not list Mayo Greenleaf Patch.

30. Will of Job Davis, Essex Probate 7278.

31. List of Inhabitants, 1804, 1805, 1806, Marblehead Town Hall (Family History Library, reel 0864082). Patch did not appear in the 1805 or 1806 assessments. The other heirs received small payments when the house reverted to the Reids in 1805. (Essex Deeds, 175:32, 172:32, 177:302, 179:15.) The dealings with the children of Nancy Barker, who each inherited one twentieth of the two houses, can be traced in Essex Deeds, 373:240–41; 379:283; 383:154.

32. The debts, court cases, and land transfers can be followed in Essex Court of Common Pleas, March 1803 (*Sawyer v. Patch*), June 1803 (*Burnham v. Patch*), December 1803 (*Dolebar v. Patch*), March 1804 (*Goodale v. Patch, King v. Patch, Sawyer v. Patch, Reids v. Patch*), June 1804 (*Totman v. Patch, Shelden v. Patch, Holt v. Patch*); Essex Deeds, Books 172:252, 175:35, 175:186. The last—the purchase of Patch's right of redemption—is dated 2 February 1805.

33. "Petition of Abigail Patch for Divorce," Records of the Supreme Court of Providence County, September 1818–March 1819, Box 39, Providence College Archives. Convict Registers for the Charlestown State Prison, Massachusetts State Archives, Boston. A check of probate and vital records in all of the counties in which Patch or members of his family had lived, and a check of heads of household in the United States in the census of 1820, turned up no trace of Patch's later life.

34. Obediah Brown quoted in Kulik, "Factory Discipline in the New Nation," 172. Slater's trips to the North Shore: Samuel Slater Day Book, vol. 3, entries for 8 December 1804, 30 April 1808, 10 October 1809, Almy, Brown, and Slater Papers, Baker Library, Harvard University. See also Kulik, "The Beginnings of the Industrial Revolution in America," 205.

35. The estate inventory of Archelaus McIntire and a letter that his widow signed with a mark are in Middlesex Probate 14481. Accounts of women's work in postrevolutionary New England begin and end with Laurel Thatcher Ulrich, *A Midwife's Tale: The Life of Martha Ballard, Based on Her Diary, 1785–1812* (New York, 1990). Studies of home life deduced from estate inventories are deftly presented in Jack Larkin, *The Reshaping of Everyday Life, 1790–1840* (New York, 1988), 105–48.

36. Quote: "Petition of Abigail Patch for Divorce." For indications that this language was indeed Abigail's, see Nancy F. Cott, "Eighteenth-Century Family and Social Life Revealed in Massachusetts Divorce Records," *Journal of Social History* 10 (Fall 1976), 32–33, which demonstrates widely varying marital expectations among divorcing persons.

37. See the accounts of the division of labor in shoemaking households in Blewett, *Men, Women, and Work*, 3–19; Dawley, *Class and Community*, 16–20; Faler, *Mechanics and Manufacturers*, 48–51; Elizabeth Abbott, *Women in Industry: A Study in American Economic History* (New York, 1910), 148–52. There is an interesting discussion of the "adaptive traditionalism" of rural shoemakers in John L. Brooke, *The Heart of the Commonwealth: Society and Political Culture in Worcester County, Massachusetts, 1713–1861* (New York, 1989), 294–303.

38. Names traced in *Vital Records of Reading* and *Vital Records of Wenham*. New England child-naming patterns are described in Daniel Scott Smith, "Population, Family and Society in Hingham, Massachusetts, 1635–1880" (Ph.D. dissertation, University of California, 1973), 340–48; idem, "Child-Naming Practices, Kinship Ties, and Change in Family Attitudes in Hingham, Massachusetts, 1641 to 1880," *Journal of Social History* 18 (Summer 1985), 541–66; John J. Waters, "Naming and Kinship in New England: Guilford Patterns and Usage, 1693–1759," *New England Historical and Genealogical Register* 138 (July 1984); Jedrey, *The World of John Cleaveland*, 78–79, 84–85.

39. Information on Archelaus, his wife, and his daughter Mehitable is from the records of the United Church of Christ, North Reading (Mrs. Arthur Diaz, Church Clerk, letter to the author dated 27 June 1979). Abigail's sister Mary lived in Salem but baptized a child in Reading, suggesting that she belonged to a Salem church. Archelaus Jr. died at the age of twenty-nine without having joined a church, but his will is drenched in religious language.

40. Here and in the following paragraphs, information is from the records of the First Church in Wenham, Congregational (Carol T. Rawston, Church Clerk, letter to the author dated 22 September 1979). Baptisms from *Vital Records of Wenham*.

41. The question of church membership reveals some of the problems with research in local and genealogical records. The manuscript records of the Second (North) Parish of Reading (now the Union Congregational Church of North Reading) were carried off by Universalists during a schism in 1802; through they allowed the Congre-

gationalists to make a list of persons who were admitted to the church between 1720 and 1802. In 1979 the clerk of the church searched that list and found no Patches. Twenty years later, while searching the Stunts and Stunters File at the Niagara Falls, New York, Public Library, I found a scrap of yellow paper on which David Coapman of Alhambra, California, claimed that Abigail Patch joined the North Parish Church at the age of twenty in 1790. (Mr. Coapman, as a schoolboy in Rochester, New York, led a campaign to give Sam Patch's grave a proper headstone; he referred to himself in 1969 as "Patch's 'Boswell.'") An exhaustive search failed to locate either Mr. Coapman or the original record book. As of autumn 2002 the new clerk and historian of Union Congregational Church stand by their predecessor's 1979 finding.

42. *Vital Records of Marblehead, Massachusetts, to the End of the Year 1849* (Salem, 1903), 1:380. The infant Isaac was baptized at Marblehead Second Congregational Church. A search of the records of that church between 1790 and 1810 turned up no Patches as members. (Record books held by the Unitarian-Universalist Society in Marblehead.) The baptisms of Abigail and her oldest daughter were recorded in "Baptist Church of Christ, August 1805 to November 1837" (First Baptist Church, Pawtucket), entries for 4 April 1807 and 12 April 1807.

43. Molly, Polly, Mary: "Baptist Church of Christ," 4 April 1807: "Mrs. Patch and her daughter Polly came forward . . ." A Mary Patch married Goodman (Edward) Jones in Pawtucket in 1809 (James N. Arnold, *Vital Record of Rhode Island: North Providence* [Providence, 1892], 32), and the *Manual of the First Baptist Church, Pawtucket, R.I., Organized August, 1805* (Providence, 1884), 28, identified Mary Patch Jones as having joined the church in April 1807. The Molly Patch born in 1789, the Polly Patch of 1807, and the Mary Patch of 1809 were definitely the same woman. Nabby, Abby, Abigail: "Baptist Church of Christ," 12 November 1810, 31 January 1811, 1 January 1829. There is another—though unlikely—way of interpreting these changing names. Nabby and Abby can be diminutives of Abigail, Molly is sometimes a diminutive of Mary, and it is possible that these women simply stepped into adult names as a part of growing up. But in all the generations of Reading McIntires, while there were many Marys and Abigails, there was not a single Nabby or Molly in the records of births, marriages, and deaths. The Wenham McIntires named girls Mary and Abigail as well. Only Greenleaf's brother Isaac named daughters Nabby and Molly. Isaac also had a son named Samuel. Greenleaf and Abigail Patch had

children named Greenleaf, Molly, Nabby, Samuel, and Isaac—perfectly duplicating the names (assuming that young Greenleaf lived there) of the Isaac Patch household in Wenham.

44. Population Schedules of the Fourth and Fifth Censuses of the United States, 1820 and 1830: North Providence, Rhode Island (Family History Library). Robert Grieve, *An Illustrated History of Pawtucket, Central Falls, and Vicinity* (Pawtucket, 1897), 66, states that Abigail moved into the Main Street house "about 1830." She did not appear as a household head in the census taken in 1830, but the "widow Mary Patch" did. Mary's adultery: "Baptist Church of Christ," 2 June 1825. Other information in this paragraph is from a letter to the author from Elizabeth J. Johnson and James L. Wheaton IV of the Spaulding House Research Library, Pawtucket, dated 16 March 1989.

45. *Manual of the First Baptist Church*, 29. Articles of the Church in the opening of "First Church of Christ." On mill owner control and the slow pace of growth, see Gary Kulik, "Pawtucket Village and the Strike of 1824: The Origins of Class Conflict in Rhode Island," *Radical History Review* 17 (Spring 1978), 15–17. The founding members of the church in 1805 included fourteen men and thirty women; the few who joined in 1806 and 1807 (including Abigail and her daughter) numbered twenty-four women and only seven men. Constituent members: *First Baptist Church in Pawtucket, Constituted Aug. 27, 1805. Covenant, Articles of Faith, Rules of Discipline* (Pawtucket, n.d.), 7. Dated admissions: *Manual of the First Baptist Church*, 20–37.

46. Schoolhouse and Abigail's death: Grieve, *Illustrated History of Pawtucket*, 29, 101. House purchase: North Providence Deeds and Mortgages, Book 8:523 (Pawtucket City Hall). Sarah Anne's troubles: "Church Meetings, January 1838 to January 1874," entries for 29 August 1853, 30 August 1853, 23 September 1853 (First Baptist Church, Pawtucket). The inventory of Abigail Patch's estate is in Probate Records, Pawtucket City Hall, Book 8:343. When she died, Abigail was broke: she had run up a debt of $931 for board, nursing, and doctors, which suggests an unusually long and hard death, and her administrator sold the furniture and petitioned to sell the real estate—the house and a vacant lot in another part of Pawtucket. The lot was sold, but it is not clear whether Mary retained ownership of the house. (Pawtucket Probate, 8:327; 8:348; 9:2–3; 9:13; 9:36.)

47. Benedict quote: *Benedict Reminiscences*, 65.

48. Emily Jones reminiscences, from an undated typescript of an article in the *Providence Journal*, which forms the first six pages of the Sam

Patch Scrapbook, Local History Division, Rochester Public Library, Rochester, N.Y. Unless otherwise cited, information in the following two paragraphs is from this article.

49. Greenleaf the lawyer: phone conversation with John Powers, Office of the Clerk of the Supreme Judicial Court for Suffolk County, Massachusetts, 2 October 1979. Sam's cotton mill: Emily remembered the partner's name as Kennedy. A search of deeds and tax lists in Smithfield (Central Falls), site of the supposed partnership, along with a search of bankruptcy petitions in the years 1820–25, turned up nothing on Patch. A John Kennedy, however, was taxed as the owner of one-fourth of the Chocolate Mill (so called because it actually had been a chocolate factory) in 1824 and 1826. Patch's partnership with Kennedy remains an undocumentable possibility. ("Estimate for 1824" and "Town Tax for 1826," in Smithfield Tax Records, stored in the attic at Central Falls City Hall.) Bankruptcy petitions searched in the Records of the Supreme Court of Providence County, Providence College Archives. On the Chocolate Mill: William R. Bagnall, *Textile Industries of the United States* (Cambridge, Mass., 1893), 1:390–94. Isaac the farmer: a search of the indexes to the manuscript census of 1850 (the first to list age and state of birth) turned up an Isaac Patch—native of Massachusetts—in Illinois, but this man had been born eleven years before Abigail's son. There were also Isaac Patches in Michigan and Pennsylvania, neither of whom fit the son's date and place of birth.

50. Emily's reminiscences and Abigail's divorce petition, cited above. The census listed Mayo G. Patch as head of the household in 1810: Population Schedules of the Third Census of the United States (1810): Providence County, Town of North Providence, 1:434.

51. A sailor: Joseph Cochran reminiscences in Jenny Marsh Parker, *Rochester: A Story Historical* (Rochester, N.Y., 1884), 185; a sailor and an orphan: A. J. Langworthy reminiscences, *Rochester Democrat and Chronicle*, 31 March 1898, in the Ashley Samson Scrapbook, 64:50, Local History Division, Rochester Public Library; a foreigner: Reminiscences of Mrs. Mary Ann Davis, *Rochester Democrat and Chronicle*, 31 January 1923, Sam Patch Scrapbook. In 1828 the *Providence Cadet* commented on the New Jersey leaps of Sam Patch by comparing them with the leaps of boys at Pawtucket—apparently ignorant of Sam's origins in that town. *Cadet* article reprinted in many places, including *New-York Statesman*, 21 July 1828, and *Niles Weekly Register*, 26 July 1828.

52. Quote: *Benedict Reminiscences*, 65. On Sunday schools and attitudes toward children among early national New Englanders, see Ann M. Boylan, *Sunday School: The Formation of an American Institution, 1790–1880* (New Haven, Conn., 1988), esp. 6–21; and Philip Greven, *The Protestant Temperament: Patterns of Child-Rearing, Religious Experience, and the Self in Early America* (New York, 1977), 21–148. The Pawtucket Sunday school is thought (with some competition from Philadelphia) to have been the first established in the United States.

53. Sam in White Mill: Emily Jones reminiscences. On the White Mill: Bagnall, *Textile Industries of the United States*, 1:253; Gilbane, "A Social History of Samuel Slater's Pawtucket," 139–40. On Pawtucket mill architecture, see Gary Kulik, "A Factory System of Wood: Cultural and Technological Change in the Building of the First American Cotton Mills," in Brooke Hindle, ed., *The Material Culture of the Wooden Age* (Tarrytown, N.Y., 1981), 312–18.

54. Unless otherwise cited, information on early child labor in textile mills presented in this and the following two paragraphs is from Kulik, "The Beginnings of the Industrial Revolution in America," 189–222; Kulik, "Factory Discipline in the New Nation"; and especially Anthony F. C. Wallace, *Rockdale: The Growth of an American Village in the Early Industrial Revolution* (New York, 1978), 136–39, 182–83, 327–29.

55. Carding accidents: *Benedict Reminiscences*, 78; Slater's discipline: White, *Memoir of Samuel Slater*, 108; Patch cuffs children: Charles Pitman Longwell, *A Little Story of Old Paterson, as Told by an Old Man* (n.p., 1901), 37.

56. Quote: "Account of a Journal of Josiah Quincy," 124.

57. There is a full and clear description of the spinning mule and its operations in Wallace, *Rockdale*, 189–92, which quotes Andrew Ure on pp. 191–92. See also Harold Catling, *The Spinning Mule* (Newton Abbot, England, 1970).

58. Kulik, "The Beginnings of the Industrial Revolution in America," 351–53. On the mule spinners, see Catling, *The Spinning Mule*; Isaac Cohen, "Worker's Control in the Cotton Industry: A Comparative Study of British and American Mule Spinning," *Labor History* 26 (Winter 1985), 53–85; Teresa Ann Murphy, *Ten Hours' Labor: Religion, Reform, and Gender in Early New England* (Ithaca, N.Y., 1992), 33–46; Cynthia J. Shelton, *The Mills of Manayunk: Industrialization and Social Conflict in the Philadelphia Region, 1787–1837* (Baltimore, 1986), 63–64; Wallace, *Rockdale*, 134–44; and Jonathan Prude,

The Coming of Industrial Order: Town and Factory Life in Rural Massachusetts, 1810–1860 (Cambridge, Mass., 1983), 186. For an overview of the questions involved here, see David Montgomery, "Worker's Control of Machine Production in the Nineteenth Century," in *Worker's Control in America: Studies in the History of Work, Technology, and Labor Struggles* (New York, 1979), esp. 11–15.

59. Timothy Dwight, *Travels in New England and New York* (Cambridge, Mass., 1969; orig. 1821), 2:14; [Margaret Hunter Hall], *The Aristocratic Journey: Being the Outspoken Letters of Mrs. Basil Hall, Written during a Fourteen Months' Sojourn in America, 1827–1828*, ed. Una Pope-Hennessy (New York, 1931), 106; P. Stansbury, *A Pedestrian Tour of Two Thousand Three Hundred Miles, in North America . . . Performed in the Autumn of 1821* (New York, 1822), 265.

60. Gary Kulik, "Dams, Fish, and Farmers: The Defense of Public Rights in Eighteenth-Century Rhode Island," in Steven Hahn and Jonathan Prude, eds., *The Countryside in the Age of Capitalist Transformation: Essays in the Social History of Rural America* (Chapel Hill, N.C., 1985), 25–50; J. Milbert, *Picturesque Itinerary of the Hudson River and Peripheral Parts of North America* (Ridgewood, N.J., 1968; orig. 1828), 240; author's on-site observations.

61. Henry Bradshaw Fearon, *Sketches of America: A Narrative of a Journey of Five Thousand Miles through the Eastern and Western States* (New York, 1969; orig. 1818), 99; "Account of a Journal of Josiah Quincy," 124.

62. Milbert, *Picturesque Itinerary*, 240.

63. *Benedict Reminiscences*, 66.

64. *Benedict Reminiscences*, 66, 103.

65. *Benedict Reminiscences*, 65; Grieve, *Illustrated History of Pawtucket*, 101; *Providence Cadet*, reprinted in the *New-York Statesman*, 21 July 1828; news clipping entitled "One of Sam Patch's Scholars, Pawtucket, Rhode Island, October 2" (no year), Sam Patch Scrapbook; 1829 jumpers: Thomas D. Clark, ed., *Footloose in Jacksonian America: Robert W. Scott and His Agrarian World* (Lexington, Ky., 1989), 34.

66. Jumpers at Yellow Mill: reminiscences of David Benedict and Edward Wilkinson, *Pawtucket Gazette & Chronicle*, 26 December 1862 and 7 February 1873. Bucklin genealogy: *Benedict Reminiscences*, 185–86, 307–16. Jumping style: *Pawtucket Gazette and Chronicle*, 27 May 1853, 26 December 1862, 7 February 1873; Sam's later technique: *Colonial Advocate* (York, Upper Canada), 22 October 1829.

II. Paterson

1. Quotations, in order: Edward C. Carter II, John C. Van Horne, and Charles E. Brownell, eds., *Latrobe's View of America, 1795–1820: Selections from the Watercolors and Sketches* (New Haven, Conn., 1985), 167–68; *Manufacturer's and Farmer's Journal* (Providence, R.I.,), 27 September 1824; Eliza Southgate Bowne, *A Girl's Life Eighty Years Ago: Selections from the Letters of Eliza Southgate Bowne* (Williamstown, Mass, 1980; orig. 1887), 180; C. D. Arfwedson, Esq., *The United States and Canada in 1832, 1833, and 1834* (London, 1834), 1:235; P. Stansbury, *A Pedestrian Tour of Two Thousand Three Hundred Miles, in North America . . . Performed in the Autumn of 1821* (New York, 1822), 16; *New-York Spectator*, 7 September 1827. On the view of Paterson from the falls ground, see Arfwedson, *The United States and Canada*, 1:136; J. Milbert, *Picturesque Itinerary of the Hudson River and Peripheral Parts of North America* (Ridgewood, N.J., 1968; orig. 1828), 260; Captain Frederick Marryat, *Diary in America*, ed. Jules Zanger (Bloomington, Ind., 1960), 80. See also Leo A. Bressler, "Passaic Falls: Eighteenth-Century Natural Wonder," *Proceedings of the New Jersey Historical Society* 74 (April 1956), 99–106.

2. The only modern history of early Paterson is Howard Harris, "The Transformation of Ideology in the Early Industrial Revolution: Paterson, New Jersey, 1820–1840 (Ph.D. dissertation, City University of New York, 1985), esp. 1–37. On Hamilton's role, see John R. Nelson, Jr., *Liberty and Property: Political Economy and Policymaking in the New Nation, 1789–1812* (Baltimore, 1987), 37–51. Newspaper quoted: *Sentinel of Freedom* (Newark, N.J.), 26 June 1827.

3. *Paterson Intelligencer*, 12 December 1827 (quotation); 28 July 1830 (war dances); 12 August 1829, 8 August 1832 (circus); 18 June 1828, 30 September 1829, 11 August 1830, 9 July 1828, 15 September 1830, 29 June 1831, 10 August 1831, 27 June 1832, 1 August 1832, 26 June 1833, 24 July 1833, 5 August 1835, 18 May 1836, 31 May 1836, 28 June 1837, 6 June 1838 (fireworks).

4. *Paterson Intelligencer*, 30 June 1830, 30 September 1829, 21 July 1830, 9 July 1828.

5. *Paterson Intelligencer*, 10 October 1827; E. M. Graf, "Passaic Falls Bridges," *Bulletin of the Passaic County Historical Society* 3 (October 1944), 14; Frank L. Byrne, *Prophet of Prohibition: Neal Dow and His Crusade* (Madison, Wis., 1961), 7, 10, 18.

6. On Patch and child workers, Charles Pitman Longwell, *A Little Story of Old Paterson, as Told by an Old Man* (n.p., 1901), 37; on Sam's candlewick mill, *Paterson Intelligencer*, 19 July 1826. Branigan stays in business: Rev. Samuel Fisher's census of Paterson for 1827, copied in a letter to the author from James G. Ward, 16 January 1984.

7. The lockup story told in Longwell, *A Little Story*, 37–38, and idem, *Historic Totowa Falls* (Paterson, n.d.), 37. It is corroborated in the *Journal of Commerce* (New York), reprinted in the *New-York Evening Post*, 7 July 1828.

8. *New-York Evening Post*, 1 October 1827; *Paterson Intelligencer*, 10 October 1827. Longwell, *A Little Story*, 37–41, and *Historic Totowa Falls*, 36–39, reminiscing at a distance of seventy years, differs in some details from the contemporary story in the *New-York Evening Post*. In Longwell's version the bridge sways dangerously after the fall of the log roller, and this near-disaster provides the backdrop for Sam's leap. Longwell has Patch's pre-jump speech as "Now old Tim Crane thinks he has done something great; but I can beat him." Given the many decades that intervened between the two accounts, they are remarkably similar. When they differ, I follow the account in the *Post*.

9. Local memories of Sam's leap: Longwell, *A Little Story*, 37–41; Longwell, *Historic Totowa Falls*, 36–39; William Carlos Williams, *Paterson* (New York, 1963), 15–17. The *Intelligencer* published a cryptic account of the leap which received this response from the writer "No Quiz": "What a pity it is, that too much modesty should ever repress the brilliant coruscations of wit and genius. O that Quiz had done justice to the launch of Timothy Crane's bridge o'er the deep and yawning chasm at Passaic Falls, and the adventurous leap of Sam Patch, Esq. from the giddy height which overlooks the aforesaid gulf! But, alas, we must now despair of ever having these memorable events, 'at which the little boys and girls did gape and stare,' given to us and embodied in the true quizzical style." He went on to what appears to be a defense of Timothy Crane against unspecified rumors: "Quiz is informed that Wormwood's ear has never been lent to such 'oft repeated tales,' but that the facts have come from other sources, and are incontrovertible. Quiz is of course at liberty to laugh when he pleases; but with all due deference, would it not be well to select a subject at which he could laugh with a better grace?—this is so confoundedly like a forced laugh, that it sounds as if 'he mocked himself.' But there is another circumstance, which I suppose will also be

laughed at by the whole attacked corps, who seem to have concentrated and marshalled all their forces, bringing up all the resources, 'little Trim' and all, which have been so sagaciously kept back, for the fatal moment when a last and desperate effort is to be made to prostrate a single individual, who, notwithstanding many sneers, does not appear to be beneath their notice: and it is this—that the individual did serve in the armies of these U. States, during the whole of the late war, with credit to himself and advantage to his country—and a part of the time under the immediate command of the lamented and gallant Pike, with whom, as I can prove from circumstances, he must have been a favorite and confidential officer. He shall stand, Mr. Editor, like a redoubt of granite, uninjured, amidst all this slanderous fire." (*Paterson Intelligencer*, 10 October 1827.) Another tantalizing and unresearchable note—possibly referring to Sam Patch—was printed in the *Intelligencer* on 10 January 1827: "The lines of 'S.P.' evince a very creditable feeling, but are not sufficiently finished for publication."

10. Longwell, *Historic Totowa Falls*, 40 (quote). Adlard Welby, *A Visit to North America and the English Settlements in Illinois, with a Winter Residence in Philadelphia* (London, 1821), 23–24; Stansbury, *A Pedestrian Tour*, 15–16; [Margaret Hunter Hall], *The Aristocratic Journey: Being the Outspoken Letters of Mrs. Basil Hall, Written during a Fourteen Months' Sojourn in America, 1827–1828*, ed. Una Pope-Hennessy (New York, 1931), 30; Marryat, *Diary in America*, 80–81; Norman F. Brydon, *The Passaic River* (New Brunswick, N.J., 1974), 109. Sam's early jump: *New-York Evening Post*, 7 July 1828. Sam advertised his second and third publicized jumps as his third and fourth.

11. *Paterson Intelligencer*, 11 May 1831, 7 July 1831, 14 July 1830, 12 August 1829; Rev. Isaac Fidler, *Observations on Professions, Literature, Manners, and Emigration in the United States and Canada, Made during a Residence There in 1832* (New York, 1833), 98.

12. Fidler, *Observations*, 96–97; *Paterson Intelligencer*, 20 June 1838, 27 June 1838, 11 May 1831 (Crane's explanation).

13. *Paterson Intelligencer*, 19 March 1828, 31 December 1828, 11 May 1831. On Christmas Night: Stephen Nissenbaum, *The Battle over Christmas* (New York, 1996); Susan G. Davis, "'Making Night Hideous': Christmas Revelry and Public Order in Nineteenth-Century Philadelphia," *American Quarterly* 34 (Summer 1982), 185–99.

14. Fidler, *Observations*, 97 (quote); *Paterson Intelligencer*, 11 May 1831.

15. On Timothy Crane: Longwell, *Historic Totowa Falls*, 38; Fidler, *Observations*, 96–97; Ellery Bicknell Crane, *Genealogy of the Crane Family. Volume I. Descendants of Henry Crane, of Wethersfield and Guilford, Conn., with Sketch of the Family in England* (Worcester, Mass, 1895), 1:102; William Nelson, ed., *The Van Houten Manuscripts: A Century of Historical Documents* (Paterson, 1894), 69–70; D. Stanton Hammond, comp., "Rev. Samuel Fisher's Census: Paterson, N.J., 1824–1832," *Bulletin of the Passaic County Historical Society* 4 (August 1958), 104; William Nelson and Charles A. Shriner, *History of Paterson and Its Environs* (New York, 1920), 2:406.

16. Albert Winslow Ryerson, *The Ryerson Genealogy: Genealogy of the Knickerbocker Families of Ryerson, Ryerse, Ryerss; also Adriance and Martense Families; all Descendants of Martin and Adriaen Reyersz (Ryerzen) of Amsterdam, Holland* (Chicago, 1916), 128; Crane, *Genealogy of the Crane Family*, 1:102.

17. Paterson bank seizes the property: *Paterson Intelligencer*, 26 March 1828 and 9 April 1828. Further legal troubles with the land: *Paterson Intelligencer*, 16 June 1830, 18 November 1835, 15 June 1836, 20 July 1836. The north bank remained contested territory for many years. In the 1850s a silk manufacturer bought the grounds and closed them off with the intention of building a house for himself. He reconsidered and turned the property into a privately owned "public" park, with the advertised intention of improving Patersonians. He too was harassed and vandalized until he quit the grounds. See Longwell, *Historic Totowa Falls*, 40, and Levi R. Trumbull, *A History of Industrial Paterson* (Paterson, 1882), 332–33. The land is now a public park, operated by the City of Paterson.

18. Fidler, *Observations*, 99–100, told the jumped-for-love story just after a conversation with Timothy Crane. Patch told his own story in the *Paterson Intelligencer*, 16 July and 2 July 1828.

19. Raymond Williams, *Culture and Society, 1750–1950* (New York, 1958), and *Keywords: A Vocabulary of Culture and Society* (New York, 1976). Williams's principal concern is with the dissociation of "art" from occupational skills (Sam Patch's definition) and its attachment to anti-occupations practiced by special people who operate apart from and above the workaday world, a redefinition that was not accomplished in the United States until at least the 1850s. A third use of the word (Timothy Crane's) stemmed from the old vocabulary used

by Sam Patch, but reshaped in ways that gave "art" new entrepreneurial and developmental meanings. Crane's "art" is fully illustrated in the historical and critical studies cited in note 25. Those studies and the works in labor history cited in note 20 establish the centrality of Patch's and Crane's definitions of art in working-class and middle-class perceptions of economic development during the crucial years 1825–50.

20. The vocabulary and ethos to which Patch's "art" was attached had been in existence for a long time, but had been codified by the experience of the Revolution and the succeeding debate on economic development. Labor historians have established their importance to working-class thinking and actions throughout the nineteenth century and beyond. That ethos among handworkers is most thoroughly discussed in Sean Wilentz, *Chants Democratic: New York City and the Rise of the American Working Class, 1788–1850* (New York, 1984). Anthony F. C. Wallace, *Rockdale: The Growth of an American Village in the Early Industrial Revolution* (New York, 1978), 211–95, discusses a very similar cluster of attitudes. Popular ideas of the value of work and workers in the shoe and textile towns in which Sam Patch grew up are discussed in Paul G. Faler, *Mechanics and Manufacturers in the Early Industrial Revolution: Lynn, Massachusetts, 1780–1860* (Albany, N.Y., 1981), 28–57; Alan Dawley, *Class and Community: The Industrial Revolution in Lynn* (Cambridge, Mass., 1976), 42–73; and Gary Kulik, "The Beginnings of the Industrial Revolution: Pawtucket, Rhode Island, 1672–1829" (Ph.D. dissertation, Brown University, 1980). David Montgomery, *The Fall of the House of Labor* (New York, 1987), places that ethos at the center of working-class life between the Civil War and World War I. The term "system of rules" is from the definition of "art" in Noah Webster, *An American Dictionary of the English Language* (New York, 1828).

21. Pawtucket jumpers: *Pawtucket Gazette and Chronicle*, 26 December 1862; Elizabeth J. Johnson and James Lucas Wheaton IV, comps., *History of Pawtucket, Rhode Island: Reminiscences & New Series of Reverend David Benedict* (Pawtucket, 1986), 65. Later technique: *Colonial Advocate* (York, Upper Canada), 22 October 1829; *New-York Evening Post*, 21 October 1829 (from the *Buffalo Republican*); *Farmer's Journal and Welland Canal Advertiser* (St. Catherine's, Upper Canada), 19 December 1829 (from the *Buffalo Republican*). Sheriff McKee: *Paterson Daily Press*, 20 May 1885. (Thanks to James Ward.)

22. Sam's jumping suit: "Colonel William L. Stone's Visit to Niagara in 1829," *Buffalo Historical Society Publications* 14 (1910), 270; *Rochester Daily Advertiser*, 7 November 1829. Spinner's uniform: *Paterson Intelligencer*, 12 July 1826.

23. *New-York Evening Post*, 7 July 1828 (reprint from the *New York Journal of Commerce*). This article included the first publication of what became Sam's motto: "Some things can be done as well as others."

24. Keith Thomas, *Man and the Natural World: A History of the Modern Sensibility* (New York, 1983), 25. William W. Campbell, ed., *The Life and Writings of DeWitt Clinton* (New York, 1849), 23. (Thanks to Steven Bullock.)

25. These conceptions of nature and art were central to writings in American Studies in the 1960s through the 1980s, beginning with Leo Marx, *The Machine in the Garden: Technology and the Pastoral Ideal in America* (New York, 1964). See Thomas Bender, *Toward an Urban Vision: Ideas and Institutions in Nineteenth-Century America* (Lexington, Ky., 1975), 73–93; Neil Harris, *The Artist in American Society: The Formative Years, 1790–1860* (New York, 1966), esp. 188–216; John F. Kasson, *Civilizing the Machine: Technology and Republican Values in America, 1776–1900* (New York, 1976), 55–106. The grandest of civilized nature parks is the subject of Elizabeth McKinsey, *Niagara Falls: Icon of the American Sublime* (New York, 1985). For the philosophical groundings of all this, see Terry Eagleton, *The Ideology of the Aesthetic* (Oxford, England, 1990).

26. The juxtaposition is analyzed beautifully in McKinsey, *Niagara Falls*, 127–77.

27. *New-York Evening Post*, 24 July 1828.

28. *Paterson Intelligencer*, 9 July 1828. See the discussions of "mechanic" in Stuart M. Blumin, *The Emergence of the Middle Class: Social Experience in the American City, 1760–1900* (New York, 1989), 31–34, and David R. Roediger, *The Wages of Whiteness: Race and the Making of the American Working Class* (London, 1999), 50–52.

29. E. T. Coke, *A Subaltern's Furlough: Descriptive of Scenes in Various Parts of the United States, Upper and Lower Canada, New Brunswick, and Nova Scotia, during the Summer and Autumn of 1832* (London, 1833), 1:142.

30. On celebrations of the Fourth of July, see Len Travers, *Celebrating the Fourth: Independence Day and the Rites of Nationalism in the Early Republic* (Amherst, Mass., 1997); David Waldstreicher, *In the Midst of Perpetual Fetes: The Making of American Nationalism,*

1776–1820 (Chapel Hill, N.C., 1997); Simon P. Newman, *Parades and the Politics of the Street: Festive Culture in the Early American Republic* (Philadelphia, 1997), 83–119; Scott C. Martin, *Killing Time: Leisure and Culture in Southwestern Pennsylvania, 1800–1850* (Pittsburgh, 1995), 71–101. More general studies of American festivities that have shaped the following paragraphs include Mary P. Ryan, *Civic Wars: Democracy and Public Life in the American City during the Nineteenth Century* (Berkeley, Calif., 1989); Ryan, "The American Parade: Representation of the Nineteenth-Century Social Order," in Lynn Hunt, ed., *The New Cultural History* (Berkeley, Calif., 1989), 131–53; Susan G. Davis, *Parades and Power: Street Theatre in Nineteenth-Century Philadelphia* (Philadelphia, 1986); Sean Wilentz, "Artisan Republican Festivals and the Rise of Class Conflict in New York City, 1788–1837," in Michael H. Frisch and Daniel J. Walkowitz, eds., *Working Class America: Labor, Community, and American Society* (Urbana, Ill., 1983), 37–77; Laura Rigal, " 'Raising the Roof': Authors, Spectators, and Artisans in the Grand Federal Procession of 1788," *Theatre Journal* 48 (October 1996), 253–78.

31. Information in this and the following three paragraphs is from the *Paterson Intelligencer*, 21 June 1826, 6 July 1826, 12 July 1826.

32. *Paterson Intelligencer*, 11 July 1827. Canal explosions at Paterson: *Montreal Gazette*, 19 July 1827. On the emerging connections between technological progress and the Fourth of July in the 1820s, see David E. Nye, *American Technological Sublime* (Cambridge, Mass., 1994), 41–43.

33. *Paterson Intelligencer*, 4 June 1828, 18 June 1828, 25 June 1828, 2 July 1828, 9 July 1828.

34. Quotation from *Paterson Intelligencer*, 9 July 1828 and 8 July 1829. In subsequent years the mechanics' associations were not listed among the planners, and none of the official toasts mentioned them. There were now toasts to an abstracted "People." In 1830 the fire companies, apparently controlled by Jacksonian Democrats, held their own banquet. There were twelve cheers for "The People," and toasts not only to De Witt Clinton but to Thomas Paine, and to the Jacksonian Democrats' libertarian position on church and state. In 1831 the official banquet included the visiting Directors of the Paterson and Hudson Railroad, which had ritually begun construction on that day. In another hotel the Mechanics Institute (which, if it was like those in other towns, was an elite organization that provided rational education for ambitious and well-behaved mechanics) held a

banquet of its own. Its vice-president toasted "The Mechanics of Paterson—May their reputation for intelligence and patriotism be equal
to their reputation for mechanical excellence; they will then assume
that rank in Society to which their industry so justly entitled them"—
a rank that they had occupied unchallenged in previous years. At the
end of the day, the elite could choose between Crane's fireworks and
a fancy-dress ball.

There was a related transformation in the official celebration of
women. Women marched in the parades of 1826 and 1827—the
schoolteachers with their children, the others apparently marching as a
group, dressed as they pleased. Women were not mentioned in 1828,
and the parade was rained out in 1829. They reappeared in the parade
of 1830 as "Ladies, dressed in white"—an abstract, feminized purity.
The thirteenth official toast was always made to women, transformed
from "Our Fair Country Women" in 1826 to "The American Fair" in
the following three years (followed in 1827 and 1828 by the playing of
"Come Haste to the Wedding) to "Woman" in 1830. Judging by what
the elite chose to celebrate, one would have to say that Paterson was
transformed in the late 1820s from a town of useful mechanics and
pretty women to a pantheon of Industry, Progress, and Woman. See
the *Paterson Intelligencer*, late June through mid-July, 1826–31.

35. *Paterson Intelligencer*, 9 July 1828. The longer piece appeared in the
New York Journal of Commerce, and was reprinted in the *New-York
Evening Post*, 7 July 1828, and other papers.

36. Sam's motto: *New-York Evening Post*, 7 July 1828. Though the exact
time for the official dinner was unannounced, its seems very safe to
assume that the exclusive festivities were still in progress when Sam
leaped at 4:30 p.m. The parade formed at 11 a.m. on that day, and
marched through all the principal streets. Services at the church included a prayer, the reading of the Declaration of Independence, numerous songs by the choir, and the performance by the Orator of the
Day, a speech that generally occupied more than an hour. There was
then the parade to St. John's Hall, more festivities, a formal banquet,
the thirteen regular toasts (each followed by a band performance),
and even more volunteer toasts. In subsequent years the parade began at 10 a.m., with the banquet scheduled for 3 p.m. For times, see
Paterson Intelligencer, 9 July 1828 (Sam's leap, parade starting time);
1 July 1829 and 4 July 1830 (parade and banquet starting times).

37. *Paterson Intelligencer*, 16 July 1828; *New-York Commercial Advertiser*, 31 July 1828, 6 August 1828.

38. This is the conclusion of Howard Harris, "The Transformation of Ideology in the Early Industrial Revolution," 296–308, and of Clay Gish, "The Children's Strikes: Socialization and Class Formation in Paterson, 1824–1836," *New Jersey History* 110 (Fall/Winter 1992), 21–38.

39. Quotes: *New-York Commercial Advertiser*, 6 August 1828; *New-York Evening Post*, 26 July 1828. On the Pawtucket strike, see Gary Kulik, "Pawtucket Village and the Strike of 1824: The Origins of Class Conflict in Rhode Island," *Radical History Review* 17 (Spring 1978), 6–35.

40. *New-York Commercial Advertiser*, 24 July 1828; *New York Statesman*, 21 July 1828. *New York Enquirer*, 4 August 1828 (crowd estimate). Money: *New-Jersey Journal* (Elizabeth Town), 22 July 1828.

41. James Epstein, "Understanding the Cap of Liberty: Symbolic Practice and Social Conflict in Early Nineteenth-Century England," *Past and Present* 122 (February 1989), 101, 110–11.

42. *New-York Evening Post*, 26 July 1828 (quote); *New-York Commercial Advertiser*, 26 July 1828, 31 July 1828 (quote); *Paterson Intelligencer*, 6 August 1828.

43. *New-York Spectator*, 1 August 1828; *New-York Enquirer for the Country*, 29 July 1828; *New-York Commercial Advertiser*, 31 July 1828; *New-York Evening Post*, 30 July 1828; *Paterson Intelligencer*, 30 July 1828.

44. *New-York Commercial Advertiser*, 6 August 1828, 8 August 1828.

45. *New-York Commercial Advertiser*, 31 July 1828.

46. Archibald Douglas Turnbull, *John Stevens: An American Record* (New York, 1928), is a detailed account of the Colonel's activities. See also *Dictionary of American Biography* (New York, 1935), 614–16.

47. See Bryan J. Danforth, "Hoboken and the Affluent New Yorker's Search for Recreation," *New Jersey History* 95 (Autumn 1977), 133–44. "Best" people at hotel (including John Jacob Astor, who stayed there while supervising completion of his Hoboken villa in 1828): W. Jay Mills, *Historic Houses of New Jersey* (Philadelphia, 1902), 46–47. "Known world": *New-York Commercial Advertiser*, 8 August 1829. Quotations: James Stuart, Esq., *Three Years in North America* (Edinburgh, Scotland, 1828), 2:23; Fanny Kemble, *Journal of a Young Actress*, ed. Monica Gough (New York, 1990), 153; Robert C. Sands, *The Writings of Robert C. Sands, in Prose and Verse. With a Memoir of the Author. In Two Volumes.* (New York, 1834), 2:286.

48. Harry F. Smith, Jr., *Romance of the Hoboken Ferry* (New York, 1931), 45–59; Charles H. Winfield, *Hopoghan Hackingh. Hoboken, a Plea-*

sure Resort for Old New York (New York, 1895), 63–69, 72–76. [A Scot], Travels in the United States of America in the Years 1821, 1822, 1823 to 1824, Vol. 3:1335, manuscript travel account, New-York Historical Society. Kemble, *Journal of a Young Actress*, 83–84; Stuart, *Three Years in North America*, 1:444; 2:306–7; *New-York Spectator*, 4 August 1829. Obelisk: John W. Barber, *Historical Collections of New Jersey: Past and Present* (New Haven, Conn., 1868), 234; the obelisk was carried off "a few years" before 1830. See [Theodore Dwight], *The Northern Traveller, and Northern Tour; with the Routes to the Springs, Niagara, and Quebec, and the Coal Mines of Pennsylvania; also, the Tour of New-England* (New York, 1830), 21. In the 1830s the writer N. P. Willis lamented that "the fashion of visiting Haboken [*sic*] and Weehawken has yielded to an impression among the 'fashionable' that it is a vulgar resort. This willingness to relinquish an agreeable promenade because it is enjoyed as well by the poorer classes of society, is one of those superfine ideas which we imitate from our English ancestors, and in which the more philosophic continentals are so superior to us." Nathaniel P. Willis, *American Scenery; or Land, Lake, and River. Illustrations of Transatlantic Nature* (London, 1840), 2:31.

49. Circus: *New-York Evening Post*, 5 August 1823. Running races: *New-York Evening Post*, 1 July 1824. July 4: *New-Jersey Journal* (Elizabeth Town), 12 July 1825; *New-York Commercial Advertiser*, 2 July 1825, 7 July 1829. *New York American*, 2 July 1828. Pigeon shoot: *New-York Commercial Advertiser*, 2 October 1829. Eclipse at Hoboken: *Albany Argus and Daily City Gazette*, 25 February 1826. Shooting range and railroad: *New-York Commercial Advertiser*, 8 August 1829 and 10 September 1829. See also Smith, *Romance of the Hoboken Ferry*, 45–59; Winfield, *Hopoghan Hackingh*, 63–69, 72–76. In later decades, John Cox Stevens turned his sporting interests from horse racing to yachting. He was the first president of the New York Yachting Club, and his boat *America* defeated British boats in a race around the Isle of Wight in 1851; the trophy awarded him became the object of the America's Cup race. On John Cox Stevens and the New York sporting scene, see Melvin L. Adelman, *A Sporting Time: New York City and the Rise of Modern Athletics, 1820–1870* (Urbana, Ill., 1986), 35–38, 41–42, 197–200, 212–13. There is a fine essay on Stevens in John Dizikes, *Sportsmen and Gamesmen* (Boston, 1981), 91–120.

50. *New York Enquirer*, 4 August 1828 and 6 August 1828; *New York*

Statesman, 6 August 1828; *New York Gazette and General Advertiser*, 8 August 1828.

51. Walter M. Oddie Diary, Vol. 2, entry for 6 August 1828, Library Division, Henry Francis du Pont Winterthur Museum. *New York Statesman*, 6 August 1828; *New York Enquirer*, 4 August 1828; *New-York Evening Post*, 7 August 1828. Pawtucket jumpers: *New York Statesman*, 21 July 1828.

52. Works near Philadelphia: Charles V. Hagner, *Early History of the Falls of Schuylkill, Manayunk, Schuylkill and Lehigh Navigation Company, Fairmount Waterworks, etc.* (Philadelphia, 1869), 76. Leap at Little Falls: *Philadelphia Gazette*, 29 June 1829. Further evidence that Sam was in Philadelphia is that the owner of a summer garden in that city challenged Patch to jump against his great "antedelluvian frog" in July 1829. *Democratic Press* (Philadelphia), 9 July 1829. (Thanks to Shane White.)

III. Niagara

1. Biographical information on William Leete Stone is from Stone, *The Life and Times of Sa-Go-Ye-Wat-Ha, or Red Jacket . . . with a Memoir of the Author, by His Son* (Albany, N.Y., 1866), 9–101, and Julian P. Boyd, "William Leete Stone," *Dictionary of American Biography*, ed. Dumas Malone (New York, 1935), 15:89–91. Stone became a "colonel" as a member of Governor De Witt Clinton's wartime staff, and used the title for the rest of his life. On gentility and genteel taste: John Brewer, *The Pleasures of the Imagination: English Culture in the Eighteenth Century* (New York, 1997); Richard L. Bushman, *The Refinement of America: Persons, Houses, Cities* (New York, 1992); John F. Kasson, *Rudeness & Civility: Manners in Nineteenth-Century Urban America* (New York, 1990); and the early chapters of Terry Eagleton, *The Ideology of the Aesthetic* (Oxford, England, 1990).

2. On scenic tourism in America see Dona Brown, *Inventing New England: Regional Tourism in the Nineteenth Century* (Washington, D.C., 1995), esp. 15–40; Patricia Jasen, *Wild Things: Nature, Culture, and Tourism in Ontario, 1790–1914* (Toronto, 1995), 3–54; Kenneth Myers, *The Catskills: Painters, Writers, and Tourists in the Mountains, 1820–1895* (Hanover, N.H., 1987); Bruce Robertson, "The Picturesque Tourist in America," in Edward J. Nygren, ed., *Views and Visions: American Landscape before 1830* (Washington, D.C., 1986),

189–211; and John F. Sears, *Sacred Places: American Tourist Attractions in the Nineteenth Century* (New York, 1989). Also valuable is Malcolm Andrews, *The Search for the Picturesque: Landscape Aesthetics and Tourism in Britain, 1760–1800* (Stanford, Calif., 1989).

3. Col. William Leete Stone, "From New York to Niagara: Journal of a Tour, in Part by the Erie Canal, in the Year 1829," *Buffalo Historical Society Publications* 14 (1910), 243–44, 245. His (unfavorable) review of Hall appeared in the *New-York Commercial Advertiser*, 15, 16, 18, 23, 25, 27, and 29 August 1829. William Dunlap, *A Trip to Niagara: Travellers in America* (New York, 1830), played a long season at the Bowery Theater in 1828–29. See George C. D. Odell, *Annals of the New York Stage* (New York, 1927–49), 3:407–8. In the *Commercial Advertiser* of 2 September 1829, in a review of Herr Cline, the tightrope walker at Niblo's Garden, Stone quoted Burke, strongly suggesting a recent reading of Burke's treatise on the sublime: " 'Night,' says Burke, 'increases our terror, more perhaps than anything else; it is our nature, when we do not know what may happen, to fear the worst that can happen.' " Niagara at Niblo's: *Commercial Advertiser*, 19 July 1825; at Castle Garden (quote): *New-York Daily Advertiser*, 22 August 1827.

4. Stone, "From New York to Niagara," passim.

5. Stone, "From New York to Niagara," 211–12, 229–30. Burke's most concentrated discussion of the sublime is in *A Philosophical Inquiry into the Origin of Our Ideas of the Sublime and Beautiful*, ed. Adam Phillips (New York 1990; orig. 1757), 36–37, 53–79. "Delightful horror:" p. 67.

6. See Elizabeth McKinsey, *Niagara Falls: Icon of the American Sublime* (New York, 1985); Jasen, *Wild Things*, 29–54; Brown, *Inventing New England*, 15–74; Eagleton, *The Ideology of the Aesthetic*, passim.

7. Stone, "From New York to Niagara," 241–42.

8. Forsyth advertisement: *Colonial Advocate* (York, Upper Canada, 9 August 1827; *Black Rock Gazette*, 5 October 1826 and 6 October 1827; Stone, "From New York to Niagara," 220, 250. On the relation between conquest/development and the American view from above, see Albert Boime, *The Magisterial Gaze: Manifest Destiny and American Landscape Painting, c. 1830–1865* (Washington, D.C., 1991). Niagara Falls, on the other hand, was maintained as an "undeveloped" sacred shrine. Tourists generally avoided broad panoramas seen from great distances and heights.

9. John Howison, *Sketches of Upper Canada, Domestic, Local, and Characteristic: to which are added, Practical Details for the Information of Emigrants of Every Class; and some Recollections of the United States of America* (Edinburgh, Scotland, 1821), 107; E. T. Coke, *A Subaltern's Furlough: Descriptive of Scenes in Various Parts of the United States, Upper and Lower Canada, New Brunswick, and Nova Scotia, during the Summer and Autumn of 1832* (London, 1833), 2:31; C. D. Arfwedson, Esq., *The United States and Canada in 1832, 1833, and 1834* (London, 1834), 2:312–13; James Stuart, Esq., *Three Years in North America* (Edinburgh, Scotland, 1828), 1:140; Travel Diary of John Fanning Watson, 1827, entry for 24 July 1827, Library Division, Henry Francis du Pont Winterthur Museum; Stone, "From New York to Niagara," 242–43.

10. Stone, "From New York to Niagara," 246.

11. Edward Allen Talbot, Esq., *Five Years' Residence in the Canadas: including a Tour through Part of the United States of America, in the Year 1823* (London, 1824), 1:129; Frances Trollope, *Domestic Manners of the Americans* (London, 1984; orig. 1839), 337; Frederick Fitzgerald De Roos, *Personal Narrative of Travels in the United States and Canada in 1826, with Remarks on the Present State of the American Navy* (London, 1827), 160; Basil Hall, *Travels in North America, in the Years 1827 and 1828* (Edinburgh and London, 1829), 1:184. "We are most delighted, when some grand scene . . . rising before the eye, strikes us beyond the power of thought. . . . In this pause of intellect; this *deliquium* of the soul, an enthusastic sensation of pleasure overspreads it, previous to any examination by the rules of art. The general ideal of the scene makes an impression, before any appeal is made to the judgement. We rather *feel*, than *survey* it." (William Gilpin, *Three Essays: On Picturesque Beauty; on Picturesque Travel; and on Sketching Landscape: to which is added a poem, on Landscape Painting* (London, 2d. ed., 1794), 49–50.

12. Stone, "From New York to Niagara," 244–45.

13. Anon., *American Sketches, by a Native of the United States* (London, 1827), 237; Emanuel Howitt, *Selections from Letters Written during a Tour through the United States, in the Summer and Autumn of 1819* (Nottingham, England, 1820), 130; John Fowler, *Journal of a Tour in the State of New York, in the Year 1830; with Remarks on Agriculture in those Parts Most Eligible for Settlers, and Return to England by the Western Islands, in Consequence of Shipwreck in the Robert Fulton* (London, 1831), 141; Stone, "From New York to Niagara," 246.

14. [Theodore Dwight], *The Northern Traveller, and Northern Tour; with the Routes to the Springs, Niagara, and Quebec, and the Coal Mines of Pennsylvania; also, the Tour of New-England* (New York, 1830), 87; [Thomas Hamilton], *Men and Manners in America* (Philadelphia, 1833), 2:162; Talbot, *Five Years' Residence in the Canadas*, 1:134; Howison, *Sketches of Upper Canada*, 98; Henry R. Schoolcraft, *Narrative Journal of Travels from Detroit Northwest through the Great Chain of American Lakes to the Sources of the Mississippi River in 1820* (Albany, N.Y., 1821), 36–37.

15. Stone, "From New York to Niagara," 246.

16. Stone, "From New York to Niagara," 246–47.

17. *Albany Daily Advertiser*, 9 July 1828; *New-York Evening Post*, 7 July 1828 (reprint from the *Journal of Commerce*). On the *Journal of Commerce*: Bertram Wyatt-Brown, *Lewis Tappan and the Evangelical War Against Slavery* (Cleveland, 1969), 54; *Rochester Daily Advertiser and Telegraph*, 5 August 1829 (reprint from the *New England Palladium*); Stone: *New-York Spectator*, 11 July 1828 and 18 July 1828. (The *Spectator* was the for-the-country edition of the *Commercial Advertiser*.)

18. Stone, "From New York to Niagara," 227, 238, 240.

19. Jackson riot: *New-York Commercial Advertiser*, 31 July 1828 (quote) and 2 August 1828.

20. Corrupt bargain parody: *New-York Commercial Advertiser*, 8 August 1828. Historians continue to argue about the validity of these charges. See Robert V. Remini, *Andrew Jackson: Volume Two: The Course of American Freedom, 1822–1832* (New York, 1981), 74–99; Remini, *Henry Clay: Statesman for the Union* (New York, 1991), 251–72; Charles Sellers, *The Market Revolution: Jacksonian America, 1815–1846* (New York, 1991), 185–201; Harry L. Watson, *Liberty and Power: The Politics of Jacksonian America* (New York, 1990), 80–83.

21. *New-York Commercial Advertiser*, 6 October 1829.

22. James Fenimore Cooper, *The Pioneers, or the Sources of the Susquehanna; A Descriptive Tale* (New York, 1823). On Hiram Doolittle, see Alan Taylor, *William Cooper's Town: Power and Persuasion on the Frontier of the Early American Republic* (New York, 1995), 290–91, 421–22.

23. Francis Hodge, *Yankee Theatre: The Image of America on the Stage, 1825–1850* (Austin, Tex., 1964), 106–9, 162–63; Leon Howard, *The Connecticut Wits* (Chicago, 1943), 262–65. On the stage Yankee generally, see Hodge, *Yankee Theatre*; Alexander P. Saxton, *The Rise and Fall of the White Republic: Class Politics and Mass Culture in*

Nineteenth-Century America (London, 1990), 116–23; Rosemarie K. Bank, *Theatre Culture in America, 1825–1860* (Cambridge, Mass., 1997), 39–42.

24. On Cooper: Taylor, *William Cooper's Town*. On Dunlap: Joseph J. Ellis, *After the Revolution: Profiles of Early American Culture* (New York, 1979), 113–58. On Hackett: Hodge, *Yankee Theatre*, 84–86, and Coke, *A Subaltern's Furlough*, 1:35.

25. William Dunlap, *A History of the American Theatre* (New York, 1832), 384–92, 400–1, and idem, *History of the Rise and Progress of the Arts of Design in the United States* (New York, 1834; reprint 1965), 1:345; Taylor, *William Cooper's Town*, 411.

26. On Jedediah Peck: Taylor, *William Cooper's Town*, 237–38, 241–49, 275–76, 284–87. Stone, "From New York to Niagara," 216.

27. Stone, "From New York to Niagara," 228–33.

28. *New-York Commercial Advertiser*, 6 October 1829 and 21 October 1829.

29. *New-York Commercial Advertiser*, 13 October 1829. All further quotes from Hiram Doolittle, Jun., are from this article. It is reprinted in full in *Buffalo Historical Society Publications* 14 (1910), 265–71.

30. Forsyth: *Colonial Advocate* (York, Upper Canada), 9 August 1827; *Black Rock Gazette*, 15 June 1826. Guest lists: *Colonial Advocate* (Queenston, Upper Canada), 16 September 1824; *Farmer's Journal and Welland Canal Intelligencer* (St. Catharine's, Upper Canada), 1 August 1827. Quote: *Syracuse Advertiser*, 15 August 1827. The Pavilion, the largest of four hotels at Niagara, could accommodate 150 guests in 1828, according to Stuart, *Three Years in North America*, 1:110. A guidebook estimated the capacity of the Pavilion at 100–150 guests. [Gideon Davison], *The Traveller's Guide through the Middle and Northern States, and the Provinces of Canada*, 6th ed. (Saratoga Springs, N.Y., 1834), 272.

31. *Rochester Album*, 14 August 1829 (from the *Black Rock Gazette*); *Black Rock Gazette*, 23 December 1826.

32. Names: Christian Schultz, *Travels on an Inland Voyage through the States of New-York, Pennsylvania, Virginia, Ohio, Kentucky and Tennessee, and through the Territories of Indiana, Louisiana, Mississippi and New Orleans; Performed in the Years 1807 and 1808; Including a Tour of Nearly Six Thousand Miles* (1810; reprint Ridgewood, N.J., 1968), 65; Hibernicus [De Witt Clinton], *Letters on the Natural History and Internal Resources of the State of New York* (New York,

1822), 202; Robert Gourley, *Statistical Account of Upper Canada, Compiled with a View to a Grand System of Emigration* (London, 1822; reprint 1966), 1:66; Anon., *A Northern Tour: Being a Guide to Lake George, Niagara, Canada, Boston, &c., &c.* (Philadelphia, 1825), 149; David W. Prall, "Journal of a Jaunt from New York to Niagara, July 1821," entry for 21 July 1821, manuscript journal, New-York Historical Society; Samuel Rezneck, "A Traveling School of Science on the Erie Canal in 1826," *New York History* 40 (July 1959), 265 (quote); John Fanning Watson Travel Diary, 24 July 1827 (quote); *Rochester Gem*, 25 September 1830. Only a few early tourists (Schultz in 1807, Prall in 1821) admitted that they "conformed to the custom of the place, by engraving our names on a rock."

33. Quote: [Dwight], *The Northern Traveller*, 86. M. Smith, *A Geographical View of the Province of Upper Canada, and Promiscuous Remarks on the Government in Two Parts, with an Appendix: Containing a Complete Description of Niagara Falls, and Remarks Relative to the Situation of the Inhabitants Respecting the War, and a Concise History of Its Progress, to the Present Day* (New York, 1813), 13; Timothy Bigelow, *Journal of a Tour to Niagara Falls in the Year 1805* (Boston, 1876), 64; Howison, *Sketches of Upper Canada*, 101–2; P. Stansbury, *A Pedestrian Tour of Two Thousand Three Hundred Miles, in North America . . . Performed in the Autumn of 1821* (New York, 1822), 112–13; [——— Mathews], *A Summer Month; or, Recollections of a Visit to the Falls of Niagara, and the Lakes* (Philadelphia, 1823), 78. Trees and boats: Peter Kalm, *Travels in North America* (1770; reprint, New York, 1964), 2:702–3; Elizabeth Cometti, ed., *The American Journals of Lt. John Enys* (Syracuse, 1976), 132; Trollope, *Domestic Manners of the Americans*, 338; Hamilton, *Men and Manners in America*, 2:166–67.

34. *The Columbian* (New York), 22 November 1810. Canoe: Clinton, *Letters on . . . Natural History*, 208. Furniture: *Ontario Repository* (Canandaigua, N.Y.), 13 November 1821; *Connecticut Courant* (Hartford), 20 November 1821; the story is retold in Talbot, *Five Years' Residence in the Canadas*, 1:136–37. Canoe and small boat: *Montreal Gazette*, 21 November 1821. Apples: *Colonial Advocate* (York, Upper Canada), 25 November 1824; *Wayne Sentinel* (Palmyra, N.Y.), 1 December 1824. Three men: *Black Rock Gazette*, 28 March 1826; *Livingston Register* (Geneseo, N.Y.), 4 April 1826; *Ontario Repository* (Canandaigua, N.Y.), 29 March 1826. Ice: *Syracuse Gazette & General Advertiser*, 4 March 1828. Smugglers: *Erie*

Gazette (Pa.), 26 February 1829. Eagle: *Seneca Farmer & Waterloo Advocate* (Waterloo, N.Y.), 27 February 1828. Deer: *Farmer's Journal and Welland Canal Advertiser* (St. Catharine's, Upper Canada), 1 April 1829. See [Theodore Dwight, Jr.], *The Northern Traveller; Containing the Routes to Niagara, Quebec, and the Springs; with Descriptions of the Principal Scenes, and Useful Hints to Strangers* (New York, 1825), 50–51.

35. See the dates to newspaper citations in note 34. Construction: Coke, *A Subaltern's Furlough*, 2:38; Trollope, *Domestic Manners of the Americans*, 344; [Davison], *The Traveller's Guide*, 271–72n.

36. Annie Fields, ed., *The Life and Letters of Harriet Beecher Stowe* (Boston, 1897), 90. On romantic death at Niagara, see Patrick McGreevy, *Imagining Niagara: The Meaning and Making of Niagara Falls* (Amherst, Mass., 1994), 41–70, and McKinsey, *Niagara Falls*, esp. 167–69. Both the nineteenth-century elite and most historians have construed the relations between common people and nature in these years as unthinking, unfeeling rape of the land. For an account which sees a more nuanced plebeian aesthetic—one with powerful echoes of the terrific sublime—see Lewis O. Saum, *The Popular Mood of Pre–Civil War America* (Westport, Conn., 1980), 174–99. On the relation of nature, physical labor, and elite leisure, see Richard White, " 'Are You an Environmentalist or Do You Work for a Living?': Work and Nature," in William Cronon, ed., *Uncommon Ground: Rethinking the Human Place in Nature* (New York, 1995), 171–85.

37. Paul E. Johnson, "Strange Cargo: The *Michigan* Descent at Niagara, 1827," presented at the Conference on Festive Culture and Public Ritual, American Philosophical Society, 13 April 1996. Quotes: *Black Rock Gazette*, 8 September 1827 (reprinted in many places); *Leroy Gazette*, 16 August 1827.

38. *Buffalo Patriot*, 8 September 1829; *Buffalo Journal*, 8 September 1829; *Rochester Daily Advertiser and Telegraph*, 1 October 1829; *Farmer's Journal and Welland Canal Intelligencer* (St. Catharine's, Upper Canada), 30 September 1829. Many, many reprints.

39. *Buffalo Journal*, 8 September 1829; *Rochester Daily Advertiser and Telegraph*, 1 October 1829 (citing *Buffalo Republican*); *Seneca Farmer & Waterloo Advocate* (Waterloo, N.Y.), 23 September 1829 (citing *Niagara Courier*); *Painesville Telegraph* (Painesville, Ohio), 15 September 1829.

40. William Forsyth spent his fortune on the court cases, lost, and left Niagara in 1832. On Forsyth and his troubles with the government, see

Robert L. Fraser, "William Forsyth," *Dictionary of Canadian Biography* (Toronto, 1988), 7:311–16; John Charles Dent, *The Story of the Upper Canada Rebellion* (Toronto, 1885), 1:151–60; Patrick Bode, *Sir John Beverley Robinson: Bone and Sinew of the Compact* (Toronto, 1984); Paul Romney, *Mr. Attorney: The Attorney General for Ontario in Court, Cabinet, and Legislature, 1791–1899* (Toronto, 1986). Willis story: Nathaniel P. Willis, "Niagara—Lake Ontario—the St. Lawrence," in *Dashes at Life with a Free Pencil*, Part 2: "Inklings of Adventure" (1845), reprinted in the American Short Story Series (New York, 1968), 30:11. Because the governor sent soldiers instead of civil authorities to tear down the fence, Canadian reformers branded the incident the "Niagara Falls Outrage," and covered the controversy in scores of newspaper stories. See especially McKenzie's *Colonial Advocate* for the years following 1827. Papers on the United States side also kept track of Forsyth's travails.

41. *Buffalo Journal*, 6 October 1829 and 13 October 1829; *Farmer's Journal and Welland Canal Intelligencer* (St. Catharine's, Upper Canada), 7 October 1829; *Connecticut Courant* (Hartford), 27 October 1829; *Livingston Register* (Geneseo, N.Y.), 21 October 1829; *New-York Commercial Advertiser*, 13 October 1829. Pigs and fireworks: *The Atlas* (New York), 10 October 1829. Circus: Barnard and Page headed the only circus troupe playing in the area. They had played in Erie, Pennsylvania, a few days earlier, and opened in Buffalo a few days after the Niagara exhibition. On this troupe, see *Rochester Daily Advertiser and Telegraph*, 21–27 November 1828; *Erie Gazette* (Pa.), 1 October 1829; *Buffalo Journal*, 13 and 20 October 1829; *Anti-Masonic Enquirer* (Rochester, N.Y.), 24 November 1829 (fullest description); *Onondaga Standard* (Syracuse, N.Y.), 21 October 1829 and 30 December 1829; Stuart Thayer, *Annals of the American Circus, 1793–1829* (Manchester, Mich., 1976), 224–25.

42. *Livingston Register* (Geneseo, N.Y.), 21 October 1829.

43. *New-York Commercial Advertiser*, 13 October 1829.

44. Hiram Doolittle locates the downriver explosion at the Indian Ladder in the *New-York Commercial Advertiser*, 13 October 1829. Accounts of the Indian Ladder: Commetti, ed., *American Journals of Lt. John Enys*, 136–39; Isaac Weld, Jr., *Travels through the States of North America, and the Provinces of Upper and Lower Canada, during the Years 1795, 1796, and 1797* (London, 1800), 2:122–23; J. Hector St. John de Crèvecoeur, in Frank H. Severance, "Studies of the Niagara Frontier," *Buffalo Historical Society Publications* 15 (1911), 356–59.

There in 1823: Talbot, *Five Years*, 131–35. Fishing: Capt. William Newnham Blane, *An Excursion through the United States and Canada during the Years 1822 and 1823* (London, 1824), 405; Mary F. Dewey, *Life and Letters of Catharine Maria Sedgwick* (New York, 1871), 132.

45. Terrapin Rocks quote: Hamilton, *Men and Manners in America*, 2:166. Other accounts: Fowler, *Journal of a Tour*, 140; Stuart, *Three Years in North America*, 1:141. Terrapin Bridge and *Michigan* Descent: *Saratoga Sentinel*, 18 September 1827.

46. *Providence Patriot*, 21 October 1829 (citing a Buffalo paper); *Farmer's Journal and Welland Canal Intelligencer* (St. Catharine's, Upper Canada), 7 October 1829; *Livingston Register* (Geneseo, N.Y.), 21 October 1829; *Rochester Daily Advertiser and Telegraph*, 13 October 1829.

47. Quotes: *New-York Commercial Advertiser*, 13 October 1829; *Livingston Register* (Geneseo, N.Y.), 21 October 1829; *Providence Patriot*, 21 October 1829; *Farmer's Journal and Welland Canal Intelligencer* (St. Catharine's, Upper Canada), 7 October 1829. The ship stayed on the rock until a storm dislodged it in late November, *Buffalo Republican*, reprinted in *New-York Evening Post*, 3 December 1829.

48. *Painesville Telegraph* (Painesville, Ohio), 13 October 1829; *Freeman's Journal* (Cooperstown, N.Y.), 26 October 1829; *Livingston Register* (Geneseo, N.Y.), 21 October 1829; *Providence Daily Advertiser*, 20 October 1829.

49. *Colonial Advocate* (York, Upper Canada), 15 October 1829.

50. *People's Press* (Batavia, N.Y.), 23 October 1829 (citing *Buffalo Republican*); *Livingston Register* (Geneseo, N.Y.), 21 October 1829; *Colonial Advocate* (York, Upper Canada), 22 October 1829. Other mentions of drunkenness: *Farmer's Journal and Welland Canal Intelligencer* (St. Catharine's, Upper Canada), 19 December 1829; *Painesville Telegraph* (Painesville, Ohio), 27 October 1829.

51. Sam at museum: *Livingston Register* (Geneseo, N.Y.), 21 October 1829; *Painesville Telegraph* (Painesville, Ohio), 27 October 1829. *Buffalo Patriot*, 10 November 1829 (portrait) and 27 October 1829 (recitation).

52. *Buffalo Journal*, 14 July 1829, 11 August 1829, 25 August 1829; *Buffalo Republican*, 25 August 1829; *Buffalo Patriot*, 25 August 1829. During the previous year, McCleary operated a similar establishment in Detroit. The *Detroit Gazette*, 6 November 1828 and 13 November 1828, printed McCleary's advertisement for a "Select Cabinet of Nature and Art" in that town. He published notices of dramatic recita-

tions in the issues of 25 December 1828 and 8 January 1829, then apparently left Detroit.

53. *Buffalo Journal*, 4 August 1829, 18 August 1829, 22 September 1829; *Buffalo Patriot*, 25 August 1829, 29 September 1829, 27 October 1829 (Patch recitation). Neither Hewitt nor Anderson appears in the detailed indexes to George C. O. Odell, *Annals of the New York Stage* (New York, 1927–47). Within a few years McCleary had left Buffalo to perform his Irish songs and comic sketches with the York (Toronto) Circus. See Edith G. Firth, ed., *The Town of York, 1815–1837* (Toronto, 1962), 344n.

54. Clothes: accounts of Sam's second Niagara leap. Bear: *Painesville Telegraph* (Ohio), 27 October 1829. W. P. Moore: *Buffalo Journal*, 13 October 1829. Frog: *Democratic Press* (Philadelphia), 9 July 1829. (Thanks to Shane White.)

55. *Buffalo Journal*, 13 October 1829; *Colonial Advocate* (York, Upper Canada), 15 October 1829; *New-York Commercial Advertiser*, 20 October 1829; many others.

56. Goat Island tolls: *Onondaga Standard* (Syracuse, N.Y.), 21 October 1829; *The Atlas* (New York), 17 October 1829. Steamboat: *Buffalo Gazette*, 13 October 1829.

57. *People's Press* (Batavia, N.Y.), 23 October 1829 (citing *Buffalo Republican*); *Colonial Advocate* (York, Upper Canada), 22 October 1829. Steamboat departure: *Buffalo Gazette*, 13 October 1829.

58. Biddle Stairs: *Buffalo Journal*, 29 September 1829; Harriet Martineau, *Retrospect of Western Travel* (New York, 1969; orig. 1838), 1:108. Crowd, weather, and ladder: *People's Press* (Batavia, N.Y.), 23 October 1829; *Buffalo Journal*, 20 October 1829; *Colonial Advocate* (York, Upper Canada), 22 October 1829; *The Gem* (Rochester, N.Y.), 31 October 1829.

59. Flag: *Farmer's Journal and Welland Canal Intelligencer* (St. Catharine's, Upper Canada), 19 December 1829 (from the *Buffalo Republican*); *Buffalo Patriot*, 27 October 1829. For a particularly startling mix of patriotism, Anglophobia, and populist racism, see Sean Wilentz, *Chants Democratic: New York City and the Rise of the American Working Class, 1788–1850* (New York, 1984), 264–65. See also Paul A. Gilje, *The Road to Mobocracy: Popular Disorder in New York City, 1763–1834* (Chapel Hill, N.C., 1987), 246–53.

60. *New-York Commercial Advertiser*, 22 October 1829 (from the *Buffalo Republican*); *Colonial Advocate* (York, Upper Canada), 22 October 1829; *The Gem* (Rochester, N.Y.), 31 October 1829.

61. *Colonial Advocate* (York, Upper Canada), 22 October 1829. The article is bylined "Andrew Todd," but Mackenzie reprints it and identifies himself as its author in William Lyon Mackenzie, *Sketches of Canada and the United States* (London, 1833), 97–100. At the Descent: *Colonial Advocate*, 15 September 1827.

62. Only fragmentary files of the *Buffalo Republican* have survived. The long article datelined 17 October 1829, however, was reprinted throughout the Northeast: see *New-York Commercial Advertiser*, 22 October 1829; *New-York Evening Post*, 21 October 1829; *Rochester Republican*, 27 October 1829; *Rochester Daily Advertiser and Telegraph*, 21 October 1829; *Anti-Masonic Enquirer* (Rochester, N.Y.), 3 November 1829; *Onondaga Standard* (Syracuse, N.Y.), 28 October 1829; *People's Press* (Batavia, N.Y.), 23 October 1829; *Manufacturer's and Farmer's Journal* (Providence), 26 October 1829; *Providence Patriot*, 24 October 1829. Most of the article is reprinted in the *Buffalo Historical Society Publications* 14 (1910), 247–49n. A reminiscence published in the *Republican* two months later (it contains Sam's admission that he nearly fell) was reprinted only in the *Farmer's Journal and Welland Canal Advertiser* (St. Catharine's, Upper Canada), 19 December 1829.

IV. Rochester

1. [Margaret Hunter Hall], *The Aristocratic Journey: Being the Outspoken Letters of Mrs. Basil Hall, Written during a Fourteen Months' Sojourn in America, 1827–1828*, ed. Una Pope-Hennessy (New York, 1931), 53; Thomas L. McKenney, *Sketches of a Tour to the Lakes, of the Character and Customs of the Chippeway Indians, and of Incidents Connected with the Treaty of Fond Du Lac* (Baltimore, 1827), 85.

2. For tourists' descriptions of Rochester in the 1820s, see Dorothy S. Truesdale, ed., "American Travel Accounts of Early Rochester," *Rochester History* 16 (April 1954), 1–24; and Pat M. Ryan, ed., "Rochester Recollected: A Miscellany of Eighteenth- and Nineteenth-Century Descriptions," *Rochester History* 41 (January and April 1979), 1–48. Paving at Four Corners: *Rochester Daily Advertiser and Telegraph*, 7 January 1829. (The name State Street is used throughout the text for purposes of clarity, although the street's Carroll section had yet to be renamed in Sam Patch's day.) See also Blake McKelvey, "The Physical Growth of Rochester," *Rochester History* 13 (October 1951), 1–24; McKelvey, "Rochester and the Erie

Canal," *Rochester History* 11 (July 1949), 1–24; and Paul E. Johnson, *A Shopkeeper's Millennium: Society and Revivals in Rochester, New York, 1815–1837* (New York, 1978), 15–21.

3. Mills obscure both ends: *The Gem* (Rochester, N.Y.), 13 November 1830. Aqueduct quotes: [Theodore Dwight], *The Northern Traveller, and Northern Tour; with the Routes to the Springs, Niagara, and Quebec, and the Coal Mines of Pennsylvania; also, the Tour of New-England* (New York, 1830), 74; Isabella Hope Wilson (1833), cited in Ryan, "Rochester Recollected," 36; Anne Royall, *The Black Book; or, a Continuation of Travels in the United States* (Washington, D.C., 1828), 1:59; A. Levasseur, *Lafayette in America in 1824 and 1825; or, Journal of a Voyage to the United States* (Philadelphia, 1829), 2:193. Lafayette quote: *Rochester Telegraph*, 14 June 1825.

4. William Leete Stone, "From New York to Niagara: Journal of a Tour, in Part by the Erie Canal, in the Year 1829," *Buffalo Historical Society Publications* 14 (1910), 254–55; Basil Hall, *Travels in North America, in the Years 1827 and 1828* (Edinburgh and London, 1829), 1:153, 160; E. T. Coke, *A Subaltern's Furlough: Descriptive of Scenes in Various Parts of the United States, Upper and Lower Canada, New Brunswick, and Nova Scotia, during the Summer and Autumn of 1832* (London, 1833), 2:18.

5. The literature on respectability, entrepreneurialism, and middle-class self-fashioning in these years is immense. Substantial recent contributions include Richard L. Bushman, *The Refinement of America: Persons, Houses, Cities* (New York, 1992); Daniel Walker Howe, *Making the American Self: Jonathan Edwards to Abraham Lincoln* (Cambridge, Mass., 1997); Joyce Appleby, *Inheriting the Revolution: The First Generation of Americans* (Cambridge, Mass., 2000).

6. On Rochester's culture wars in the 1820s, see Johnson, *A Shopkeeper's Millennium.*

7. Recess: *Rochester Daily Advertiser and Telegraph*, 17 July 1829; *Anti-Masonic Enquirer*, 20 October 1829; Jenny Marsh Parker, *Rochester: A Story Historical* (Rochester, N.Y., 1884), 184–85.

8. See *Rochester Daily Advertiser and Telegraph*, 29–31 October and 2 November 1829.

9. Partnerships: *Rochester Telegraph*, 12 July 1825, 28 June 1828; Edwin Scrantom, "Old Citizen Letters," newspaper scrapbook, Rochester Public Library, Letters Nos. 4 and 8; Parker, *Rochester: A Story Historical*, 184–85; Herbert A. Wisbey, Jr., "J. L. D. Mathies: Western New York State Artist," *New York History* 39 (1958),

133–50; Paul E. Johnson and Sean Wilentz, *The Kingdom of Matthias: A Story of Sex and Salvation in 19th-Century America* (New York, 1994), 84–87. Practice at Recess: *Rochester Daily Advertiser and Telegraph*, 30 January 1829.

10. Band roster and stories: Scrantom, "Old Citizen Letters," Letters Nos. 2–10. They are identified (once) as the Clinton Band in *Rochester Daily Advertiser and Telegraph*, 30 January 1829. Celebrations: *Ontario Repository* (Canandaigua, N.Y.), 11 October 1823; *Rochester Telegraph*, 14 June 1825. Concerts: *Rochester Album*, 14 March 1826; "Diary of E. Maria Ward," 3 January 1819, in *Rochester Historical Society Publications 11* (1932), 49; *Rochester Daily Advertiser*, 24 March 1832.

11. Scrantom, "Old Citizen Letters," Letters Nos. 2–10. Monroe Garden: *Rochester Telegraph*, 21 June 1825; *Rochester Daily Advertiser and Telegraph*, 15 July 1828. Utica trip: *Rochester Daily Advertiser and Telegraph*, 28 September 1829. Band occupations and anecdotes: Scrantom, "Old Citizen Letters"; Sylvester J. H. Clark, *Early Rochesterians Index* (Syracuse, N.Y., 1969).

12. Drinking episode: Scrantom, "Old Citizen Letters," Letter No. 4. Monroe Garden: *Rochester Telegraph*, 21 June 1825; *People's Press* (Batavia, N.Y.), 9 July 1825. Saturday practice: *Rochester Daily Advertiser and Telegraph*, 30 January 1830. Buffalo and Niagara trips: *Rochester Telegraph*, 11 September 1827; *Rochester Gem*, 25 September 1830.

13. Utica trip: *Rochester Daily Advertiser and Telegraph*, 28 September 1829. Band occupations and stories: Clark, *Early Rochesterians Index*; Scrantom, "Old Citizen Letters," Letters Nos. 1–10.

14. Joe Cochrane and O'Donohue: Parker, *Rochester: A Story Historical*, 184–88.

15. Drake is identified as having been personally acquainted with Sam Patch in *Rochester Evening Times*, 13 November 1909 (Sam Patch Scrapbook, Local History Division, Rochester Public Library, cited hereafter as SPSB). Bible: Scrantom, "Old Citizen Letters," Letters Nos. 129–30; relation to Peck, Letter No. 51. On Peck, see Johnson, *A Shopkeeper's Millennium*, 43–44, 45, 98.

16. Scrantom, "Old Citizen Letters," Letter No. 52.

17. See Susan G. Davis, *Parades and Power: Street Theatre in Nineteenth-Century Philadelphia* (Philadelphia, 1988), 77–96. Pluck's tour: *Albany Argus and Daily City Advertiser*, 19 March 1827 (elephant); *Wayne Sentinel* (Palmyra, N.Y.), 10 August 1826; *Manufac-*

turer's and Farmer's Journal (Providence), 28 August 1826; *Livingston Register* (Geneseo, N.Y.), 12 September 1826.

18. Parker, *Rochester*, 133–34; Mrs. Elizabeth J. Varney, "Panorama of Rochester in Its Early Days," *Rochester Historical Society Publications* 8 (1929), 222; [Lyman B. Langworthy], *Desultory Notes and Reminiscences of the City of Rochester: Its Early History, Remarkable Men and Events, Strange Revelations of the Murders, Mysteries, and Miseries, Casualties, Curiosities and Progress of the Young and Growing City for the Last 50 Years* (Rochester, N.Y., 1868), 33–35. Langworthy and Parker both claim that the Fantastical farces in New York State began in Rochester, though exact dates are provided in none of the sources. Leaders' occupations: Clark, *Early Rochesterians Index*. Robinson's barbershop: *Rochester Telegraph*, 2 April 1822, 12 August 1823, 3 September 1828; *Rochester Republican*, 29 December 1829; Landlord's Appendix to Clark, *Early Rochesterians Index*.

19. Scrantom, "Old Citizen Letters"; Parker and Varney, note 18; Stone, "From New York to Niagara," 220. The literature on working-class and sporting male social life, amusements, and organizations in antebellum America places Sam Patch's Rochester friends somewhere between the rough and respectable extremes. On the rough, see Richard B. Stott, ed., *History of My Own Times: or, the Life and Adventures of William Otter, Sen., Comprising a Series of Events, and Musical Incidents Altogether Original* (Ithaca, N.Y., 1995), especially the editor's "Commentary," 181–223; and Elliott J. Gorn, *The Manly Art: Bare-Knuckle Prize Fighting in America* (Ithaca, N.Y., 1986). On the respectable: Warren Goldstein, *Playing for Keeps: A History of Early Baseball* (Ithaca, N.Y., 1989), 17–63; Amy S. Greenberg, *Cause for Alarm: The Volunteer Fire Department in the Nineteenth-Century City* (Princeton, N.J., 1998), esp. 41–79.

20. Of the nine men identified as ringleaders of the militia Fantasticals, only the master saddler C. G. Lathrop was a church member (St. Luke's Episcopal Church, admitted in 1827). The fifteen who formed the traveling squad of the band in 1829 included the housepainter Jerry Selkrig (First Presbyterian Church, 1824, transferred to St. Paul's Episcopal, which became a haven for anti-evangelical churchgoers during Charles Finney's revival). The newsman Edwin Scrantom joined the Second Presbyterian Church during that revival in December 1830, and thereafter sold his newspaper to become a merchant and miller. The printer's apprentice E. O. Hall converted under Finney and became a missionary to Hawaii. Sources for church mem-

bership: Johnson, *A Shopkeeper's Millennium*, 152–58. Drake's toast: *Rochester Republican*, 12 July 1831. Free-thought advertisers: *The World as It Is* (Rochester, N.Y.), 2 April 1836; *Liberal Advocate* (Rochester, N.Y.), 13 October 1832.

21. This section has been shaped by Walter Benjamin, "A Berlin Chronicle," in *Reflections: Essays, Aphorisms, Autobiographical Writings*, ed. Peter Demetz (New York, 1978), 3–60, and Michel de Certeau, *The Practice of Everyday Life* (Berkeley and Los Angeles, 1984), 91–110.

22. Stuart Thayer, *Annals of the American Circus, 1793–1829* (Manchester, Mich., 1976), 135–36, 144–45, 224–25. George M. Elwood, "Some Earlier Public Amusements in Rochester," *Rochester Historical Society Publications* 1 (1922), 19–20. Bernard and Page advertisements: *Rochester Daily Advertiser*, 21–24 November 1828; 27–28 November 1828; 19–23 December 1828; *Rochester Telegraph*, 26 November 1828; *Anti-Masonic Enquirer*, 24 November 1829 (fullest description). Village restrictions: *Records of the Doings of the Trustees of the Village of Rochesterville* (typescript, Rochester Public Library), entries for 15 April 1828, 2 December 1828, 14 April 1829, 24 November 1829. Anti-circus editorials: *Rochester Observer*, 8 May 1829, 20 June 1829, 26 June 1829.

23. Riots and murders: *Spirit of the Times* (Batavia, N.Y.), 3 January 1823; *Ontario Repository* (Canandaigua, N.Y.), 7 January 1823, 14 January 1823; *Sandusky Clarion* (Ohio), 26 February 1823, 28 August 1824; *Lyons Advertiser* (Lyons, N.Y.), 24 August 1825; *Rochester Telegraph*, 17 May 1825. Bearcup: *Rochester Album*, 19 September 1826. Peddlers, etc.: *Rochester Gem*, 18 July 1830. Celtic airs: William Lyon Mackenzie, *Sketches of Canada and the United States* (London, 1833), 6. On Erie Canal disorder, see Blake McKelvey, "Rochester and the Erie Canal," *Rochester History* 11 (July 1949), 10–11; Roger E. Carp, "The Limits of Reform: Labor and Discipline on the Erie Canal," *Journal of the Early Republic* 10 (Summer 1990), 191–219; Carol Sheriff, *The Artificial River: The Erie Canal and the Paradox of Progress, 1817–1862* (New York, 1996), 138–71, and Peter Way, *Common Labour: Workers & the Digging of North American Canals, 1780–1860* (New York, 1993), esp. 163–99.

24. *Rochester Daily Advertiser and Telegraph*, 23 September 1829. Reprinted in *Rochester Observer*, 25 September 1829; *Onondaga Standard* (Syracuse, N.Y.), 7 October 1829; *Western Intelligencer* (Hudson, Ohio), 20 October 1829; *Cherry-Valley Gazette* (Cherry

Valley, N.Y.), 29 September 1829; *Paterson Intelligencer*, 7 October 1829; *New-Jersey Journal* (Elizabeth Town), 6 October 1829; *United States Gazette* (Philadelphia), 29 September 1829; *Manufacturer's and Farmer's Journal* (Providence), 4 October 1829; *Boston Patriot & Mercantile Advertiser*, 1 October 1829; *Albany Daily Advertiser*, 28 September 1829.

25. Quotes: *Rochester Observer*, 15 November 1829; *Rochester Album*, 8 January 1828 and 6 June 1826; *Records of the Doings of the Trustees*, 16 September 1828. Trustees' attack on first company: ibid., May–July 1826. On early Rochester theater, see Elwood, "Some Earlier Public Amusements in Rochester," 23–25; McKelvey, *Rochester: The Water-Power City*, 144–45.

26. Hill: *Rochester Telegraph*, 24 October 1828. Vilallave: *Rochester Daily Advertiser and Telegraph*, 1–11 September 1829. Theater companies seldom advertised in newspapers after 1826, but they were licensed regularly in 1826 and 1827: *Records of the Doings of the Trustees*, 1826–29. Restrictions: entries for 12 December 1826, 26 December 1826, 4 January 1827, 9 January 1827, 27 March 1827, 15 May 1827, 29 May 1827. Peace officers and closing time: 18 September 1827. The trustees granted no theater licenses from late 1827 through the end of 1829, but theater companies clearly played in Rochester. Hooting and howling: *Rochester Album*, 8 January 1828. Batavia: *Rochester Observer*, 29 January 1828.

27. Fights: *Rochester Post-Express*, 20 August 1892, in Ashley Samson Scrapbook, 52:14–15 (Rochester Public Library); Harriet A. Weed, comp., *Autobiography of Thurlow Weed* (Boston, 1884), 30–31; *Anti-Masonic Enquirer*, 14 April 1829; *The Craftsman* (Rochester, N.Y.), 8 September 1829, 13 October 1829, 20 October 1829. On Whittlesey, see Johnson, *A Shopkeeper's Millennium*, 24, 74, 76, 78, 91, 128. His wife and Female Charitable Society: [Elisha Ely], *A Directory of the Village of Rochester . . . to which is added a Sketch of the History of the Village from 1822 to 1827* (Rochester, N.Y., 1827), 105. His theater poem was published in the *Rochester Album*, 23 May 1826. Whittlesey's Antimasonic colleagues Thurlow Weed and Henry B. Stanton (who soon dropped such frivolities to become a Presbyterian, an abolitionist, and the husband of Elizabeth Cady) also supported the theater. See Weed, *Autobiography of Thurlow Weed*, 206–7; Henry B. Stanton, *Random Recollections* (New York, 1887), 26–27.

28. On Frankfort: Johnson, *A Shopkeeper's Millennium*, 63–64; Howard L. Osgood, "The Struggle for Monroe County," *Rochester Historical*

Society Publications 3 (1924), 127–36; Ruth Rosenberg-Naparsteck, "Frankfort: Birthplace of Rochester's Industry," *Rochester History* 50 (July 1988), 1–23. Militia quote: Langworthy, *Desultory Notes and Reminiscences*, 34. McCracken's Tavern: references in *Rochester Historical Society Publications* 6 (1927), 343–44; 4 (1925), 237; Charles Hastings Wiltsie, "Reminiscences of McCrackenville as Related by Mrs. Hiram Lavira Blanchard," *Rochester Historical Society Publications* 6 (1927), 129–34. Horse races: *Liberal Advocate* (Rochester, N.Y.), 22 March 1834.

29. A. J. Langworthy reminiscences, *Rochester Democrat and Chronicle*, 31 March 1898 (SPSB).

30. Henry O'Reilly, *Settlement of the West: Sketches of Rochester* (Rochester, N.Y., 1838), 381; Catherine Josephine Dowling, "Dublin," *Rochester Historical Society Publications* 2 (1923), 233–49.

31. Journal of Mary O'Brien (1828), in Ryan, "Rochester Recollected," 21; Stone, "From New York to Niagara," 254–55.

32. Fanny Kemble, *Journal of a Young Actress*, ed. Monica Gough (New York, 1990), 192; Nathaniel Hawthorne, "Rochester," in *Tales, Sketches and Other Papers* (Cambridge, Mass., 1883), 17; Nathaniel P. Willis, *American Scenery; or Land, Lake, and River. Illustrations of Transatlantic Nature* (London, 1840), 1:89.

33. *Farmer's Journal and Welland Canal Intelligencer* (St. Catharine's, Upper Canada), 7 February 1827 (original story in the *Rochester Daily Advertiser and Telegraph*); *Rochester Album*, 13 May 1828 and 17 June 1828; *Republican Advocate* (Batavia, N.Y.), 17 March 1826 (original in the *Rochester Telegraph*) and 13 January 1826 (from the *Monroe Republican*); boys and raceway: Scrantom, "Old Citizen Letters," Letter No. 108.

34. Bunnell: Scrantom, "Old Citizen Letters," Letters Nos. 129–30 (rattlesnake); Parker, *Rochester: A Story Historical*, 134 (Fantastical).

35. "Tinselled theatricals": *Rochester Republican*, 4 January 1830. Clinton portrait: *Rochester Album*, 8 July 1828; *Rochester Daily Advertiser and Telegraph*, 31 July 1829. Julius Catlin: *Rochester Observer*, 26 September 1828; Henry O'Reilly, *Settlement of the West*, 384; Parker, *Rochester: A Story Historical*, 115–16. On the Franklin Institute in Rochester (which failed for lack of membership soon after 1830), see McKelvey, *Rochester: The Water-Power City*, 124–25; notice in *Rochester Historical Society Publications* 16 (1937), 26–29; *Directory of the Village of Rochester*, 110–11; *Rochester Republican*, 1 June 1830.

36. Quote: Trollope, *Domestic Manners of the Americans*, 333.
37. Crowd: *Albany Evening Advertiser*, 10 November 1829; *Rochester Daily Advertiser and Telegraph*, 7 November 1829; *Farmer's Journal and Welland Canal Advertiser* (St. Catharine's, Upper Canada), 18 November 1829 (reprint from the *Auburn Free Press*).
38. *Albany Daily Advertiser*, 10 November 1829.
39. *Albany Daily Advertiser*, 10 November 1829. Langworthy reminiscence: *Rochester Democrat and Chronicle*, 31 March 1898; *Rochester Post Express*, 11 April 1903; unidentified clipping dated 14 November 1909 (all in SPSB); Parker, *Rochester: A Story Historical*, 186–87, recounts this as a dubious but enduring part of the local Patch legend.
40. *Albany Daily Advertiser*, 10 November 1829; *Rochester Daily Advertiser and Telegraph*, 7 November 1829 ("Large as was the concourse"); *Farmer's Journal and Welland Canal Advertiser* (St. Catharine's, Upper Canada), 18 November 1829 ("No Mistake").
41. *Rochester Daily Advertiser and Telegraph*, 12–13 November 1829. The advertisement appeared in far fewer papers than did the notice of Sam's first Rochester leap, but the handbills circulated widely. Sam and his friends were learning that handbills were the cheapest and most effective way to advertise shows.
42. Schooners: Parker, *Rochester: A Story Historical*, 187. Bets: *Rochester Daily Advertiser*, 2 March 1833 (SPSB).
43. Crowd estimate: *Colonial Advocate* (York, Upper Canada), 19 November 1829. Five-year-old: John Haywood reminiscences, *Rochester Evening Times*, 13 November 1909 (SPSB), identified as the son of village trustee John Haywood in Anah B. Yates, "Early Records of St. Luke's Church: Marriages, Baptisms and Deaths, 1821–1847," *Rochester Historical Society Publications* 5 (1926), 167. Other crowd descriptions: *The Gem* (Rochester, N.Y.) 14 November 1829; Weed, *Autobiography*, 357; *Rochester Gem and Ladies' Amulet*, 23 January 1841 (SPSB); *Manufacturer's and Farmer's Journal* (Providence), 10 December 1829 (quote "romantic station," from the *Boston Evening Gazette*).
44. Pebbles: *The Gem* (Rochester, N.Y.), 7 January 1837 (SPSB). Collections in the crowd: A. J. Langworthy reminiscences in *Rochester Democrat and Chronicle*, 31 March 1898, in Ashley Samson Scrapbook 64:50 (SPSB), and an account written in pencil, dated 1879, in Samson Scrapbook 2:94–95 (SPSB).
45. Sam's jumping suit: Parker, *Rochester: A Story Historical*, 188.
46. Procession: Parker, *Rochester: A Story Historical*, 188; *Rochester*

Daily Advertiser, 2 March 1833 (SPSB). Cheers: *Rochester Gem*, 14 November 1829 and 7 January 1837; *Rochester Gem and Ladies' Amulet*, 23 January 1841 (all in SPSB). Journalists: Stanton, *Random Recollections*, 27; *Manufacturer's and Farmer's Journal* (Providence), 10 December 1829.

47. Woman in window: John Haywood reminiscences, *Rochester Evening Times*, 13 November 1913 (SPSB). Baby: *Rochester Democrat and Chronicle*, 3 January 1923 (SPSB). Citizen and old woman: Parker, *Rochester: A Story Historical*, 188.

48. Joe's story: Parker, *Rochester: A Story Historical*, 188. Gin: John Haywood reminiscences in *Rochester Evening Times*, 13 November 1913 (SPSB), which follows Cochrane's story closely in all other respects. Quotes: Ashley Samson reminiscences, *Rochester Daily Union*, 13 April 1855 (SPSB); Stanton, *Random Recollections*, 27; A. J. Langworthy reminiscences in *Rochester Democrat & Chronicle*, 31 March 1898; handwritten account dated 1879, in Samson Scrapbooks, 2:94–95 (all in SPSB).

49. Langworthy, *Desultory Notes*, 18; Weed, *Autobiography of Thurlow Weed*, 357; Stanton, *Random Recollections*, 27; Parker, *Rochester: A Story Historical*, 188.

50. *Albany Daily Advertiser*, 17 November 1829. Most eyewitnesses agree that Sam was clearly out of control in the air. But the correspondent of the *Boston Evening Gazette* watched Sam's descent from the island and insisted that "he appeared to rush thro' the air with the straightness of an arrow, and his white costume contrasted finely with the dark precipice behind." (Reprinted in the Providence *Manufacturer's and Farmer's Journal*, 10 December 1829.) The Englishman James Boardman, who unwittingly disembarked from a canal boat on the day of the last leap, also recorded that Patch "kept himself perfectly upright" in the descent. [James Boardman], *America, and the Americans* (New York, 1974; orig. 1833), 166.

51. Parker, *Rochester: A Story Historical*, 189. Once again, there is disagreement on how long the crowd stayed. Most agreed that they left after "several minutes," after "some time," or "in less than five minutes." But the eyewitness Henry Stanton remembered that the crowd waited "for hours," while a later reminiscence insisted that they "waited until dark." In order: *Rochester Daily Union*, 13 April 1855 (SPSB); *Rochester Daily Advertiser*, 14 November 1829; Langworthy, *Desultory Notes*, 18; Stanton, *Random Recollections*, 27; *Rochester Post Express*, 11 April 1903 (SPSB).

V. Celebrity

1. Patch alive: *Rochester Daily Advertiser and Telegraph*, 28 November 1829. Sightings: *Albany Daily Advertiser*, 1 December 1829; Jenny Marsh Parker, *Rochester: A Story Historical* (Rochester, N.Y., 1884), 189. Jacob Graves: [Lyman B. Langworthy], *Desultory Notes and Reminiscences of the City of Rochester: Its Early History, Remarkable Men and Events, Strange Revelations of the Murders, Mysteries, and Miseries, Casualties, Curiosities and Progress of the Young and Growing City for the Last 50 Years* (Rochester, N.Y., 1868), 18; Edwin Scrantom, "Old Citizen Letters," Scrapbook, Local History Division, Rochester Public Library, Letter No. 8. Boston: *American Traveler*, 24 November 1829. (All of these stories were widely reprinted in northeastern newspapers.) Nathaniel Hawthorne, "Rochester," in *Tales, Sketches, and Other Papers* (Boston, 1883), 17–18. Hawthorne's tour of western New York is dated 1832 in Elizabeth McKinsey, *Niagara Falls: Icon of the American Sublime* (New York, 1983), 308n.

2. *Geneva Chronicle*, cited in *New-York Commercial Advertiser*, 27 November 1829; *New-York Evening Post*, 28 November 1829; *Connecticut Courant*, 1 December 1829; *Providence Daily Advertiser*, 1 December 1829; *Manufacturer's and Farmer's Journal* (Providence), 26 November 1829; *Albany Daily Advertiser*, 30 November 1829; *Boston Patriot & Mercantile Advertiser*, 1 December 1829. Second rumor: *Rochester Daily Advertiser and Telegraph*, 16 February 1830.

3. Details in this and the following paragraph are from *Rochester Daily Advertiser and Telegraph*, 18 March and 19 March 1830; *The Gem* (Rochester, N.Y.), 20 March 1830; *Rochester Republican*, 22 March 1830. Alcohol: *Painesville Telegraph* (Painesville, Ohio), 30 March 1830. Charlotte reminiscences: *Rochester Post-Express*, 11 April 1903 (Sam Patch Scrapbook, Local History Division, Rochester Public Library, cited hereafter as SPSB).

4. Much of this material is presented and cited in Richard M. Dorson, "Sam Patch, Jumping Hero," *New York Folklore Quarterly* 1 (August 1945), 133–51, and in the pages below. Sentoro: F. Calvin Parker, *The Japanese Sam Patch: Saga of a Servant* (Notre Dame, Ind., 2001). Dream book: *The Dreamer's Sure Guide, or the Interpretation of Dreams, Faithfully Revealed* (Baltimore, 1831) 27–30, which tells us that Patch dreamed that he was a huge frog before his last leap. (Thanks to Karen Halttunen.) Minstrel song: "Jim Crow Complete in

150 Verses" (n.p., n.d.), Nineteenth-Century Song Sheets, Library of Congress, Making of America Web site: memory.loc.gov. (The Patch verse went like this: "Dar was one Sam Patch / Who took de ugly leap / He'd better stay in New-York / And be a chimney sweep.") Cigar box (label copyrighted 1886) in author's collection.

5. See Leo Braudy, *The Frenzy of Renown: Fame and Its History* (New York, 1986). On the Founders, the seminal treatment is the title essay in Douglass Adair, *Fame and the Founding Fathers* (New York, 1974). Well-wrought examples are strewn throughout Joseph J. Ellis, *Founding Brothers: The Revolutionary Generation* (New York, 2000), and Joanne B. Freeman, *Affairs of Honor: National Politics in the New Republic* (New Haven, Conn., 2001).

6. John William Ward, *Andrew Jackson: Symbol for an Age* (New York, 1953), is the classic rendering of Jackson's mythical-celebrity status.

7. On the origins and preconditions of modern celebrity, see P. David Marshall, *Celebrity and Power: Fame in Contemporary Culture* (Minneapolis, 1997), 3–50; Richard Dyer, *Stars* (London, 1979), 7–32; Braudy, *The Frenzy of Renown*, 315–598; Chris Rojek, *Celebrity* (London, 2001), esp. 101–41. On the folklore/fakelore controversy as it applies to Sam Patch, see Gerald Parsons, "Second Thoughts on a 'Folk Hero': or, Sam Patch Falls Again," *New York Folklore Quarterly* 25 (June 1969), 83–92; Herbert A. Wisbey, Jr., "Reply to Gerald Parsons' 'Sam Patch,'" *New York Folklore Quarterly* 26 (March 1970), 78–80; Kathleen M. Kavanagh, "The Limited Fame of Sam Patch," *New York Folklore Quarterly* 28 (June 1972), 118–34. There is a useful discussion of such matters in Robin D. G. Kelley, "Notes on Deconstructing 'the Folk,'" *American Historical Review* 97 (December 1992), 1400–8.

8. *Saturday Evening Post* (Philadelphia), 14 November 1829; *The Constellation* (New York), 21 November 1829. Some patricians, in their bemused way, shared the popular interest in Sam Patch. The genial New Yorker Philip Hone, for instance, recorded Sam's death and copied the *Albany Daily Advertiser*'s account of the last leap (with commentary that was neither positive nor negative) in his diary. See Allan Nevins, ed., *The Diary of Philip Hone, 1828–1851* (New York, 1927), 1:17–18 (entry for 18 November 1829).

9. "A Monody" appeared in the *New-York Commercial Advertiser*, 2 December 1829. It reappeared in Robert C. Sands, *The Writings of Robert C. Sands, in Prose and Verse. With a Memoir of the Author. In Two Volumes* (New York, 1834), 2:347–52. Review: *American Trav-*

eler (Boston), 8 December 1829. "Columbia man": Van Wyck Brooks, *The World of Washington Irving* (New York, 1944), 192.

10. Flaccus, "The Great Descender," *Knickerbocker Magazine*, January–February 1840, reprinted in [Thomas Ward], *Passaic, A Group of Poems Touching that River: with other Musings: by Flaccus* (New York, 1842), 17–41. Reviews: *The North American Review* 51 (July 1840), 231–32; Edgar Allan Poe, "Thomas Ward" and "William Ellery Channing," in *Essays and Reviews*, ed. G. R. Thompson (New York: Library of America, 1984), 994, 459. On the Knickerbocker Circle, see Perry Miller, *The Raven and the Whale: The War of Words and Wits in the Era of Poe and Melville* (New York, 1956), 9–68.

11. Review of Mr. Green, *The Work of Aerostation*, in the *International Monthly Magazine of Literature, Science, and Art* 2 (December–March, 1850–51), 17; Senex, "The Corinne, or Italy, of Madame De Staël," *Southern Literary Messenger* 15 (July 1849), 380–81; "My Lost Darling," *Continental Monthly* 4 (August 1863), 160; "General Grant and the President," *The Living Age* 95 (12 October 1867), 126; "The Imperial Sam Patch," *Appleton's Journal: A Magazine of General Literature* 4 (22 October 1870), 504; "Popular Lectures," *New Englander and Yale Review* 8 (May 1850), 193–94. (These and subsequent citations from nineteenth-century magazines were collected from the Making of America Web site: http://cdl.library.cornell.edu/.)

12. Lloyd McKim Garrison, "Robert Habersham, A Young Harvard Poet," *The New England Magazine* 17 (September 1894), 57; "Editorial Notes—American Literature," *Putnam's Monthly Magazine of American Literature, Science, and Art* 4 (October 1854), 450. Mark Hopkins, *Baccalaureate Sermons, and Occasional Discourses* (Boston, 1862), 16. (Address delivered in 1850.)

13. Some sample anti-entertainment and anticrowd editorials: *Rochester Telegraph*, 26 November 1828 (shooting matches). *Rochester Album*, 6 June 1826; *Rochester Observer*, 4 July 1828, 11 July 1828, 19 June 1829 (July 4 and militia parades); 8 January 1828, 11 January 1828, 15 November 1829 (theater). *Rochester Daily Advertiser and Telegraph*, 15 October 1829; *Rochester Republican*, 29 November 1829; *Rochester Observer*, 7 November 1828, 31 July 1829 (public executions). Joseph Penney, *The House of Mirth: A Discourse Preached in the First Presbyterian Church in Rochester, December 20, 1829* (Rochester, N.Y., 1830). On Rochester's culture wars of the 1820s and 1830s, see Paul E. Johnson, *A Shopkeeper's Millennium: Society and Revivals in Rochester, New York, 1815–1837* (New York, 1978).

Guilty audience: Mary B. A. King, *Looking Backward, or, Memories of the Past* (New York, 1870), 118; *Rochester Observer*, 20 November 1829; *Anti-Masonic Enquirer*, 17 November 1829; *Albany Daily Advertiser*, 17 November 1829; *Freeman's Journal* (Cooperstown, N.Y.), 23 November 1829 (quote); *New-York Commercial Advertiser*, 18 November 1829; *Providence Daily Advertiser*, 21 November 1829.

14. *Providence Daily Advertiser*, 21 November 1829. Englishman: *Rochester Daily Advertiser*, 2 March 1833 (SPSB). "Loafer": *Rochester Daily Union*, 11 November 1852 (SPSB). Robert B. Thomas, *The Farmer's Almanack . . . 1836* (Boston, 1835), unpaginated, but the Patch reference is for October 1836.

15. *Portland Courier*, 13 October 1829 (no lotteries); 21 December 1829 and 1 January 1830 (museum). On Seba Smith and Jack Downing, see Mary Alice Wyman, *Two American Pioneers: Seba Smith and Elizabeth Oakes Smith* (New York, 1927), and Milton Rickels and Patricia Rickels, *Seba Smith* (Boston, 1977).

16. The issue of the *Courier* in which the poem appeared has not survived, but the piece was picked up by other papers. For instance, *United States Gazette* (Philadelphia), 9 February 1830. Major Downing is revealed as the author in [Seba Smith], *The Life and Times of Major Jack Downing, of Downingville, Away Down East in the State of Maine. Written by Himself.* (Boston, 1835), 261–67.

17. Henry J. Finn, ed., *American Comic Annual* (Boston, 1831), 216–20.

18. [William Haliburton], *The Clockmaker; or the Sayings and Doings of Sam Slick, of Slickville* (Halifax, Nova Scotia, 1836), 39–40; anon., *The American Joe Miller* (Philadelphia, 1839), 49–50.

19. Falconbridge [Jonathan Kelly], *Dan Marble: A Biographical Sketch of that Famous and Diverting Humorist, with Reminiscences, Comicalities, Anecdotes, etc., etc.* (New York, 1851), 77–79 (Canada).

20. Unless otherwise cited, information on Dan Marble's Sam Patch is from Frances Hodge, *Yankee Theatre: The Image of America on Stage* (Austin, Tex., 1964), 221–39. Uncle Sam: Joseph Jefferson, cited in Richard Moody, *America Takes the Stage: Romanticism in American Drama and Theater, 1750–1900* (Bloomington, Ind., 1955), 112–13. The first announcement of the play that I have found is in the *Rochester Daily Democrat*, 13 December 1836 (SPSB). On the enduring popularity of Marble's portrayal, see Dorson, "Sam Patch: Jumping Hero," and Constance Roarke, *American Humor: A Study of the National Character* (New York, 1931), 74.

21. Kelly, *Dan Marble*, 89, 90–94.

22. George C. D. Odell, *Annals of the New York Stage* (New York, 1928), 4:321. Kelly, *Dan Marble*, 109. The conversation between Sam Patch and Frances Trollope has not survived, but Kelly (22–27) tells of a (staged) conversation on a steamboat between Trollope and Dan Marble. Marble overwhelms the Englishwoman with western tall tales about the "big slantendicular puddle" of Niagara Falls, and the fountain of brandy hidden in Kentucky's Mammoth Cave. He concludes: "You should have been born in America, my dear Ma'am: but as you were not, you may possibly die here, and that's some consolation for you."

23. Anon., "Sam Patch, the Jumper," Plays Submitted to the Lord Chamberlain, Catalogue (Add. Mss.) No. 42979 (2), the British Library, London (microfiche). "Monsieurs": *Working-Man's Advocate* (Rochester, N.Y.), 14 March 1840 (SPSB). Marble's combination of the Yankee and Western characters is central to Hodge, *Yankee Theatre*, which includes a chapter entitled "Dan Marble and the Western Hybrid." The hybrid, transregional democratic hero was a source of some concern (as well as fundamental misunderstanding) for critics who thought that the vernacular speech of Yankees, frontiersmen, and other regional types should be rendered with ethnographic precision. A New York critic had this to say about "Down East," a Yankee farce that appeared in 1830: "In order to depict local manners the author would have been bred on the spot; or at least should have spent some years among the people whom he attempts to represent. That the author of Down East is not well acquainted with New-England peculiarities of language, is very evident from the fact of his putting into the mouth of his Yankee hero, Major Joe Bunker, such words and phrases as 'corn-cob,' 'I reckon,' 'rowing up Salt River,' &c. which everybody knows are Southernisms." *The Constellation* (New York), 24 April 1830.

24. Composition Book of Charles C. Brown, 1835–38, Chautauqua County Historical Society, McClurg Mansion, Westfield, New York. Spelling and punctuation in the original. (Thanks to Katherine Martinez.)

25. "The Nicaraguan Question," *United States Democratic Review* 41 (February 1858), 117; "Gossip of the Month," Ibid. 20 (January 1847), 96. On the *Democratic Review*, see Miller, *The Raven and the Whale*, 104–17.

26. Hawthorne, "Rochester," 18. The sketch first appeared in the *New England Magazine* 9 (December 1835).

27. Herman Melville, *Redburn, His First Voyage* (1849), Chapters 15, 24. (Thanks to Sean Wilentz.)

28. "Andrew Jackson at Home. Reminiscences by his Granddaughter

Rachel Jackson Lawrence," *McClure's Magazine* 9 (July 1897), 793. Robert V. Remini, *Andrew Jackson: Volume Three: The Course of American Democracy, 1833–1845* (New York, 1984), 432. Quote: John Dizikes, *Sportsmen & Gamesmen* (Columbia, Mo., 2002; orig. 1981), 10. Phone conversation with the Research Department at the Hermitage, 20 September 2001. We cannot know whether Jackson named the horse himself, or whether the horse was named Sam Patch when Jackson received him. If the latter is true, it is interesting to note that Jackson did not change the name.

29. Anon., *The Wonderful Leaps of Sam Patch* (New York, ca. 1875); William Dean Howells, *Their Wedding Journey* (Bloomington, Ind., 1968), 68. Howells's novel was originally serialized in *Atlantic Monthly* 28 (1871).

30. Richard Dorson's first (annotated) Sam Patch essay appeared in the *New York Folklore Quarterly* 1 (August 1945). He revised this for a series of popular accounts: "The Story of Sam Patch," *American Mercury* (June 1947), 741–47; "Sam Patch: The American Mock Hero," in John A. Garraty, *The Unforgettable Americans* (New York, 1960), 183–89; "The Wonderful Leaps of Sam Patch," *American Heritage* 18 (December 1966), 12–18; "Sam Patch the Mill Hand," in Dorson, *America in Legend: Folklore from the Colonial Period to the Present* (New York, 1973), 92–98. Children's books: Arna Bontemps and Jack Conroy, *Sam Patch, the High, Wide, and Handsome Jumper* (Eau Claire, Wis., 1951); Irwin Shapiro, *Sam Patch, Champion Jumper* (Champaign, Ill., 1972); Carol Beach York, *Sam Patch, the Big Time Jumper* (Mahwah, N.J., 1980). Sam is also featured in a reader intended for home schoolers: Morrie Greenberg, *American Adventures: True Stories from America's Past, 1770–1870* (Northridge, Calif., 1991), 30–35. Novel: William Getz, *Sam Patch: Ballad of a Jumping Man* (New York, 1986). A recent privately published novel is built around Sam's undying love for an Indian maiden: David Tinling, *There's No Mistake in Sam Patch* (Xlibris, 2000).

31. Anon., *A Visitor's Guide to Passaic Falls* (Paterson, 1859), 32. Devlin: "One of Sam Patch's Scholars," typescript from a Providence paper dated October 2 (the year was not transcribed, but internal evidence suggests 1890), in SPSB.

32. The 1830 edition of one of the principal guidebooks included a hurried insertion about Sam's Niagara leaps: [Gideon Minor Davison], *The Fashionable Tour: A Guide to Travellers Visiting the Middle and Northern States, and the Provinces of Canada,* 4th ed. (Saratoga

Springs, N.Y., 1830), 272n. For later examples, see D. W. Clark, "Two Days at Niagara," *Ladies Repository* 16 (September 1856), 560; Mrs. S. S. Colt, *"The Tourist's Guide through the Empire State. Embracing all Cities, Towns and Watering Places, by Hudson River and New York Central Route* (Albany, N.Y., 1871), 194; J. Disturnell, comp., *Sailing on the Great Lakes and Rivers of America: embracing a description of lakes Erie, Huron, Michigan & Superior, and rivers St. Mary, St. Clair, Detroit, Niagara & St. Lawrence* . . . (Philadelphia, 1874), 306. Philip Mason, *Niagara and the Daredevils: The Story of the Niagara River and the Men and Women Who Defied It* (Niagara Falls, Ontario, 1969), n.p.

33. Attempts to rebury Sam: *Albany Daily Advertiser*, 25 March 1830; *New-York Commercial Advertiser*, 25 March 1830. Pictures in boats and taverns: *Rochester Daily Advertiser*, 2 March 1833 (SPSB). Bear at hotel: Frances Trollope, *Domestic Manners of the Americans* (London, 1984; orig. 1839), 334. Travelers: Davison, *The Fashionable Tour*, 250; John Fowler, *Journal of a Tour in the State of New York, in the Year 1830* (London, 1831), 104–5; Henry Tudor, *Narrative of a Tour in North America: Comprising Mexico, the Mines of Real del Monte, the United States, and the British Colonies; with an Excursion to the Island of Cuba. In a Series of Letters, Written in the Years 1831–32* (London, 1834), 1:222; Rev. Isaac Fidler, *Observations on Professions, Literature, Manners, and Emigration in the United States and Canada, Made during a Residence There in 1832* (New York, 1833), 122; C. D. Arfwedson, *The United States and Canada in 1832, 1833, and 1834* (London, 1834), 2:302–3; [Rev. S. Gilman, comp.], *The Poetry of Traveling in the United States. By Carolina Gilman* (New York, 1838), 103. Clam shells: reminiscences of Mrs. Mary Pollard, *Rochester Post-Express*, 11 April 1903 (SPSB). Sam Drake: *Rochester Evening Times*, 13 November 1909 (SPSB). Hollenbrook: *Rochester Daily Democrat*, 17 June 1848; *Rochester Republican*, 22 June 1848 (SPSB). Sam Scott: Ricky Jay, *Learned Pigs & Fireproof Women* (New York, 1986), 147–54; Jenny Marsh Parker, *Rochester: A Story Historical* (Rochester, N.Y., 1884), 190.

34. Author's on-site observations. Railroad: Wisbey, "Reply to Gerald Parsons' 'Sam Patch,' " 79. Marker in parade: *Rochester Post-Express*, 11 April 1903 (SPSB). Grave: David Coapman, "The Grave of Sam Patch," *New York Folklore Quarterly* 5 (Winter 1949), 291–95. The canal boat is operated by Cornhill Transportation; Sam Patch Nitro Porter is produced at Rohrbach's Brewery.

INDEX